The Many
MIZNERS

An Autobiography

ADDISON MIZNER

Pineapple Press
Palm Beach, Florida

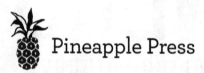

Pineapple Press

An imprint of The Globe Pequot Publishing Group, Inc.
64 South Main Street
Essex, CT 06426
www.globepequot.com

Distributed by NATIONAL BOOK NETWORK
Copyright © 2025 The Globe Pequot Publishing Group, Inc.

British Library Cataloguing in Publication Information available

Library of Congress Cataloging-in-Publication Data available

ISBN 978-1-68334-462-9 (paperback)
ISBN 978-1-68334-463-6 (electronic)

ADDISON MIZNER
THE MANY MIZNERS

ADDISON MIZNER was born in 1872 in Benicia,
California, one of seven siblings. After numerous
documented adventures in his early adult life, some-
disputed by biographers and historians, he later lived
in New York City, and provided humorous illustrations
to works by Ethel Watts Mumford.

His lasting fame came when he moved to Palm Beach,
Florida, at the age of 46, and became the definitive
architect of the city, despite no formal training. He
also developed Boca Raton into a luxurious resort
community, using a similar approach to Spanish
Revival architecture.

A long-time socialite and bon viveur, he died at the age
of 60, in February 1933.

FOREWORD

HE CLIMBED into his roadster and settled his three hundred pounds behind the wheel. Ching, that incomparable Chow, nuzzled him questioningly. Nettie, the monkey who must be left behind, chattered an anguished farewell. He placed the electric fan securely; there would be hot nights in the desert and one must be cool. He sprayed himself with a Flit gun, as a last defiant gesture to the mosquitoes, stepped on the starter and he was away, away from that Palm Beach which he had found a sandy, jungly strip of land, and which he had transformed into the queen of all resorts.

Only himself and his brother remained of the many Mizners, but one was to be born of another name but of the Mizner blood, and he was off to San Francisco to greet the child who would carry on the fun-loving tradition of the clan.

As I write this, I can visualize him, urging the infant to hurry up and become old enough to hear of the hell that Grand-uncle Wilson raised from Nome to New York, and the ructions that Granduncle Addison created from Honolulu to London.

I wonder if he, the artist, the wanderer, the wit, the bon vivant, the gay Bohemian, the capitalist, the builder, will drop everything to help raise a child.

For where his affections are concerned, nothing else matters. He has given of his time, his great ability, and his money, to help others. His greeting has always been, "Move in." He has entertained the great and the lowly, and made them all at ease. A great host and an equally great guest.

There are those, of vast ignorance, who would call him fat. He is merely large, of brain and heart as well as body, and every ounce of him is concocted of roguery and gayety and mischief and laughter. It needs a great frame to contain tremendous mirth.

Drop in at Palm Beach, some lovely February day, and listen for the sound of gayety. And where it is, you will find Addison Mizner. He will be ensconced in an enormous chair; there will be drinks; there will be hospitality such as you have never known.

"Stay to dinner."

"But there are twenty of us."

"Stay to dinner."

And you will stay, and grow weak with mirth, as I have done a thousand times. And as you will now, when you read this gorgeous book about the Many Mizners.

ARTHUR SOMERS ROCHE.

Chapter I
THE MANY MIZNERS

I was neither the fattest nor the thinnest; the blondest nor the blackest; the oldest nor the youngest; I was just the next to the last; and the last was something that mother evidently had not put her mind upon.

Papa Mizner was the best wrong guesser the world had probably ever produced, and when he moved from San Francisco to Benicia (which was still the State Capital), he crowned his misjudgment with mud to the ears. God evidently made Benicia late Saturday afternoon, and must have had a tea date with a chorus girl and was in a hurry, for it was a mess.

He started sprinkling alum on it when we arrived. Mama and Papa Mizner tried to keep the population up by having the "Many Mizners," but the shrinkage was so rapid that they sort of lost hope and gave it up with Wilson's birth.

I don't think anyone could describe the Mizner house. The original parlor, sitting room, hall, and three bedrooms had been brought around Cape Horn, each piece marked and set together by more or less unskilled labor. Additions were rapidly added at the back, each one larger than the first. From the air it must have looked like a telescope, with the smaller end toward the street. The porch was entirely covered with vines, and the planting of great trees and shrubs crowded it in on either side. After luncheon when the front door (with a coffin plate inscribed "L. B. Mizner") opened and vomited forth the family, people must have thought it was a subway exit. Tons of the family oozed forth, and strangers passing must have gasped in wonderment as to where in hell they could have come from. As time went on, cottages sprang up in the shadow of the foliage.

When years later somebody asked me where I was born, and I told them Benicia, they said, "For God's sake, where was your mother going?"

I think perhaps right here is the place to tell where mother came from, and how the Mizners came to California, because the only thing that could be of interest in this yarn is: that two dignified, respectable people could have been the parents of so many outlaws.

The first Mizner we know anything about was a tax collector under Henry the Eighth. He evidently got his fingers jammed in the cash register, for he seems to have left England for Ireland between two days. They came to America early in 1700.

To excuse Papa Mizner's judgment of Benicia, the Mizners were among the first founders of the town of Elizabeth, New Jersey.

Lawrence Mizner must have been full of larceny, for he left a fortune of three hundred thousand dollars, which, in 1788, was considered very large. He left it all to my grandfather, who married Mary Bond, and moved to Illinois.

The family were always pioneers, and it makes one wonder if the police were not just behind them, because they were always moving West.

My grandfather died at the age of twenty-three, leaving two children; Lansing Bond Mizner (Papa Mizner), and Mary Mizner, who later became Mrs. Floyd-Jones.

My grandfather's widow promptly married one General Semple, who was appointed minister to the United States of Colombia, where Papa Mizner learned Spanish.

He left Shurtleff College in Alton, Illinois, at the age of seventeen, to go into the Mexican War, where he was made a major before he was eighteen. He translated the surrender of some of the most important battles.

The following letter was received from his uncle upon his return to Illinois:

"San Francisco, California, January 4, 1847.

"Dear Nephew:

"I did not write to you last Spring, not for want of a disposition, but for want of time and paper.

"Permit me now to remind you that California is under the United States Government, and that everything has changed much since I left St. Louis.

"I arrived in California the twenty-second day of December, 1845, little more than one year ago, with *one little horse*, no money, and no clothes but a suit of leather.

"What a change one little year can make. Without a friend to urge me forward, I went to work at *carpentering*; then I took half of a farm and sowed wheat.

"On the ninth day of June, last, I joined a party of revolutionists. On the tenth we took about two hundred horses and eighteen prisoners. The prisoners were released. On the fourteenth we took the fortified town of Sonoma, with thirty-three men. I continued in the service until the fifteenth of August; got a printing press and commenced publishing the 'Californian,' and within the last few days purchased and paid for a site for a city on the Bay of San Francisco (five miles); one-half in partnership with General Vallajo, the wealthiest and best educated man in California; and have about four hundred dollars in cash left, and owe no man anything but good will.

"I have the confidence of all in power except one or two, and I have got them afraid of me, with my industry and knowledge of business. My property is worth two hundred thousand dollars, and popularity enough to get into any office in the gift of the people.

"Now, my dear boy, if you have finished your studies and can get to this country, with a small library and your knowledge of the Spanish language, and my influence, you can make ten thousand dollars a year at the practice of law.

"I will take much pleasure in forwarding your interests.

"Still your uncle,
"ROB'T SEMPLE."

"L. B. Mizner, Esq.,
"Vandalia, Illinois."

Mama Mizner's people were Watsons, from County Clare. My great-grandfather arrived in Pennsylvania in 1753. Grandfather John Watson married the grandniece of Sir Joshua Reynolds. She became the mother of Ella Watson, later to be known as Mama Mizner.

Lansing Bond Mizner and Ella Watson were married on the twenty-second day of September in 1855.

It was during the reign of the Vigilantes, who were cleaning up the criminal element of California, and San Francisco was in a "ferment."

Mother has often described to me the slanting light on three bodies that had just been hanged at the street corner, and I often wonder if it had any pre-natal influence.

It was years later when Mama Mizner was reproving us for some misdemeanor that she said, "Lord, Lord, when you were all young I had some ambition for you; I thought at one time you would be presidents of the United States, bishops, and men of ability and respect; but, now the only ambition I have for you is to keep you out of State prison."

CHAPTER II
CHILDHOOD

I AM QUITE sure that I remember things that happened eight or ten years before I was born, but there are those who do not seem to think it possible; therefore, I think it better that I depend upon "eye say" rather than "ear say."

It was the nineteenth day of May, 1876, that a great hubbub was going on in the Mizner household. I had been tied with a long clothes line to a century plant early in the morning; Ying was beating up a birthday cake in a big yellow bowl; Mary Hamilton came into the kitchen in great excitement. In a moment Ying stepped out on the kitchen stoop and, looking up at the skies, announced to the world "another keed."

I knew, instinctively, that he would not have made any such announcement if it were a girl, for the Chinese have a lack of appreciation of daughters.

Simultaneously, a grim-visaged nurse appeared and did more bustling. The doctor's buggy, with an old bay horse, had been tied to the hitching post for hours. Some time later Papa Mizner appeared with the little doctor.

I wondered then, and we have wondered ever since, why he congratulated my father.

Wilson was making his vocal debut, which would prove in later years that he could win any argument by out-yelling his opponents.

The tribal roll call now read: Lansing, Mary Ysabel (known as Min), Edgar, William, Henry, myself, and Wilson. There were two or three of the older ones that "cooled off" when they were kids, and Murray, who was older than Lansing, "snapped to the Great Beyond" when he was seventeen years old, when I was less than two.

Ying Lee was the cook, who at this time had been with us for over twenty-five years. Mary Hamilton, who had brought us all into the world, had been with us even longer.

The dear little childish pranks that mother had sighed herself through were those that might make a reformatory gasp; but her placidity was never ruffled for long, for behind it was the most divine sense of humor that I have ever known.

Some years must have passed.

I well remember having a tortoise shell cat named Portia, which I loved dearly. As the barnyard was full of chickens, and "Offty Goofty" (one of the stable men) was constantly setting hens, it gave me an idea.

I wrapped Portia up very carefully in a newspaper, which I thought resembled a shell, expecting to sit on her until I had kittens. I did not sit on anything else for days, and I don't think Portia and myself ever understood each other again, because after that I liked dogs better.

The older boys spent much of their time hunting, as the surrounding tubes were covered with ducks and geese; the chaparral was full of quail; and the hills were thick with deer.

The first sporting event I remember was at the time of the Gordon Bennett balloon race, which started from San Francisco. It was late in the afternoon when I sighted the first balloon with a loud yell. William rushed in to get his rifle to prove what a good shot he was, but before he got his second aim Papa Mizner had hit him a good clip and admonished him in no mean terms.

The cemetery hill rose to a height of two or three hundred feet, about three hundred yards from the house. Mrs. Linch's tomb stood on top. It was composed of three great blue granite blocks, one set upon the other, with the single name "Linch" in raised letters on the middle block.

When father was out of town it made the most wonderful target, and to this day is covered with great blue blotches and several of the letters have disappeared.

Edgar was the best rifle shot but William could bring in a buckboard full of ducks and geese that would swamp the Mizner tribe for a week.

At this time Benicia was the educational center of California. Across the street from the front door stood St. Catherine's Convent; across the street to the right, St. Mary's school for girls; across the corner was St. Augustine's Military Academy; and there were two other girls' schools in the town. Fifty percent of the parents of the "inmates" knew the family, so that Mama Mizner always felt it her duty to have ten or fifteen, or even twenty, of these brats in for a "squared." No one ever consulted Ying as to supplies, and how he ever kept the trough full for these razorback hogs, no one will ever know.

There was a slide between the kitchen and dining room (this was before the days of pantries). After a run on waffles or hot biscuits had tried Ying's energy to the last, he would open the slide just a crack and holler, "No more!" slamming the slide to again before he was hit with a plate.

Mother was giving a very formal dinner. There was a long wait after the roast and Mary Hamilton and the butler whispering, and occasionally peeking through the slide. Finally, Ying snapped back the slide; there was again more whispering. The argument was getting heated, and in a disgusted voice Ying shouted, "The cow ate it!"

The tank house was a heavy trestle, supporting a huge V-shaped iron tank, which was taken from the bow of a deserted sailing vessel. It had numbers painted on the side, and a weight attached to a floating powder keg showed you that it was nearly empty, and that the wind had better "come up." If the wind did "come up" it overflowed. The lower part had been clapboarded in—this was the "tank house."

It was where juvenile court was held. On one side was a work bench, where tools were kept; on the other side big racks for vegetables; and in the center was space to "fight it out."

When arguments grew too violent, mother would merely say, "Take your disputes to the tank house." No reference was ever made to the outcome.

Although we were on the edge of the village, we owned several ranches, which were in the near vicinity, and the home-place itself took up a couple of blocks. At the bottom of the hill a stream ran through the place, and on the edge of it stood a very large arbor, or trellis, with fig trees and vines. In the center was a large circular fountain with a bowl-shaped bottom, where we used to keep terrapin we caught in the marshes.

I must have been about five when I over-reached myself and slid in. Without making any effort to save me, Henry started yelling bloody murder, which finally brought Ying and Mary Hamilton to the rescue. After they were through wringing and squeezing me out, somebody inquired of Henry why he had not saved me, and his answer was a perfect excuse: "I had on my best suit."

Further down the gulley there was a windmill, which was sufficiently high to make a splendid vantage point for throwing rocks across the back road onto the Chinese vegetable man's shanty. If we made a hit, we could jump off the top into a pear tree. For years father wondered why the pear tree was always broken down.

Although I never saw mother take a stitch of sewing, I never met the woman after a misdeed that she did not have a thimble on to rap me on the dome with.

I must have been about ten when some distant cousins of my father's arrived to spend the weekend. They stayed nineteen months. When they left they gave us a silver-plated soup tureen, with goat heads for handles.

Cousin Edgar was just a pompous little old ass, a General in the United States Army, who was always posing for photographs, and wanted to have his picture taken with every new plume, braid, or medal.

Cousin Emma was a thorn in our side, because she loved these two nasty, impossible brats, who became members of the household.

We were all brought up with written laws, that were placarded in the dining room. The first and foremost was on the subject of tattling. If I tattled on Wilson for stealing apples out of the convent yard, I got a clubbing that went with that crime, and Wilson went free. But, our rules and regulations could not hold guests to account.

Hector and little Emma, our two "dear little cousins," could not keep their traps closed on any subject, good or bad, and, although we were not punished physically, we were in bad odor. This leakage of information did not make them any more popular. They had been billeted upon us six months. Hector had his birthday. Dear Cousin Emma gave him a gold-mounted black riding whip, which she spent much of the rest of the time wearing out on him. She always dressed him as Little Lord Fauntleroy, with a big red silk sash about his middle.

Several weeks later Hector was taking the clubbing with loud shouts and screams, when suddenly the bright idea came into his mind to throw the whip down one of the holes in the old-fashioned "Chic Sales." I don't know why anyone should have seen it, but someone discovered it. The hushed excitement, and the sight of the red sash being removed from his waist and tied under his armpits so that he could be lowered down the hole to recover his beautiful birthday present, pleased us no end.

At the end of a year and a half's visit he had so gotten on our nerves that we began to plot against him. It was a rainy, miserable afternoon, and mother had stood us all in the house as long as possible, so she suggested that we go to the barn to play hide and seek.

The barn was an enormous thing, stabling thirty or forty horses, with many traps, et cetera, and this allowed for a very large loft above, which made an ideal place for us kids. The hay was baled on one of the ranches, driven up to the end of the barn, and from there hoisted into the loft by means of block and fall. There was a large door at the end of the loft which was held fastened from inside with an iron hook, and just above the door were the pigeon houses.

We chose the door as the base, having first taken Hector's attention to the other end of the building, while Mitty McDonald attached a little brown fishing line to the hook on the door and pulled it through the bottom of the pigeon house, where he hid. We had selected Hector as "it," and one of us was to give the signal when we thought he had enough weight against the door to make it worthwhile tripping the latch. Of course, the idea was to drop him out about fifteen feet onto a manure pile. I have never quite understood why he shot out over the stable yard, as though from a catapult, and hit the stone watering trough twenty odd feet away.

He started hollering as he flew through the air. He sang his solo so loud that it brought his mother and the entire household. We kids scattered like a lot of rabbits for cover. I remained hiding for hours down in a culvert, with water above my knees, while they brushed him together as much as possible and carried him into the house. It was weeks before they could move him; then was when we got the tureen.

Perhaps we judged Hector too harshly, for a year or two later he was removed from an eighty-five foot tapeworm.

Mrs. Eyres, a very dear friend of mother's, had decided to go to Europe for several months, and thought as long as Mama Mizner had such a herd already that it would be nice to leave Bobby with us while she was away.

There was a bell on top of the tank house and each one of us had our number; first, mine tolled out, and then Wilson's. We appeared promptly before Mama Mizner to meet Bobby. He was dressed in a black velvet suit, with real lace collar and cuffs, silk stockings, and patent leather pumps. We roughnecks started snickering and nudging one another, taking great care that no one but Bobby should see us—we wanted to make him comfortable at once.

"Now, my dear children, go out and play nicely with Bobby," said mother.

Hand-in-hand we tripped out. We had received velocipedes for Christmas. The great stunt was to ride rapidly down the hill. At one place it was so abrupt that you were lost to sight until you shot up on the other side waving cheerily. Bobby begged to have a try at it; of course, we very graciously loaned him the velocipede, but neglected to tell him there was a plank over a gulley at the bottom of the hill, which, if it was not hit accurately, you broke your neck. Therefore, Mrs. Eyres did not go to Europe, but stayed for a couple of weeks to nurse her child.

Mother was giving a Mother Goose lancer for the benefit of St. Paul's Episcopal Church, which she had built in Benicia. All the darling little children were rehearsing madly for it.

Of course, Wilson and myself were to take part. Bobby Chisholm was to be "Ole King Cole," and Wilson, appropriately, "Simple Simon." After one of the rehearsals, Wilson, Bobby, and myself, with several other kids stopped to play a little game of tossing a ball into a hole. The loser was to lean over and be the next target. Wilson thought that Bobby was too strenuous and too accurate in his aim, and with sobbing and jumping around threatened Bobby. Bobby started to run and Wilson picked up a rock and whanged it at him. Wilson was a wonderful shot.

The cast of the lancers had to be entirely changed, for the crown would not fit Bobby any longer, and he had to take the part of "Simple Simon," which called for a great big red sock well stretched to cover his bandages. Shows like these were the top notch of excitement for the town.

The Presbyterian Church gave a very serious play a few weeks later; but, owing to some slight misdemeanor (probably arson or murder), Wilson and myself were not allowed to go. I asked Mitty McDonald the next day what he thought of it. "Not so good—the only excitement was when Dickey Duval, sitting in the front row, got slapped out for belching." Nothing else seemed to have made any kind of a hit with him.

We got up a circus, for which we charged pins, and invited all the girls from the seminaries to see our acrobatic feats. I cannot claim any distinction as a performer, except as a bareback rider in a mosquito net skirt. Joe Jewett really made the hit of the day, by bending the crab and picking up a handkerchief with his mouth. It would have been a perfect performance if his tights had not split, which immediately emptied the arena.

Later on we gave "Bluebeard" as a play in the loft of the barn. Fortunately, there was only a medium audience. Three or four bales of hay had been stacked one upon the other to form the tower. Three boards nailed together and whitewashed, with windows painted on it, stood on the floor and leaned against the bales, standing enough higher to form a battlement for me to lean on. (Even then, I was building scenery.)

I was "Fatima," the last wife of "Bluebeard." In this scene I thought it unnecessary to use anything except the top part of one of Min's ball gowns for a costume. When I screamed to Sister Ann on the next tower to inquire if she saw anybody coming to the rescue, and he answered, "Nothing but a cloud of sheep and a flock of dust," it so embarrassed me that I leaned a little too far forward. It was as though the tower had been hinged to the floor. Slowly at first and then faster and faster I described my quarter circle into the audience like a comet. The result was neither pretty nor modest. No one stayed to see if I were hurt. Mother closed the "opera house."

For some unknown reason, father was "your father," and all the way through, it was "your brother," or "your sister," and always as though it was a shame to acknowledge them as your own.

Days when Mama Mizner was going to the City we were all kissed goodbye and admonished to keep our noses clean and be careful of fire.

As soon as the phaeton had been driven away from the door we decided to sweep out the gun room. We were very successful, for we got together a heap of powder much too large to go into the tin can we had; therefore, we decided to take mother's best punch bowl which was much larger. There must have been two or three quarts of slow-burning black powder. It made a wonderful pyramid in the middle of the bowl. We sneaked out to the long arbor, which was hanging ripe with grapes. At first, we lit matches and threw them at the bowl, but none seemed to have any effect. Little by little we got nearer and nearer, and I decided that if I lit a match and held it to the edge of the powder it would surely go off. I was right—it did! Grapes splashed on St. Mary's Convent, and I think even on Mrs. Linch's monument. It certainly cleaned our noses, and left us as bald as fish, innocent of eyebrows and eyelashes, to say nothing of putting an end to the punch bowl.

My hair had grown out again, when Lizzie Lander asked mother if I would precede her wedding cortege with Carole Crockett on my arm. So up the aisle of the church we were to go, and open the floral gates. I had a little black velvet suit, silk stockings, and patent leather slippers, which I was terribly ashamed of because it made me look like Bobby Eyre and cousin Hector. I sneaked out early and was playing in the duck pond trying to teach little chickens to swim, when Ying caught me and dragged me back to the house. I had to have a black eye painted out and rush to San Francisco, where the wedding was to be held at twelve o'clock. Everything was exceptionally tight, as I was a growing child, and the suit looked more like it had been tattooed on me than made by a tailor. When it came to getting into the pumps no one had a shoe horn, and a struggle with a tablespoon trying to get my feet into them was agonizing.

Carole was dressed in a Kate Greenway gown. I was glad that none of the Beniciaites could see her on my arm, as it was just the age when sex was beginning to dawn. Everything went well until we started down the aisle again, and some old lady said, "He looks just like a cupid," which so enraged me that I took a good kick at her. The crowd covered up so quickly that it only made a few enemies for my mother.

All the old linen sheets were torn into different width bandages; bottles of Pond's extract and arnica, and other aids to the injured, were always in the closet in the sitting room. After the shriek of agony, the first one by was grabbed and doctored.

The dear little children were playing out in the backyard. Some of the rabbits had gotten out and were under the barn. The aperture was very small; the head room nil; and fleas by the millions. As a great favor, they allowed Min to wriggle in. She was in the first attitude, when the curate from St. Mary's Episcopal Convent saw a bird on the fence from the other side. Loud shrieks followed the report of the gun, and the screaming procession fled to the house.

Mama Mizner and Mary Hamilton spent hours picking out bird shot from Min's rump and she lay face down for several days, while the poor curate sent stick candy as a solace.

Mother had been ill for several days. My father, being Speaker of the Senate at Sacramento, was away on duty. He left Grandmother Watson and a big Colt revolver to take care of Mama Mizner.

It was a clear October night, with a waning moon. About three o'clock in the morning mother called softly to Grandma Watson that she thought she heard a noise in the dining room; as a matter-of-fact, she knew damn well she did, for there was clanking of silver going into gunny sacks.

Grandma Watson slipped her feet into her slippers and took the enormous Colt revolver and crept down the front stairs.

"Throw up your hands," she said as she threw open the dining room door. Two men sprang to their feet and stood with their backs to the wall; their hands in the air. Whether more astonished to see the Colt, or the old lady in the nightgown, they were never able to figure out.

Grandma Watson started giving orders at once. "Keep your hands up! Step out here! I'll be right behind you! Keep nearer together!" and down the street they marched to the firehouse, where the long rope connected with the fire bell swayed in the breeze.

Suddenly, the loud clanking of the bell rang out, which spilled every bed in Benicia. Everybody rushed to get the fire engine. With great dignity Grandma Watson turned the two burglars over to the crowd. The sheriff congratulated her, and said, "You were very lucky that you did not have to shoot them." Grandma Watson said, "I could not—the gun wasn't loaded," and the two bad men wilted in disgust.

I know very little about Grandfather Watson, as he "cooled off" long before I was born, but I inherited his key-winding watch and found that for years he had never hit the keyhole once in a hundred shots; and somewhere I have the impression that he got to liking his toddies.

Henry was Grandmother Mizner's favorite, and, although we did not realize it at the time, she was the one that headed him for the church—we all thought it was for the stage.

One afternoon mother said, "Your father is arriving on the five-forty. Henry, will you take the phaeton and 'Sam' down to meet him?" A little after six o'clock father came in on foot, not having seen Henry.

It seems that he was driving down Main Street when he ran into a cow and broke both the shafts short off.

"My son, how did you happen to do that?"

"Well, I was driving along and the cow wasn't looking."

He never got further with his explanation, and for the rest of his life we could get a "rise" out of him with, "The cow wasn't looking."

CHAPTER III
BOYHOOD

IT IS HARD to know just where "childhood" melted into "boyhood," but I suppose it was when I was taken out of the cradle of refinement and flung into the jaws of public school.

I had had a couple of years at St. Mary's Seminary for girls. There were four or five other boys that attended this school, but we were of such tender age that we were supposed to be harmless to the opposite sex. Papa Mizner, being a "pupil of the old school," had taught us that we should never talk about ladies. However, I was in a constant blush most of this time.

I learned very little, though it started an interest in Latin which was far beyond the depths for the other kids.

I was blond, blue-eyed, and pink and white. I had already learned the value of an innocent expression, even to the most stupid "blank." Through the rest of my life this has proven of great value.

I'll never forget my first day at public school. I suppose the family had made some previous arrangement, for I was sent alone to report to the first reader, which was presided over by Miss Shipman. As I turned through the stile it hit me on the chin. I had to run gauntlet of a lot of jeering boys of my own age and up.

One sturdy-looking brat stepped forward and criticized my general appearance, which caused enmity to rise mightily, and set up a great babble of laughter from his audience. Then, looking me up and down, he said, "I'll take a fight with you!" Without waiting to give him a written acceptance, I swung right on his "smeller," which so surprised him that he fell down, with blood spurting from his trumpet. Just at this time the bell rang and we were marched into our different classes.

Having been taught at home not to tattle, I was surprised to hear the brat say that I had picked the fight and made his nose bloody. I was promptly beaten up for this with a ruler. At the noon hour I was unable to find the tattle-tale, so I went home to lunch. After school I outran my erstwhile opponent and gave him another beating. I had hardly gotten home before the news had reached my mother, and I was again well trounced.

During the two or three years that I spent at the public school I generally had a black eye. At this tender age I learned that life was just one damn thing after another.

Within a few weeks I was moved up to the second reader in Miss Driscoll's class; and life went on, with arithmetic, fighting, spelling (which was always worse than fighting), and a great deal of snickering, for which I was constantly slammed into the corner with my face against the blackboard.

Actual school days were rather dull, but the vacations made up for it.

It was about the end of the second year of public school that Edgar (one of my older brothers) fell violently in love with Tessie Fair. Edgar was twenty—the "courting age." He was six feet two inches in height, very strongly built, blond, and second in looks in the family. He had charm (sex appeal not being known at this time). He never became stoop-shouldered carrying his brains about. Society pronounced him witty, but the family said "not"; although they said he was sentimental, even sloppy.

It was about the year 1885. Many millions were being dug out of new mines. The Mackay's, Fair's, and O'Brien's homes were among the many houses silhouetting against the cloudless blue sky on "Knob Hill," San Francisco.

Money had made a rift in the Fair family. The old man lived apart, and made a collection of women, who later sued his estate as "widows." Mrs. Fair lived on Bush Street with her two beautiful daughters. Tessie, being the oldest, was possibly eighteen. She had blue eyes, black, wavy hair, and exquisite classic features. Edgar went off the deep end the minute he saw her. Mama Mizner spoke of them as Catholics; however, narrowness was never a failing that lasted long with her.

A house party was arranged for a week at Benicia, There was a great bustling, particularly on Edgar's part. The older brothers kidded; the younger ones snickered. The barnyard and the back road were in an uproar, and dangerous. Edgar had decided to hitch up six horses from some of our nearby ranches. He had selected them for beauty's sake. None of them had ever met before. They all had different ideas; some wanted to turn around and talk to those behind; others had an opposite complex and wanted to kick the stuffing out of their mate, or anyone else. Edgar was a good horseman. Out of chaos he finally made a ribbon of order with long, flowing manes and tails.

The small station "brake" only seated six, and as there were going to be twelve, the stagecoach was hired from the livery stable. It was a very high thorough-brace; that is, swung on leather straps, with little or no other springs. Proudly, he made the change and climbed up on the driver's seat, and drove off with a loud crack of the bull whip, touching this colt, flicking that, to gallop the first vigor out of the team.

Up the street and around the corner he went, headed for our barn. So far everything had gone well, but his idea of proportion was at fault, for the top of the barn door was eighteen inches lower than the top of the stage. He discovered this "slight error" in the nick of time and ducked, but was too late to stop the charging horses. With a crash it skimmed off the top of the stage like a pan of milk.

The effect, which at first seemed a disaster, turned out to be rather an improvement. It turned the old "pumpkin" into an attractive open "chariot." Needless to say, the family's ridicule and comment were both humorous and scathing.

Fortunately, this slight accident occurred a few days before the arrival of the house party, so that some of the criticism had died down. It had also given Mama Mizner a chance to swear us all to secrecy. Edgar was made miserable by signs, gestures, or grimaces. The wreckage was neatly trimmed off and painted. It was splendid.

The next few days were taken up by dinners, parties, picnics, and sailing, all leading up to the great climax, which was to be the Catholic fair at "The Willows."

"The Willows" was about four miles out of town, and consisted of a half-mile track. Boxes and booths had been added to the old grandstand for the occasion.

An early lunch, and the house was deserted, leaving Wilson and me behind. Edgar was to drive Fanita in the main race, and several of our horses had been entered.

Father and mother left in the phaeton. All the servants, except Ying, who was neither a Catholic nor a sportsman, had gone forth in almost every conceivable kind of trap.

The silence was appalling. The whole town was at "The Willows." Our minds and our feet carried us to the stable-yard. Sam was the only thing left. He was seventeen hands high, with a razorback, and had seen the light of day for over twenty years. His teeth were long. Great sunken cavities were over his eyes. He had a malicious look on his face. Apparently, he, too, wanted to see Fanita win over Nick Fitzpatrick's "Silver Heels." Nothing else had been talked of for weeks. We were both ready to cry, but each ashamed to start the "breakdown." We simply had to see the race. If only we could arouse Sam's enthusiasm as well and get him to see it in the same light. With rope in hand, I ventured timidly forth with a handful of oats. As I feared, Sam charged, showing his long buck teeth. I narrowly escaped an untimely end by sliding on my belly under the barn. Had he stepped on me I would have busted open with a loud explosion. Wilson, having more subterfuge than I, and being quite a bit thinner, decided that he would venture through the bars of the corral and entice Sam for another charge. I was stationed on top of a fence with a slip-noose with which to catch him. Our deceitful efforts were rewarded, after many lunges.

Everything in the way of saddles or bridles, or even horse blankets, had been used, or loaned, for the big annual fair; so with two halter ropes we devised a bridle.

By climbing on top of the pig pen, we were able to drop simultaneously upon Sam's razor as we dragged him alongside. Sam galloped for a couple of blocks and then settled down to a ghastly and agonizing trot, and then into a long, jarring walk.

We had not gone a mile before Wilson began to complain about the nearness of Sam's spine, and long before we reached the fair grounds he was whimpering in agony. For that matter, we were both chafed from knee to knee.

We had neglected to take into consideration the small matter of gate money, and between sobs decided to tie Sam to a fence and sneak over the hill, avoiding ticket collectors.

As it was a charity affair for the Catholic hospital, we must have felt that we were both in need of charity and hospital, for I do not remember "conscience" entering into the matter of ethics. Walking was agony. We had to walk with our legs far apart to keep our underclothes from rubbing against our skinless loins. Finally, Wilson refused to go any further and I had to ride him "piggy back." After having fallen down twice, I threatened to leave him, so he followed on.

Fortunately, the last two hundred feet were thick with willows and concealed us until we had reached the crowd, where we quickly gained confidence and forgot all about the gate receipts.

We kept well away from Mama Mizner, who was seated in the front row of the "royal box." Beside her sat Tessie, looking lovelier than ever, in soft, blue "toque," trimmed with forget-me-nots, perched on the top of her head. Army and navy officers fluttered about the other girls; but, Tessie was all attention, for Edgar had just appeared in his high-wheeled sulky.

Fanita was notorious for her hard mouth; so Edgar had big loops riveted to the reins, through which he had thrust his wrists to give him a firm clutch on the reins.

Gee, they looked beautiful! The other horses were all lining up for the start. Edgar thought he would give Tessie an extra thrill, and drove down the track past the grandstand. Fanita was the favorite, and a great shout went up as a tribute to her. But, she did not understand this, and besides, the biggest crowd she had ever seen before were the half dozen bums in front of Philipson's Candy Store. She gave a lunge and wheeled suddenly. The turn was so abrupt that the sulky did a "flop." Breaking off the shafts, they left the frail wreckage behind.

A terrific shriek went up from the crowd and again Fanita wheeled and came down the track at a gallop. Naturally, Edgar could not get his "mits" out of the loops, and there he dragged, whipping back and forth like the tail of a kite. They passed Wilson and me in a cloud of dust, Edgar bouncing along on his belly. Around and around they went. There was a shout of "Head her off!" which merely made Fanita turn and run in the opposite direction, whipping Edgar against the fence.

The excitement was intense. We had never seen anything like it and, forgetting our stiffness, jumped up and down with delight.

Finally, a cowboy lassoed her. Edgar had worn off his vest, shirt, undershirt, and a couple of layers of blubber from his "tripe" covering, and the track was swept clean.

Some were leaving the track and we were able to hook a ride back to the house.

So ended Edgar's house party.

It was a year later that the New York and San Francisco papers announced the splendid ceremonies of the marriage of Tessie Fair to Herman Oelrichs, and the best we can say for Edgar is that he was one of the ushers. It had been like a man holding on to a live electric wire—he could not let go.

CHAPTER IV
PAIRING OFF

IT WAS PROBABLY in the summer of my twelfth year that we definitely realized that the tribe had "paired off."

Lan had finished at the University and was reading law with my father. Edgar and William were a team, and seemed to pal together entirely. Henry and Min (although very different in ages), were inseparable pals. Therefore, it left Wilson and me to "gang" together.

It was at the table where we all foregathered and fought for rich and fattening foods, and a chance to butt in with an idea, that we learned that brevity was always the keynote of any discussions or remarks, for you couldn't get in otherwise. These gatherings did more to make or break character and destiny than I can explain. Any remark was taken and torn to pieces and thrown back and forth across the table. Unless you happened to be the wittiest you were vanquished and driven into silence.

William made some remark in his childhood which was so quickly snapped up that for the remainder of his life I never heard him open his trap before the family.

It was one day, when I had ten cents, that I had gone downtown to treat a couple of kids to an apricot pie. We had been kept waiting at the window, while Mrs. Inglebretson turned the pie around in the oven. As we peered in through the window I saw that half of the pie was a beautiful brown and the other half platinum blond. Mrs. Inglebretson had to turn it around to brown the other half; and, in so doing, she burned her finger.

Putting deep thought to work, I went back to the tank house and worked out a scheme with heavy, twisted wire, which when pinched opened three claws, and when released the claws closed on the pie plate. The weight of the pie turned it half around on a screw.

When I appeared at the table somebody said, "What is the matter with Addison, we haven't heard a peep out of him during dinner?" With no little pride, I answered, "I have just invented a pie lifter." A shout went up. "What in the name of heaven do you need a pie lifter for when you have two hooked onto you for life?"

The result was that I invented a dozen other things later in life which brought other people fortunes and, of course, I never got a red cent out of any of them.

Everything was discussed at the dinner table. Ninety percent of my education was received across the board. Pronunciation of words, their derivations, and enunciation, were corrected and insisted upon by my father, who was considered one of the greatest extemporaneous speakers of the day. He taught us the value of words of one syllable; the colorfulness of similes; and from the mob, we had brevity stamped forever upon us.

An example of this followed many years later when San Francisco burned down and a train full of bankers left the stricken city to go to New York and float a loan for the purpose of rebuilding. All the great New York bankers were represented at the banquet given to receive the San Francisco delegation in

New York. One tiresome old bore was called upon for a speech. For three-quarters of an hour people wriggled around and wore water blisters on their chairs. His subject was banking. Finally, out of sheer exhaustion, he sat down, among sighs of relief. The toastmaster sprang to his feet to fill the gap, and called on Lansing to respond to "this great speech." Lan rose to his feet. The toastmaster asked him to tell them what he thought made a great banker. Lan said, "Circumcision," and as quickly sat down. There was a terrible silence for half a minute, and then a roar went up; for after all, they were all bankers.

At the dinner table Wilson, being "Mama's Angel Birdie," was allowed to criticize and cut in at any time, and Mama Mizner always protected her last born.

The dining room, though much added to, was a very low ceiling room, with a great mahogany sideboard, upon which stood many decanters. For the mere reason that claret was always served with dinner and we could have anything to drink that we wanted, none of us ever cared for it and, until prohibition came in, seldom used it.

One night Edgar told about some drummer offering him five dollars to drive him over to Vallejo, which was the next town, seven miles from Benicia. Mother immediately said, "I hope you do not make a hack driver of yourself." Father made some terse remark. "Of course, I didn't accept the five dollars, but I drove him to Vallejo with Fanita in twenty-one minutes." Although I may have doubted the veracity of his word about the five dollars, it was typical of the family's attitude that only the highest professions were dignified enough for the Mizner tribe.

This bred a contempt for the business world at large, and perhaps is the reason for a lot of bums who hated work. Especially if there was to be no pay.

It was about this time that the first complete, modern bathroom was installed in the house. It included three pieces of furniture. The third and most important piece became a marvel of the countryside. People arrived and waited in lines to see "it" flushed.

Mother, who had ridden on the first railroad, and father, who had seen the first steamboat go up the Hudson, kept impressing us about the great inventive era that we were living in; therefore, when the first electric lights, which were two carbide points burning together, and called the arc light, sprang into a blaze in Benicia, we were all lined up to "Oooh" and "Ahhhh."

Although the telephone had been used for short distances for a year or so, there was another great celebration when Benicia was connected up with San Francisco thirty miles away. Father spoke over it, to congratulate the new marvel of the age.

But our whole lives were not devoted to science, for sometimes we were very naughty.

There was a Republican campaign on, and one of the "most important headliners" had been imported from the East to stump the State with Papa Mizner.

On this particular night he was put up in one of the guest cottages, and was to be fed in state. Wilson and I were ruled out as being too young. The neighbors were terribly impressed with our guest. Wilson and I wanted to see what an "impressive personage" looked like. We sneaked out and tiptoed to the shutter of his room and peeked.

He had just finished shaving. To our horror, we saw him powder his face. No resident of Benicia could get away with that. The worst was yet to come—he used perfume on his handkerchief!

We waited until he went over to the house, and saw other guests arriving; then, after "a council of war," we sneaked over to the kitchen and stole some powdered sugar. We knew that the coast would be clear. We stole into the room and emptied half the powder box, filling it up again with sugar. Now for the perfume. Half was poured down the drain; then, from a "spicket" that we had with us, we filled the bottle. It was the same in color, if not in aroma. Replacing the articles, we slipped out again.

I don't think I have ever been "impressed" by anybody since.

Poor Henry, from the beginning, seemed to be one apart. He was serious, studious, and kind, to a fault. These three qualities made him the question mark in the family, and laid him open to all the annoyances that could be applied to one we did not understand.

He was preparing to recite a poem for commencement at St. Augustine's College. Alone, each day, he went to his favorite fig tree, where he declaimed with gestures. At the climax there was one gesture that took in "high heaven." William and myself, having killed a six-foot king-snake, thought it would be cute to twine it around a limb just in line with the final gesture. We hid breathlessly in a patch of artichokes. We were rewarded by a startled expression, as the hand swept up and struck the dangling snake on the head. For a full half minute Henry was paralyzed in his attitude, with gaping mouth and bulging eyes. A moment of dead silence, then a screech, and he had collapsed on the ground. The act had gone over perfectly.

Henry was a high-strung, nervous person. We should have been ashamed to take slight advantage of him. Jumping out at him in the dark; throwing a blanket over his head; and screaming at him. This was the height of comedy for us.

Henry, being the neatest and most studious, was given the best room at the end of the corridor. He gathered together trinkets and made the room much more attractive than the rest of us did ours.

For sanitary reasons, mother only allowed one small rug by the side of the bed, to say our prayers on. We would go in and hide on the rug at night and grab Henry by the legs as he came in to light his lamp. Although he knew that nine chances out of ten it would occur, we could always get a scream out of him. He developed the habit of opening his door and listening; then, instantly jumping from the door onto his bed. William and myself thought it would be awfully funny to move his bed. Half way in his flight he knew instinctively there was going to be nothing to light on, and started screaming before he was hurt. Mother, Mary Hamilton, and Ying all arrived at once. Although they found William and myself sound asleep in bed, they also found that Henry had broken his collar bone. They also discovered that William and myself were still fully clad. There was some unbuttoning before we were punished.

I was in the parlor one afternoon, when two old ladies came to call on mother. Their sole purpose seemed to be to state that they had seen William and Edgar down at Philipson's Store at eleven o'clock the night before. Mama Mizner smiled sweetly and overlooked their remarks. Just then William and Edgar came in, spoke to mother, and seeing that she had company, slipped out. "My dear Mrs. Mizner, why didn't you ask them where they were last night and what time they got in?" Mother folded her hands on her empire stomach and smiled sweetly. "Because I do not wish to make liars of my sons."

Min had the snap of the family and, being the only girl, we all had to wait on her, hand and foot. Believe me, she was a "Simon Legree." If she had said, "Take the kitchen stove up into the attic, and while you are up there you might as well bring down the grand piano," we would have had to obey her.

Wilson and myself were able to play even. If Min had a suitor we always hung around until we were paid off. We really knew better than the family how generous or well-fixed the prospects were—all the way from a dime to a dollar, we had them pegged up. There was one poor lieutenant from the arsenal who was hard-boiled, and who was on to us. In some way or other, in which we never quite understood, he could get rid of us without financing the deal. I think we liked him better than most of the others.

In the early days of California, when people thought that the state was a mere desert, the government imported a couple of hundred dromedaries, and stocked the arsenal up with equipment. Many years had passed and they found that the camel family was not appropriate. The few remaining animals had been sold, and would occasionally be seen driven in phaetons or in buckboards, ambling along in the most jerky, seasick fashion.

The government decided to have an auction sale at the arsenal. It was advertised extensively. Edgar, having sold a horse or two, had his pockets bulging full of cash. One of his best purchases was to buy two hundred camel saddles, because they went for ten cents a piece. Try as you would, nobody could figure out just what use they could be put to. Among his other purchases were a thousand bayonets, without the guns, and several thousand rounds of ammunition for muzzle loading guns, which had been out of style for some thirty years. When Edgar died he did not leave a big fortune.

Corrections generally came from Mama Mizner, who always misrepresented things by saying, "It hurts me as much as it does you"; however, I suppose she really thought so, because she was quite a truthful woman, as far as I know.

CHAPTER V
HOME BREAKING

I HAVE TOLD you of my blue-eyed, innocent look. But, after all, why wear your thoughts on your sleeve. I had found out a few things at St. Mary's, and my elders, thinking I was innocent and dumb, had added much to my store, by talking before me. Public school was a library of guesses and bragging.

It was the end of June; and "on the springs a young man's fancies lightly turn to thoughts of love."

I was eleven, inquisitive, shy, and bashful. Mabel was twelve, and the opposite. I was betrayed in a manger in a deserted barn, out by the waterworks. For days I couldn't make up my mind between shame and a certain pride.

At school I had learned (out of class) that if I was going to have a Lord Byron career, I would have to accomplish it all before I was fourteen, or leave a path of deserted mothers in my wake.

School had started again, without any further romance, and I began to feel that I was dropping behind in my duty.

For "two bits" I had bought from an older boy a French picture that really wasn't nice. I had been looking across the aisle at Annie for days, making eyes, and otherwise making myself fascinating, when the picture came into my possession. I scribbled on the back a request, couched in no uncertain terms, and passed it over to Annie.

It goes to show that you can never trust a woman, for she rose instantly and took it to Miss Moore. Miss Moore grabbed it, and me, and hurried us to Lew Wyman, the principal. Oh! What a beating I got! It cured me like a Virginia ham. I shrank up, and played marbles, mumble peg, duck on the rock—and hated girls for two or three years.

My first love affair was with Esther Kress (the daughter of a Major at the arsenal). Gawd! It was pure. I used to sit around and "moon," but if she looked at me, I ran to cover like a quail.

Judge Campbell held court over his bar on Main Street. He had long, white whiskers; in fact, so long that he had to tuck the ends into his trouser band. The whiskers had a yellow streak down the center, and took the place of both collar and cravat. It gave a very patriarchal appearance to the "Majesty of the Law."

Court was convened every morning at ten o'clock. Although we children were not allowed in a saloon, we could hang over a window sill, or peak under the swinging doors.

As prisoners were led to the bar the Judge would draw himself up and then lean on his finger tips, with that "what's your pleasure, gentlemen" pose. Then the police cases would come up and the sheriff state his case. The Judge would ask them if there was any reason why he shouldn't "mete out justice as it should be met." With an exceedingly stern look, he would scowl at the prisoner, as he turned to take a cigar box off the back counter. With a quick shake he turned the box over and then back again. Opening the lid he would squint in at a pair of dice and pronounce sentence according to the spots uppermost to view, using his own judgment as to whether a four and a one meant five months or five days.

As most offenders had started their sprees in his "joint," he was generally lenient, as he would have cut off trade altogether if he had sent them away for long.

A black-visaged bum was shoved forward. The Judge took his pose and, without waiting for charge or defense, started the summing up.

"Here you are again, Padie McAlony, lazy, lousy, and shiftless; with no more destination than a balloon in mid-air, and less visible means of support. Take a six spot in the house."

The prisoners were led out, and the more lucrative business of the day was immediately begun.

In May, 1888, Min announced her engagement to Horace Blanchard Chase.

She had had many suitors. From the family standpoint, there was something the matter with all of them; so there was a sigh of relief at a definite decision. The wedding was to be in July.

There were many trips to the City for fittings. The house was full of sewing women, running up creations. All this sank into insignificance for us, because the Fourth of July was at hand.

The Phoenix Fire Company had new helmets that shone and glistened in the sun. The Solanoes had new red shirts with white letters on the bosom. There were speeches in the park (a dirty, vacant block); the greased pole to climb; the greasy pig to catch; the parade (I've seen coronations since that could not compare).

The "horribles" were more horrible. There were more drunks and more fights than I have ever seen since. It was splendid—and the day drew to dusk, amid a deadening roar of firecrackers.

We dragged ourselves home, tired, dirty, and greasy, trying not to show how fatigued we were. Fifty kids were to arrive at eight to see the fireworks and dance around the bonfire; finally, to smear themselves with ice cream and cake.

The custom was for each kid to bring a box, a stick, or anything that would add to the glory of the Fourth. Papa Mizner had made this rule to instill patriotism. He never knew that we had added an Eighteenth Amendment, and that all inflammables had to be stolen, which made a much more exciting game of it.

By ten o'clock the fireworks were finished. We had all been slapped for picking up "unexploded" Roman candles, or skyrockets; a record number of hands had been burned, and bandaged. It had been a perfect day and night. There was nothing left to do but the final "jumping over the fire," which was "goodnight." I was one of the first through, and, with my usual grace, I got my foot in a rut and fell down. Eight or ten jumped on top of me, and I fainted. They carried me into the house. The stupid old army doctor came and said it was a sprain.

I was carried down for Min's wedding ten days later.

By the end of July my ankle had turned a fearful color, that made it look like a derby hat. They called in doctors from San Francisco, who at once decided to amputate. Mother said she would rather have had my leg off, than heard the names I called them. I threw everything I could reach at them. I was afraid to faint for fear they would slip in on me and get my leg while I was "out."

William, who was studying medicine at Lane's Medical College, grinned. His nickname was "William Grin Mizner."

No one in the family had ever seen me really angry—"I won't have it off. I'd rather die than go floating through life on a cork leg."

William agreed, "Let's take him to Dr. Lane." That was a long conversation from William, and impressed the family. I was carried to the train in agony, and arrived at Dr. Lane's office.

He was a wonderful looking old man, with white hair and a perfectly detached expression, and few words.

"Lay him on the table. Strap the leg. Get me this. Get me that."

William, assisted by a junior doctor, moved like lightning— the grin never left William's face. Finally, they got out a scimitar and, without apologies, slashed deep. The result was messy and horrible. "Green stick fracture. Necrosis has set in." With tongs, crowbars, and pickaxes, they worked rapidly, taking out splinters of bone. The agony was terrible. I gripped the table until my nails hurt.

We stayed three days at the Occidental Hotel, and went back to Dr. Lane, where the torture was repeated. This went on for weeks. Finally, Dr. Lane asked me if it hurt. "Yes, sir," I answered. "Well, why don't you cry? It will relieve the nervous strain." He could never have regretted a speech more, for I let a yell out of me that rattled the doors and windows.

Of course, I was flat on my back, on a litter, or in bed, all this time, and was finally taken back to Benicia.

For many months I lay flat amid my poultices, unable to move from the waist down. Healing time was tedious. I read for hours. Henry gave me a water color paint box. I "daubed" everything in sight. Ying said I looked like a setting hen, and laughed loudly, as he always did at his own jokes.

I had forgotten my sad experience with Portia, and got Ying to get me a dozen fresh eggs from the barnyard. Placing them against my leg and turning them every little while, I waited like an expectant mother. Twenty-one days later I was overjoyed to find I was a parent. I woke in the morning with two little "dear ones" nestled against my hip. I had five more babies during the day. The other five eggs were taken from me, without pain. Ying operated on them, reporting, "No good."

For several days they let me keep them, but when they began eating my bread and milk poultice, they were kidnapped. No mother could have been more brokenhearted.

I was in bed about a year. One book I got hold of was about Dickens and how he trained his power of observation, and his study of character. They became games with me that I have played ever since. I think what I learned from that book has been of more value to me, and more fun, than anything in my life.

Papa Mizner had been campaigning for that poor dish-faced old ass, who became President Harrison, and sat in front of Blaine.

We had been a devoted, home-loving family, who adored Mama Mizner; loved and respected Papa Mizner, with a touch of awe; squabbled among ourselves one minute, and worshipped the next.

This could not last, of course, and when Papa Mizner (having taken the electoral vote to Washington) telegraphed us he had accepted the envoy's folio to Guatemala and the other four countries of Central America, we were flabbergasted. This meant leaving dear old Benicia. Breaking up the family.

Excitement was mingled with tears.

I was learning to hobble about the house on crutches, when mother and father returned from the East.

Deciding who was to go, and who was to stay; packing and buying clothes; took my mind off the heartbreak.

None of us had the haziest idea about Central America. Father had to point it out on the map.

Edgar was to go as First Secretary; Lan to stay in Benicia and attend to the business, and father's practice; William had another year as intern in the Lane Hospital; Henry was already at West Point, in his third year; Wilson and I were to go, as we were of the tender years of ten and thirteen. Papa and Mama Mizner had travelled a lot, while Mary Hamilton had ruled us with a strict and loving hand. But, she had died a year ago. So five of us were to go and the other four were scattered.

I sobbed quietly in the corner seat of the train as we left Benicia. The entire town turned out to see us off, bringing a band, and making speeches.

My beloved Benicia. "The loveliest village of the Plain." I'd never seen anything else, but San Francisco. That was different—That was "The City."

After thirty-five years I visited Benicia. Dirty, squalid, and dilapidated. The smelting works across the straits had deposited a thin solution of cyanide on the grass, and killed every living creature, save the remaining population. No "lowing herds;" no singing birds—not even a crowing rooster to wake you. Where the biggest ferryboat in the world (the *Solano*), which could swallow two overland trains and carry them across the straits, had been, there was a decaying wharf. The boat had been replaced by a huge bridge three miles out of town, and now there wasn't even a railroad station.

Had it always been as unattractive? I wonder!

Search as hard as I could, in the few hours I was there, I couldn't find a soul who had ever heard of a Mizner. The Mizners, who had thought themselves the reigning family, and still owned over half the town.

CHAPTER VI
DIPLOMACY

IN SPLITTING up the family I left out the most important member—Ying. Quite unperturbed he had packed up the utensils he needed, served lunch for about twenty, and got on the train, as calmly as though he had done it every day of his life. With us it was quite different, for the hubbub had approached a riot.

The few days in San Francisco are rather a blur, except a farewell dinner at Mrs. Wilson's the night before we sailed. Wilson and I had never been to such a swell affair with strangers. We had three helpings of strawberry ice cream, which was very unbecoming to the lower deck the next morning as we sailed out the "Golden Gate."

At the pier there was a great send-off. Everybody brought presents (all perfectly useless things).

As the wharf drifted away from the boat, people waved and shouted. The last thing I could see was Min sniffling on her husband's shoulder. We kids were too excited to be depressed. The rooms were jammed with flowers—even more than at Mrs. Hasting's funeral.

The steamer probably was not large, but we thought it enormous. It had a cargo for West Coast of Mexico and Central America, stopping to discharge merchandise and take on coffee on its way to Panama.

The first day we weren't very hungry and, besides, we had plenty of ammunition with the strawberry ice cream. As a matter-of-fact, I have been a human geyser on a gangplank ever since, and can "throw up" off a wharf at the drop of a hat.

As Mama Mizner had a "headache" for the first few days, we had the run of the ship; though we kept a watchful eye on Papa Mizner to see that he got into no mischief.

We had the "President's suite," so called because some Central American President had escaped from his beloved country with all its hard funds stacked in a couple of cracker boxes.

There were the usual number of drummers; a few natives returning home; and Mrs. Emmett with two young daughters. Bay (who since has become one of our greatest portrait painters) gave me my first lessons in the use of water color and pencil. Not then being an expert on crutches, I was glad to sit down and "daub" with her. We were about the same age. I fell desperately in love with her; however, Lew Wyman's beating had made me very shy, and, of course, I never told her of my passion.

Mama Mizner was on deck again, and as everyone on board was eager to please Papa Mizner, he had the captain change his course and go in as close as possible on the coast of Lower California, so that we could all see quite clearly Margaretta Island.

Part of the wreck of the *Independence* was still in sight. Although I had never seen Grandma Watson's letter at that time, I knew vaguely about the wreck and was much impressed. It was a forbidding and awful place. Cliffs, mountains, rocks, and sand, without even a bush or a blade of grass.

After a week we reached Mazatlan, one bright, hot morning. I saw coconut trees and tropics for the first time. Shimmering snowcaps rose in the distance. I had never seen snow before either.

It probably was the greatest day of my life, for there lying white in the sun was my first Spanish town.

We went ashore as soon as the lighters came out. The others had to wait for the customs and quarantine. Gosh! I felt important.

Papa Mizner spoke Spanish to everyone, while we gaped in amazement. We had never heard him use a word of a foreign tongue before; and as a matter-of-fact, he gave Min hell for interlarding her conversation with French words, saying, "English is given us to convey thought, and not to confuse it. Few enough understand even the simplest English."

In the late afternoon we went to see an old church, which had been built in the last of the fifteen hundreds. There was a large door fifteen feet high, all studded with huge iron nails. In the door itself was a small one, which father stopped to explain.

"When the Bible said 'It was easier for a camel to enter the eye of a needle than a rich man to sneak into heaven,' it really meant to enter this small door, when the great gates of a city were closed—(for the small door was called 'the eye of the needle')."

Mama Mizner evidently had heard all this many times before, for she stepped through the very low "eye" into the church. Papa Mizner was quite pleased with himself for having imparted this information to his "brood." Pointing out an old stone cross in the plaza, he drew himself very erect and turned to follow Mama Mizner.

He was several inches taller than the opening and hit his head a terrible wham.

"Jesus of Nazareth!" said the old man. "Where?" said mother, as in a daze he stumbled into the church. Father made a wild gesture. The place was jammed with saints; you could take your pick.

We never dared laugh at Papa Mizner at the wrong time—and Mama Mizner let him get away with it.

For a week we touched at a port every morning, spending the day ashore, and going on again in the evening.

There is no port at San José de Guatemala, and we dropped anchor a half mile at sea. This time, bag and baggage, we left the ship for good.

A derrick had been rigged up, with an arm chair attached. One sat in it, and was snapped into the air, and swung over the ship's side. The great lighter that had come out to meet us was one minute right under you and the next far below, as the ship rolled. They had to put blinkers on Ying to get him out; but, Mama Mizner sat down in the awful machine as though she were in her box at the opera.

It was worse landing. The long steel pier was on the edge of the breakers, which made the ups and downs worse. There was a special train waiting for us, with a little, dark man, in feathers, braid, and medals, that would put a Knight Templar to shame, and make a Shriner envious. I thought he was the president, but found out that he was in command of ten barefoot soldiers in ticking uniforms.

From behind this display a darker little man, in a Prince Albert coat, stepped forward and bowed to the ground. This was the Secretary of State.

Boarding the train was a ceremony, as Papa Mizner and Mama Mizner sat down on either side of His Excellency.

We were off! The rails ran straight into the jungle for twenty miles. The growth was so dense one could not see a hundred feet into it. Trees were pink with the Rosa de Montana vine. Orchids hung in great lavender clusters from the trees. The whole world smelled like a hot house, and felt like one.

At twelve o'clock we had finished the straight track at a little town called Escuintla. Breakfast was laid out under a banyan tree, that covered several acres.

This was the land of coffee, and I was allowed to have it much diluted in goat's milk.

The day was steaming hot, and father was beginning to lose a little of his dignified appearance, by sticking to his new white linen suit. Mama Mizner fanned herself gently.

An hour or two later we boarded the train again, and began to climb the mountains. Little by little the growth changed. Chattering monkeys gave way to squirrels; and squawking parrots and macaws to mocking birds. Nothing I have ever seen since is more astonishingly beautiful than that trip. We climbed over five thousand feet, and just before sunset got our first glimpse of Guatemala City, lying like an opal, with its great expanse of colored houses and churches.

We stayed for a week or so at the Grand Hotel. It was big, but otherwise the name was flattering. There were no bells. One merely stepped into the cloister and clapped one's hands. The rooms were enormous, with eighteen-foot ceilings.

The first night a vampire got into mother's room. The picture of Papa Mizner trying to kill it, prancing around in an old-fashioned night shirt, and jumping at an eighteen-foot ceiling, was wonderful. Mama Mizner laughed until the tears ran down her cheeks.

It was the only time that I ever saw Papa Mizner give her even a look that was not one of adoration.

The next two weeks we were busy moving into an old palace opposite the Plaza Concordia.

None of us spoke Spanish except father, and he was much too busy to be bothered, although he did interview the servants.

Valets were four dollars per month. As boys of the richer class were not supposed to carry even a book on the street, we were given Paulino. Poor soul—he was only a few years older than we were, and what a time we gave him. Even Señor Ying got onto this, and you would see him, with the greatest pride, stalking home from market with two or three women following; their arms swinging, and balancing huge and heavy flat baskets on their heads.

We had a silly-looking little old man come for two hours a day to teach us Spanish; mother, Edgar, Wilson, and me. He wrote English quite well, though you couldn't understand him except for one sentence, which he dragged out every time we did not come "up to scratch." It was, "I am a Castilian grandee." I have long forgot his name, for we all called him "Cassie Grande." It was one time that we worked at our studies, for without the language we could make no friends.

Within a couple of months I knew a lot of worthless sentences, but when anyone spoke to me I couldn't understand a word. Suddenly, my ear became tuned up, and I began throwing words together, at a greater rate, not caring for tense or gender. Wilson was a little slower, for he thought you had to be correct.

Ying used to squat on his haunches in the market square and jabber away, long before we did; and then he would say, "The kids are stupid." But, when we learned Spanish we found he had been jabbering Aztec Indian, which, he insisted, was very much like Cantonese Chinese. He did all the marketing and never learned a word of Spanish.

We were entered at the Instituto Nacional, where we learned that boys fought with knives and not with fists. We learned little else except the language.

By this time we knew everyone in the City, or they knew us.

When Wilson found that anyone from the Legation could not be arrested for anything less than murder, that's when my paternal cares began.

At the ten o'clock revolution, one morning, they lined up five poor Indians in front of my window and shot them. It was the first time I had ever seen murder done, and I did not like it.

Father had to present his credentials to the other four republics and revisit the various capitals from time to time. On the first trip he took Edgar and me. In Managua, the capital of Nicaragua, an official gave me a huge spider monkey, who, from the first, loved me devotedly. The donor explained that the soldiers had teased her so that he was afraid she might get mean if he kept her; so I convinced Papa Mizner to let me accept the present. The old man was so busy having conferences he would have said "yes" to anything.

The words: canal, boundaries, and treaties, were used over and over again in these "speak-easy" conversations, held in the great drawing room of our suite. But, of course, they didn't register with me until later.

It was on this trip that he drew up the treaty for the Nicaragua Canal, and had it ratified.

The itinerary read for a visit to San José de Costa Rica, via the East Coast, returning along the Pacific.

A messenger was dispatched down to the coast to have the steamer wait a few hours, because there had to be a big banquet to celebrate the final signatures.

When we arrived late in the afternoon at San Juan del Norte, the steamer had left. The messenger had stopped to see some friends and got full of "aguardiente," arriving an hour after we did.

There was hell to pay! It would be an anticlimax to go back to the capital of Nicaragua; no steamer would touch for two weeks; there was no hotel; so, what the hell. All the Costa Rica officials would be waiting at Limon to meet father. It was a dilemma. Finally, someone found a thirty-foot dugout with a little mast in it.

"The American Envoy, a dignified old boy with whiskers, arriving after eighteen hours at sea, in a dugout."

"Gawd!" It would have baffled an ordinary man, but not Papa Mizner. Into the nameless craft we were piled, bag and baggage.

My monkey had been christened "Deuteronomy," but this had been condensed to "Duty."

Duty climbed on top of the baggage and squatted contentedly with a large banana. She was the only one who could "down the food" at hand.

It was a beautiful, starry night, with all the warm, delicious smells from the jungles blowing offshore. In an hour or two the breeze brought a low land mist, like steam. We had no compass; but, as the crew of two natives would not have known how to use it, it didn't matter. Most of the night we were in the trough of a rather good sea; and once we heard the boom of the surf on some rocks just ahead.

There was no place big enough to lie down, so we huddled here and there, where we might, until morning.

But the night was nothing to the day. The blazing, tropic sun, in an open boat, with a monkey that had a hold of the other end of everything you touched and pulled against you. The sun blazed down from above, struck the sea, and bounced back into your eyes. The wind gave out. We rolled around like a roulette ball, while I hung over the side until I thought I had "thrown up" my toe nails.

The "two crew" worked at the oars and, finally, we rounded a coral reef, fringed with coconut trees. There were a few palm thatched shacks; the railway terminal; and the Custom House—it was Limon.

As we drew near a long, narrow wharf, people waved us away. As we drew nearer, a soldier raised a rifle to his shoulders, shouting that the Customs were closed for the day.

Father gave orders to hoist the American flag. As the only one we had with us was the same length as the boat and twice as high as the mast, this was difficult. Shouting back and forth for fifteen minutes, we made them understand that the American Envoy was not subject to Customs. One of the soldiers had been sent to inform the commandante that the port was stormed, and so brought help, in the shape of a gaudy official. He shouted that we would have to wait half an hour until the reception got ready.

This was almost too much; but it gave us a chance to change our soiled clothes, behind the protection of the flag, and make a more presentable front.

Finally, a long line of barefoot soldiers marched down the wharf. They had evidently been drilled in their work, for they filed down in double file, separated, and presented arms. Through the gap came marching the band. Then several generals and officials got up for the third act; took up a position at the end of the wharf and began bowing.

Slowly, we drew near, with Papa Mizner standing in the bow, hat in hand. Now, only a few feet separated us from the pier; when suddenly Duty took a flying leap from the top of the mast onto the top of one of the general's plumed hats.

The result was appalling. It stampeded the army. There was only one direction for them to retreat, and they did this en masse; pushing one another overboard, and chattering for gangway. In the confusion someone broke the bass drum and started a war dance.

Finally, someone hit poor little Duty on the head with a trombone and she fell overboard and was drowned. It was terribly sad, but tears must not stand in the way of diplomacy; so, we went on to the Capital and had Costa Rica ratify the Canal Treaty. The San Juan River (which was to form the basis of the canal) was the boundary line between Nicaragua and Costa Rica.

CHAPTER VII
FESTIVITIES

UPON RETURNING to Guatemala City we found that Mama Mizner had become "the idol of the hour."

There had been an unusually strong and long revolution, lasting over ten days. People were barricaded in their houses;

sand bags were thrown across several of the streets; and the town had been in confusion and terror.

A bright idea had occurred to President Barillas, and he had sent a message to Mama Mizner asking her if she would appear on the balcony if the national band was sent to serenade her. It had never occurred to her to say anything but "with pleasure."

News of the first concert in two weeks mystified the insurgents. To make the picture more convincing, mother, without consulting anyone, ordered her little "victoria" to be harnessed and kept ready, with its prancing horses, just inside the great San Juan door.

As the band ceased playing in the deserted park, the enormous doors were thrown open and Mama Mizner, sitting bolt upright, and holding a tiny marquise parasol, was suddenly driven out into the cool of the afternoon. For two hours she drove about the vacant streets. At first, people peeked through cracked shutters; then, in astonishment, they opened wide their blinds and leaned out to see where she was going. They chatted from window to window, and then, timidly, took down the bars from their doors and stole out to gossip.

Surely, the revolution must be over, or Señora was crazy; but, somehow they knew that the old girl was far from that. By the time she had returned home the streets were crowded with people shouting, "Long live Barillas!" "Long live the Presidente!"

From that time forward the populace called her "Señora Sin Quidado" (lady without fear).

She had put down the most serious revolution in years, with a parasol.

Fourth of July no longer meant greased pigs and bonfires; but, in their place, a stately reception. All the officials, diplomats, Americans, and others, were to file by and "pump-handle" mother and father.

The national and military bands alternated in the first patio.

"William Grin," who had arrived for his vacation, was to assist Edgar in seeing that everyone had dancing partners, and I was stationed behind the punch bowl. All Mizners were noted for their hospitality, and I did not want to be outdone, so I "clinked" glasses with everyone I served.

The crowd had thinned out to the thirty people who were to stay for dinner. The marimba players were getting ready to take the place of the bands. William had moved the huge iron piano lamp, with its Tiffany glass shade, to give the musicians more light.

The room was revolving and tossing in the most sickening fashion. I dimly remembered seeing pictures of men clinging to lamp posts, so I lurched for the piano lamp.

I've always hated that type of standard ever since. Instead of giving me support, it took me and snapped me with great violence into the marimba. There was an awful crash. William laughed. He got hell for it afterwards; but the matter was too grave to be mentioned to me, and for a week I avoided the family.

Father was a great lover of history, and was constantly digging into the records of the country. He was especially interested in pre-Spanish civilization.

We set out on an expedition to re-discover Copan, on the borders of Honduras. It was an arduous excursion. It took a small army of carriers and machete wielders to cut our way in. No one knew exactly where it was, and once or twice we were all for giving up; but the old man was a persistent "summer squash" and one afternoon, when we cut through the last tangle of jungle, we were well rewarded.

The ruins were so scattered, and so enormous, that in three days, climbing and hacking, we only saw a fraction of them. Stevens had found it nearly fifty years before, and had been the only other white man to set foot on the temple steps in three hundred and seventy years, or more.

It was so sultry that we made our investigations at sunrise, and again at sunset, lying in our hammocks under mosquito net during the heat of the day.

On our last evening there, just when the sun had turned to blood, and spattered the forest with every glorious color, a pair of gorgeous macaws flew across what had once been the great Plaza. They flew low, and then swooped to the top of one of the highest pyramids and perched on the huge sacrificial stone before the temple.

It has left an indelible picture on my mind of what was once the glory of a great and vanished civilization—a city that must have housed a half million souls, with all its pomp of royalty, and priesthood. It faded into the dusk, and was gone.

Having lived on frijoles, tortillas, and fruit for weeks, we almost swamped Ying when we got home. He stuck his head in the dining room door to ask if "we were leaking."

There were no fireplaces, so we could not hang up the Christmas stockings; we fell back on a mangy old pine tree and let it go at that. The Christmas fiestas made up for our forlorn tree. The pageant, giving the scenes of the birth of Christ, winding up with the manger in the cathedral, was superb. The whole show would have gone off without a hitch except for Wilson.

The three kings of the Orient were appropriately mounted, except the king on the camel, for it was really a tall, scrawny, old horse, with a false head and humps. But, even at that, it would have gotten by if Wilson hadn't thrown a bunch of fire-crackers under it.

Sunday was always a funny day. It started with the different masses and the clanging of a thousand bells. At eleven o'clock everyone went to the Cathedral. The girls all filed in, dressed in black, with their mantillas over their heads, followed by a servant carrying a pillow and prayer book. There were no seats, and the women all knelt down in the center aisle, with their servants behind them. The men all tiptoed up and down the side aisles, and flirted, and made eyes at the praying virgins.

Three minutes before the end of the service, all the boys sneaked out and formed a gauntlet for the girls to pass through. No one ever spoke, and to show your ardor, the best you could do was to follow the adored one at no closer than half a block.

As I thought I was in love with the half-breed daughter of the president, I had a short stroll, because the Palace was only at the opposite end of the Plaza.

From mass until four everyone took their siestas, and the streets were deserted. Promptly at four the San Juan doors flew open, and the victorias clattered into the Calle Real. Young men rode splendid horses, with silver-mounted saddles, and pranced beside the carriages, making "goo-goo" eyes over the heads of the sad-looking old duennas. The glittering parade of many colors and flowers lasted until five o'clock, when people began seating themselves at the bull ring.

Being the national dish, someone from the Legation had to occupy our box each Sunday. Mama Mizner didn't like them, and would only go on important occasions. As a matter-of-fact, I didn't like seeing the horses killed myself, and much preferred going to Guardaviejo to see the half-breeds get drunk and cut one another to pieces with machetes.

We now spoke Spanish more often and with greater ease than we did English, and I began to whimper about going back to America to school. I had first thrown away one crutch and then the other, and now tried to get along on a cane, pretending swank, like the young men.

I was nearly sixteen, and a head taller than anyone else in town—I thought I was a man of the world. To shut me up, Papa Mizner took me to San Salvador with him and Mama Mizner.

There was to be the usual big banquet given by the President, and Mama Mizner was dressing in her best. Our rooms were on the ground floor, with the usual huge, grilled windows directly on the street. As mother was sitting at her dressing table with Silvania doing her hair, someone slipped a note under the shutter.

"Please hand me that paper."

Silvania obeyed, and mother spread it out on the dressing table. Of course, I had to peer over her shoulder, as she made no explanation. Suddenly, I picked up the cheap scrap of paper, and read:

"Señora Sin Quidado,
"Don't go to the Palace tonight. It is very dangerous."

There was no signature. I looked at Mama Mizner, who was polishing her nails complacently, "Surely, you won't go."

"Go? Why, my dear son, I wouldn't miss it for worlds."

She held her hand up to the light to see if the nails were sufficiently bright.

By eleven-thirty I began to get worried.

I hobbled down the street and across the Plaza, arriving just in time to see the family drive out of the Palace gates.

They had hardly struck the center of the street when there was the most awful explosion, and seventeen people came through the roof of the Palace.

I jumped on the carriage step.

"Why did you go, Mother?"

"Why did I leave, is more to the point. I nearly missed the whole thing."

In an instant the deserted streets filled with dancing, delighted people, shouting, "Viva the new President!" The revolution had been a perfect success, and a good time was enjoyed by all!

CHAPTER VIII
ON MY OWN

I FELT terribly important when I arrived alone in San Francisco without a lot of family to guide me. It's true, Min was at "Stags Leap," in the Napa Valley, and I expected to spend my vacations with her on the vineyard—but that was fifty miles away.

Lan, too, was in California, but at Benicia, which was thirty miles, so I did not feel that these connections would hamper me much.

I had met a young English ensign in Guatemala, whom I liked immensely, and as he was transferred to a ship in San Francisco, we came up on the steamer together. This boy of twenty later became the famous Captain Scott, who was lost at the South Pole.

In Guatemala everyone was small and daintily made; but Mama Mizner had an entirely different idea, for the family were all built on the North German Lloyd lines, and wherein I had been an important monster among the Pygmies, I was now just one of a multitude, for my six foot, two inches, mingled unnoticed with the crowds in San Francisco.

Of course, thinking myself a roué, I wanted to show Scott the town. After getting set at the hotel, I made some excuse about "important business" and sneaked down to the desk to ask some questions of the porter. He looked at me askance, and referred me to a bell boy of about sixty, who passed me on to a nobby youth of about twenty-one. Even he had his doubts as to my age (although he did not say so), but after a good tip he got a pencil and paper and gave me some addresses.

We dined at the Poodle Dog—and strolled down the street to get our creme de menthe.

When I had left California I was just a crippled, sobbing kid; but now I thought I was a man. Three years of sharing import-ance had veiled my vision.

We drifted into a brightly lighted saloon and ordered our liquors. I almost had my hand on it; when, turning slightly, I saw Lan.

"Don't you know that you could get this place pulled?" he yelled. "Selling drinks to a kid! You'd better scram while the wind is with you!"

I was able to stammer the name "Scott" and then, in great shame, I slunk out.

The next day I was packing up, hoping to sneak out before Scott, who had the next room, woke up. I couldn't bear facing anyone who had seen my shame of the night before. The door between the rooms opened and the cheery voice of Scott, with-out preliminaries, started telling how glad he was that I had decided not to go on. It had been terribly boring, and the places were unspeakably disgusting. He bulled me around until I almost forgot my shame.

He was the nicest, most thoughtful fellow, I think, I have ever known, and I was awfully sorry to see him join his ship. Although we wrote to each other up to the time of his last exped-ition, neither of us ever referred to my shame.

Min had made arrangements, and entered me at Bates in San Rafael. It was called "a school for young gentlemen," but then you see they had not seen me.

I roomed with a boy named Salazar, who couldn't have been nicer.

After my life in Guatemala, where we had a box at the opera, the bull fights, horse races, and other worldly things, it was irksome, being treated as a child again.

It was rather drear until father's health broke down, and he and the family came back; then Wilson was entered at Bates. "Mama's Angel Birdie" had never been away from the wing before, and he spent the first day locked in his room crying. I had to climb in a window to see if he was dead, for I got no answer from the door. He became a great responsibility to me from then on.

He was a strange looking boy, with thin legs. He wore a number seven collar, and a number eight hat. Where I was fair, he was black; I had a pointed nose, and an oval face; he had a pug nose, and a bullet-shaped head.

He could start more trouble (and get caught at it) than anyone in the world; whereas, I could look blue-eyed and innocent, he had a criminal look that convicted him at once.

In three months he was fired, and Mama Mizner (who was strong in all else) would not let me stay where her "Angel Birdie" had been so grossly insulted.

We got the "bum's rush" from three or four other schools, and then father stepped in and separated us. Wilson was sent to Santa Clara College, a Catholic school run entirely by priests. The wall about it was ten feet high. At night they let bull-dogs loose in the yards, which acted as a moat. It was managed like a penitentiary, and you couldn't get fired, just locked up. But Wilson accomplished the impossible. One night he stole a couple of beefsteaks that were meant for the Fathers' dinner and tied them to the dangling rope of the alarm bell.

The dogs were not turned loose until the boys went to bed, and then it took them half an hour to find the meat. The lights were all out, when fire, earthquake, and every disaster rang out with fierce clanging, as the dogs jumped for the viands. The five hundred boys were all ready, and pandemonium broke loose.

It was Wilson's guilty look that convicted him. He got ten days on bread and water.

But when he smuggled the "shot" from the gym and heated it in the stove and rolled it off the end of a shovel down the aisle of the dormitory, knowing that Father Kelly (whom everyone hated) would catch the bouncing, noisy, bombardment, that was too much. They took him to the gate the next morning. After he had knelt down in the infirmary and asked Father Kelly's forgiveness, and received a blessing from the burned and bandaged hands.

Wilson bears the distinction of being the only person ever expelled from Santa Clara. Imagine being expelled from a penitentiary.

At this time I was at "Boones," in Berkeley, being brushed up for the University of California examination. I was naturally stupid and slow—and above all I couldn't spell three words correctly.

I floundered around for a year, having had no foundation to build an education on, and took the examinations. When I got into the vast, rustling scales of learning, I realized, before they told me, that I had not even passed water.

Father had been taken ill with complications and dropsy. They had to stick a spigot in his stomach once a week and bail him out.

We had no home, so we lived at the Occidental Hotel in San Francisco.

Mrs. Catherwood had the suite next to us, and being an old friend, thought she had the privilege of talking father out of his mind. She was a woman with grandchildren, and full steam ahead. Captain (I can't think of his name) was beginning to be attentive to her, for she was rich, and he could play the piano.

I met Colonel Hooper (the proprietor of the hotel) in the hall, storming and fuming.

"What the hell does she think this is?" he spluttered. "'Send up a piano at once.' You would think she was ordering ice water."

Mrs. Catherwood came in to ask Mama Mizner and me in to hear the Captain play. "Listen—they are rolling in the piano now. He will be here at four."

At a few minutes after the hour, we foregathered. There was the upright in the corner of the sitting room. Tea was served. The coy old girl said, "Captain, won't you play something on this for me?" She turned a key in the front of the rosewood, and slowly but surely, the spring worked. It was a folding bed.

The family sent me to schools and universities, far and yon; but there was no use. I was just dumb.

When William took his first trip to China as ship's doctor, I was sent along to prevent me becoming an artist, which the family said was the lowest form of long-haired, flowing-cravat ass extant. I stayed over a couple of trips and had a wonderful time. But this is not a travelogue, so I will skip that.

When I returned I found that the doctors thought a year in Honolulu would do father good. Again I was left alone, with instructions to be a mother to Wilson.

Without further ado, I went in to Willis Polk, who was a young architect of great taste and little work, and applied as an apprentice draftsman.

Perhaps I needed a mother to guide me myself. I was twenty now, and could "get in" anywhere.

It was in the back room of Gobie's saloon that I first met Peter Martin. Harry Pringle and I had a couple of girls in one of the booths, when Peter stuck his head in through the chenille portières and made some funny crack. So we invited him to join us.

As the night wore on, and we were making sprightly, someone suggested we take a buggy ride.

Peter said he knew a swell girl for me if I would let him escort mine. Being always the sucker, and on the generous side (and besides I didn't like her much), I agreed.

We stopped at a house to pick up my new girl. I recognized it as a place where the chaperone gave the girls wrappers and first names; but, you couldn't be fussy at four-thirty in the morning.

Eula had charm, and something else; but I didn't know that until three or four days later.

At about six, as day was breaking, we arrived at Uncle Tom's Cabin, on the outskirts of what is now Burlingame. We were given a cottage with three rooms. About noon we had breakfast under the apple trees. None of us had dressing gowns, so we used sheets; but, as these were hard to keep on, we decided to play "Adam and Eve."

Eula had caught the roving eye of Uncle Tom, and under the pretense of getting a hot bath, she went into the main house. They forgot to lock the door, and Mrs. Uncle Tom was furious.

The first I knew of the scandal was when I saw our surrey driven to the door and our clothes dumped in.

The outraged wife ordered us out. She knew Peter's and my name, and told us we would be haled into court as divorce witnesses.

Driving up the road we must have been a strange sight, for it is awfully difficult to dress in a bouncing surrey, driven at top speed; with three in a seat, everybody's elbows were in each other's eyes.

That night Peter and I, being thoroughly scared, left for Chicago to see the World's Fair of 1893.

I have often wondered whether Uncle Tom found out what Eula had besides charm.

Thank "Gawd!" It wasn't "cupid's eczema."

CHAPTER IX
BROKE

THE WORLD'S FAIR was wonderful. There were hundreds of people I knew, and through them I met many more.

Mrs. Grace Greene Alexander (mother of Mrs. Theodore Roosevelt, Jr.) took me under her wing and taught me to use "I say!" rather than just "Say!" I wonder how she would have sung the Star-Spangled Banner? "I say, can you see, et cetera?"

Miss Greene, "Lady" Grace's sister, arrived with Helen Benedict. I became their official chaperone.

Richard Harding Davis was in hot pursuit of Miss Benedict; hence, I was thrown in constant contact with him. Through my yarns of Central America he first became interested in Latin America. I gave him the underlying plot of "Soldier of Fortune," which was a personal experience, only without the "love interest," as I was only a kid.

The story, in tabloid, was that elections were coming up in Guatemala. These were always farces, where the man in power just marched the army around in circles; voting them as many as ten times; therefore, the man in power always won re-election.

But this time it was a little different. They had had enough of the present regime. A young man named Refino Barriose had become very popular. He was the nephew of a former president, who had been assassinated, making room for the present incumbent, who had been third vice president; also, he had been lucky enough to be in the Capital and able to fortify it against the first and second vice presidents.

Barriose had married an American girl, and one night she came to the Legation sobbing out the tale of her husband's arrest. Father was busy and there was no one else available, so he called me to him, and said, "Addison, will you see what Señora Barriose wants. And do anything you can for her, my son."

Feeling that this gave me full authority, I took it upon myself to straighten things out.

I entered Señora's carriage and drove down to the palace with her, and ordered the president to sign a release from prison for Barriose, whom they had planned to shoot at daybreak, as an insurrectionist.

Señora had told me that they had no proof of Refino's being implicated in any insurrection, but that it was a little ruse for eliminating a candidate.

Knowing the palace guard and the layout of everything, I had had the coachman drive into the inner court and park directly in front of the president's private office.

My love affair with the president's daughter had given me a complete knowledge of the run of things.

Señora leaned back in a dark corner, while I went in to make my demands, and no one knew she was there.

The president was much surprised, and shocked, to hear of the arrest, and said he would see that Barriose would be released in the morning. I knew that "in the morning" he would be as cold as a bottle, so I insisted that he should write out a release and give it to me, and I would take it within an hour to the prison. This, he finally did, and bowed me to the door of the carriage.

He had beckoned a guard to his side, and as I was getting in he said something to him in an Indian dialect, which I did not understand. I leaned out to bid the president á Dios, and direct the coachman to drive to the Barriose house, which was in the opposite direction from the prison.

As the horses started up, Señora clutched my arm. "Did you hear what he told that soldier?"

I answered that I had not understood, and she hastily told me that she spoke the dialect well, and that the president's instructions were to hasten to the prison and countermand the release, which I held so proudly in my hand.

I leaned out to the coachman, as we reached the gates, and told him to drive at once to the prison.

We got Refino out, and passed the messenger several blocks from the prison.

The bluff had worked, and I got them into Mexico.

After three months at the fair, absorbing architecture, and life in general, I went on to New York to visit Henry.

He, always having secretly loved God, naturally hated war; and so on the eve of graduation from West Point had resigned and gone into the Episcopal Seminary in New York.

It was a lovely old place, covering a couple of blocks, starting at Ninth Avenue and Nineteenth Street.

I was quite religious myself, and enjoyed the atmosphere thoroughly.

My life befitted a guest of the monastery, with the exception of one slip perhaps.

I had written to Peter, at Jamestown College, and received a telegram that he was coming up to see me.

I met him in the Old Holland House with two other boys. We dined in Peter's suite, where champagne was the principal course, and went to see Hoyt's "Trip to Chinatown."

At the end of the second act, which was laid at the Cliff House, a man stumbled in, all out of breath, and when asked what was the matter with him, said that the bottom had dropped out of the hack, and that he had run all the way.

As we went out on the sidewalk for the entire act, we saw an old four-wheeler and decided to charter it and see whether it really could be done.

Peter and his friends tried it first, and laughed with delight. Finally, they let me try, and when I got my feet on the street they cheered the driver to greater speed, and wouldn't let me up.

It seemed as though they had run me halfway around the town, when we turned into Fifth Avenue.

It was a drizzly, slushy night, and we were a mess from the knees down.

The Waldorf was new, and the chic place for supper. Peter ordered the coachman to draw up to the curb. He opened the door just as we were passing a lamp post. There was a horrible, ripping crash, as the door tore off, with half the side of the hack.

This started an argument with the owner, and he cleaned us as clean as snowbirds, in settlement. The argument had lasted long enough to have our straw hats melt in the rain, and this added to our bedraggled appearance.

We didn't have five cents among us, and I was for going home. Peter was insistent that we have supper at the Waldorf.

"How are we going to pay for it?" I queried. "I'll show you," he said, sidling up to an old man getting out of a carriage with a pretty girl. He mumbled something to the dotard, who reached in his pocket and slipped Peter something, and moved on into the hotel. It was five bucks. So we all took our beats, and in almost no time had made a collection of nearly twenty dollars. This was enough, so we strolled, in and as no one looked kindly upon us we took the best table and sat down.

There was silver, linen, glass, and a great floral decoration. There were covers for eight. Head waiters whispered together, but no one came near us for a while. I was sitting with my back to the beautiful, red plush portières, and instinctively I knew by the clatter of the curtain rings that it was the bouncer.

The others left more or less quietly, but I had gotten my hand tangled up in the tablecloth, and in some way landed on Thirty-third Street, with a paper chase of wreck and ruin in my wake, with the tablecloth still in my hand. Police whistles were blowing, and a black carriage backed up. It had side benches and no windows, and in state we were driven off to the old Tombs.

With the money we had so pathetically begged we were able to bribe a policeman to go to the Holland House (where Peter had unlimited credit). We got the manager over, and although he knew the captain on duty, he couldn't get us out, for at this time there was no night court.

We got permission to have supper sent in, and they transferred us from a cell to the captain's office.

It's the only jail I have ever been in where the service was good. We had a marvelous supper and three cases of champagne, and got half the faculty drunk.

The next morning, sadder, wiser, and feeling like hell, we were led into police court and fined ten dollars apiece, and costs, which the hotel charged to Aunt Annie as C. O. D. packages.

It's funny that I very seldom got in jail, except when I was with a Martin.

When I returned to California I found that father was very ill, and that the family were all at Stags Leap.

He died on his sixty-seventh birthday, and was buried on my twenty-first birthday. Needless to say, I did not get the usual gold watch.

His long absence in Central America and his prolonged illness put finances on the rocks.

He left a lot of real estate, but taxes ate most of the revenue. It was all willed to Mama Mizner, and I never took a cent again. The income would have been ample for mother, but the rest of the family had a little way of "borrowing" from her.

She went back to live in Benicia for awhile, where Lan was living.

Wilson had an allowance of one hundred fifty dollars per month; which, then amounted to three times as much in value as now. One day he wired her, "Please send me five hundred at once."

She turned the sheet over and wrote her answer, "Sorry did not receive your telegram."

She had never refused her "Angel Birdie" anything before, and it came as a great shock to him. So he became the guest of a girl by the name of Bell Emmett.

He had grown up to his head by now, and the women thought he was wonderful looking. Six feet and four inches, straight, with big shoulders, and a slim body, and very dressy.

One day he met a friend who said, "Bill, do you want to make a wad of money?"

Wilson was never a "how" man. At once they got down to business.

"You know Catherine Murphy, don't you? The one that married big Black Dan Murphy. Well, she wants to get two or three hundred thousand in life insurance. None of us can reach her. Now, if you can get the insurance, I'll give you four thousand on each hundred thousand."

"I'll go up and see her at once."

Having gotten himself up like "one of those," he rang the bell. The butler showed him into the reception room.

Mrs. Murphy came down, looking exquisite. She was young, slender, and dark.

After a lot of preliminaries, he came to the point.

It seemed that Dan (though very rich) was such a gambler that they thought, as he was in poor health, it would be well for her to take out the insurance on herself, as he had been refused by the companies. They had decided that she better take out two hundred and fifty thousand, and Catherine was delighted to give the business to Wilson.

Everything was all set. Wilson swelled up like a pouter pigeon. He stopped in to tell the great news to Bell. "That means ten thousand for us! We will go around the world," he told her. He left her to go on to the insurance office and see his principal.

The office was full of congratulations. "Now, Wilson, take this application blank, and this (they handed him a small milk bottle), get the first signed, and the other filled. As soon as we get the analysis we will slip you the ten thousand dollar check."

Wilson left, in some embarrassment, and made for the Murphy mansion, with his bottle neatly done up.

Leaving his hat and package in the hall, he spent the afternoon with Catherine. He got the signature, but finally left with an empty bottle. Several times he called, always with the same modest result.

Finally, he and Bell had a consultation—the conclusion was that maybe there was some difference between male and female samples, and that she had better fill the pint.

The next day I called to see Wilson and found Bell with her head in a trunk packing up for the trip around the world. She explained that Wilson had gone to the office to get the check and would be back any minute. So I waited.

In a few minutes the door burst open and Bell, taking her head out of the trunk, said, "When do we start?"

"Start? You summer squash! You couldn't 'wee' your way to Oakland."

The analysis had shown that Bell hadn't got "housemaid's knee," at any rate.

Willis Polk was a genius, only spoiled by having read Whistler's "Gentle Art of Making Enemies." He became a genius at this as well. The result being even less work than ever.

I was working hard, and took architecture very seriously. Willis had a good, though small, library; and wherein I had not been a worker at school, I became an absorbed student. Even through later frivolities, I put in a specified amount of labor at the drawing board, and at all odd moments you could find me with a book in my hand.

Strange to say, I liked good things, and mentally had plenty of "whys" and "whens?" When was the chimney place invented, or what did the barber pole represent; all intrigued me immensely.

Today I don't know a half dozen architects who know anything about history, or why everyone in the Middle Ages had sore eyes from sitting over smoking braziers, or creeping about under the flicker of pitch torches.

My salary was microscopic, and half the time unpaid. So Willis took me in as a partner, and I got first one and then another good job.

It took money and time to get out the plans, so Willis suggested that I keep house with him on top of Russian Hill, to cut expenses.

It was a funny house; one story on the street, and seven stories in the back, for it was built over the edge of a cliff.

We were very poor, and sometimes lived on beans for days. It was a cold winter, and we had no firewood. The man far below at the back had been adding to his house, and had the most luscious pile of lumber you ever saw. Fashioning the tongs and poker into a grappling iron, and with the use of the clothes line, we were able to fish on dark nights and "keep the home fires burning brightly."

One night when our pile was becoming low, and a dense fog was hanging thick, we decided to make a "haul." The first thing we hooked was so heavy that it took three of us to "haul." There was an unusual jerking and swaying to our load, but on we "hauled." There was a queer strangling sound below. We all wondered what it could be, but on we "hauled." Suddenly, a huge bulk came into view. It was a dog house, and the poor dog was dangling from it, choking to death. The others let go; but, not wanting to wake the neighbors, I burned my hands as the rope slid through. It was awful—trying to unhook, but we couldn't leave a trail right to our windows.

"The Lark," a monthly pamphlet, was written on our dining table. Gelet Burgess, Willis Polk, and others, subscribing, while I acted as sub-editor.

But as the "Purple Cow" was more broke than we, and used our telephone (which was at the head of my bed) at all hours of the night, we soon pooled up the drawbridge.

Of course, I was in love. I always was; I was the prize "mush" of the world. Aileen Goad was the beauty of San Francisco. I couldn't work or sleep, and was either in the clouds, or in the dumps.

One night, when something went wrong between us, I decided to commit suicide. I went all the way to the most dramatic spot I could think of—and there I remembered that I had a hole in my drawers. By the time I got home I had forgotten about it. And, besides, I don't think I had a pair that didn't.

CHAPTER X
THE MARTINS

PETER MARTIN had two brothers, Walter and Andy, and a half brother, who was much older, named Downey Harvey. They also had a mother, and an aunt. The two old widow ladies were always called by us Eleanor and Annie.

At this time we had become inseparable, and had formed a pact, that when they were in good standing with the family, I would live with them; but, when they were at "outs" they would move in with me.

The old ladies hated me, but maintained an armed neutrality. We would generally have breakfast with them while they were having lunch, and this irritated them no end. For awhile they would make cutting remarks over our heads to each other, not noticing us any more than if we had been chairs or plates. Try as you might, you couldn't politely break into the conversation.

Andy thought of the scheme of talking dirty among ourselves. When they had to stop us, with great indignation, he would apologize and say, "Mother, I didn't know you and Aunt Annie were here." That broke the old ladies of their impudent ignoring, for after that they would start battling the minute we sat down.

One day the blessing was hardly over when Annie said, "Peter, what time did you and the boys get in this morning?"

Peter stretched a little and shrugged his shoulders. "I don't know exactly," he said, "but it must have been about twelve."

"Twelve, indeed! I heard the dog barking at six-thirty."

"Very well, Auntie, if you would rather believe the dog than me, I can't say any more."

With great dignity he put down his napkin and left the table. We all filed out after him. They stayed with me for a week, until auntie's letter of apology included largess.

So we moved back, without too much meekness.

One evening we were having a fine time upstairs at the "Poodle Dog" in a private suite. We all decided to stay and have dinner. Our acquaintances in the feminine world were divided into two groups; the girls of the best families, and the girls of the best houses. We were entertaining this evening the latter. Andy remembered that we had promised to be home for dinner, so we were all asked for a new excuse. As far as we knew they were all used up. Andy, with a sudden bright look, went to the telephone and rang the number.

"That you, Mother? We are out on Billy Whitier's yacht, and he thinks it is too rough to send us ashore, as the rowboat is so small he thinks it might swamp. He says we can stay all night if it doesn't get calmer."

"That's good, Mother dear. We will be careful; but, of course, we will try it if you really want us to. You know how sick we will all be in a little while. Goodnight." We were.

One day Andy hurried in. "Get a move on. I'll help you throw some things in a bag."

"What's the matter?" I inquired.

"We've got a private car, and going to Los Angeles. We have to catch the five o'clock boat—hurry up."

He didn't give me much time for questions, and we hurried off.

On the boat we met Annie and Eleanor, two pyramids in crêpe. I turned to look at Andy and noticed for the first time he was in black—so were Downey, Peter, and Walter. I drew Andy aside. "Uncle Downey has 'cooled off.' We will have a lot of fun at the funeral," he whispered.

We arrived next morning, and had time to fix up a bit for the long and trying services. It was far from fun. By eight-thirty that night we had finished dinner in Mrs. Martin's sitting room at the hotel.

Downey Harvey, being the oldest, made the first move, and said he had such a bad night on the boat that he thought he would go to bed.

"Why don't you send the boys to bed too, Aunt Annie, so you and mother can get a little rest."

It worked, and in a minute we were bolting down the hall. Downey knew where we could get a good glass of beer, so we hurried off down the street, and dived down some steps into a music hall. A big German waiter, carrying a tray of brimming steins above his head, was just ahead of us.

"You wouldn't think I could kick that tray, would you?" said Downey.

"I bet you five dollars you can't," wagered Peter.

Wham! The beer went hurtling over all those for a radius of twenty feet. Everyone was cursing, and a riot followed, with everyone wanting to lick the waiter.

Under cover of the excitement we crawled out, but they pinched Peter, and it cost fifty dollars to get him out. This was difficult, as he had given another name; and, of course, we didn't know what it was.

It was nearly eleven when we were able to go on romping. Being in such deep mourning, we did not want to be conspicuous; for out of respect for the dear departed, who had been a governor of the State, we thought it best to frequent places where "secrecy" was the watchword.

About four in the morning we passed a vacant lot where a tired looking old horse was looking over the gate. Andy was always tender-hearted and thoughtful. He knew at once that he wanted a drink, so we took him to the next saloon and bought him a bucket of beer. As he still seemed thirsty, we bought him two or three more.

It did not seem to agree with him after a while, for he sat down in the middle of the floor and refused to get up. He had such a silly expression on his face, Andy sat down alongside him and tried to feed him pretzels, but he wouldn't eat them. About five-thirty a milkman came in and accused us of stealing his horse. As he had a cop with him, all the pleas of belonging to the humane societies wouldn't go. He insisted that we were horse thieves. We were marched off to jail, in a body. This left us without anyone to bail us out.

The Los Angeles' hoosegows of forty years ago were very poor, and the service was almost nil. We were slapped into a big cage with a lot of common drunks; but our indignation impressed no one.

They had searched us, and taken everything we had, at the desk; so there was no chance of bribery. Finally, Peter got the eye of a kind-faced civilian and promised him worlds unconquered if he would go to the hotel and get the manager to bail us out. He was to swear the manager to secrecy, of course. But, he forgot to swear the envoy, who turned out to be the police reporter for the biggest paper in town. To our horror, as we reached the hotel we heard the newsboys crying, "All about the drunken orgy of the Martin boys! Nephews of the late Governor Downey, land in jail!"

The horrors of that day! We spent the time waiting on the old girls, answering telephones, guarding the doors, delecting newspapers—it was horrible.

Back in San Francisco we were very good for a couple of weeks, busy making character.

It couldn't last long, and little by little we drifted back into late hours.

One morning at lunch (breakfast) the girls were unusually stiff. With icy hardness Eleanor addressed Peter, "My son, you are twenty-four years old, and you ought not to keep your brothers out all night. You should be an example to them."

He always had been, but not in the way she meant.

"You should have something to do. I have spoken to Mr. Crockett, the head of the gas works (she owned controlling interest), and you are to report to him right after lunch and he will set you to work."

Peter looked meek and compliant, and said he thought that would be fine—he was tired of loafing.

A month flashed by, and again we were at our midday meal.

"Peter, you are looking terrible. I don't see how you can live, working all day and out all night—it's awful."

"Mother dear, I haven't wanted to complain, but the work is very hard."

"What do you mean—what is your job?"

"They made me gas light inspector, and I can't come home until every light in town is put out."

The old girl was full of indignation and spluttered with sympathy.

After lunch we all moved to my place, before she found that Mr. Crockett had never seen Peter.

We were all more or less indebted socially to the ladies of the first houses; so, when Annie and Eleanor announced that they were going to Los Angeles on the following day to see about brother Downey's estate, we decided to snap a party.

We hired two bands and invited everybody we shouldn't have known.

At four-thirty we escorted the old girls to the five o'clock boat and Walter crossed with them to put them on the train. Peter, Andy, and I hurried back to the house to get ready for the festivities, instructing the caterers, seeing about the wine, et cetera.

At seven Walter returned to report that the girls had been locked in their stateroom and were on their way.

The guests were invited from ten on for the next three days.

At nine-thirty a carriage stopped at the gate, and Eleanor and Annie got out. There had been a washout on the railroad and no train would get through for several days.

The horrors of the next few days will never leave me. Night and day we had to be on guard to keep guests from breaking in, for everybody thought it just a "Mizner-Martin" joke. One old madame got mad and I had to throw her down; she was getting the better of me when she saw a policeman, which saved my life, but not my suit.

The old ladies never got on to it, but they began to realize that the boys weren't preparing for the priesthood, so they were shipped east to college.

CHAPTER XI
A CHANGE OF LIFE

FINANCES WERE in a desperate state, when Señora Barriose arrived in town. I had heard that Barriose had marched back across the border, gathered up an army against Barillas and become president, and then made himself Dictator.

Just getting him out of prison; hence, saving his life, and helping him over the Mexican border had been such a trivial thing that I had never thought of gratitude.

Señora sent for me and laid her proposition before me. The old palace, which only covered a block, had become inadequate and they had decided to build a two million dollar one. I was to be the architect, draw the plans, and superintend it, going to France, besides, to get the furniture. The fee was to be magnificent. She gave me the contracts to sign, so they could catch the boat leaving next day. It would take two weeks to reach Guatemala and two weeks to get back—a little over a month. I was to receive my retainer of twenty-five thousand dollars in gold.

I didn't know there was that much money in the world. I went drunk with excitement. I ordered a tropic trousseau, gave dinners, and sent flowers—all charged, of course.

Four or five weeks had passed like a shot. The Panama boat steamed in through the Golden Gate and I rushed down to the dock to meet it.

Barriose had been assassinated the night before the boat had left Guatemala.

So that was that!

I dropped into William's office to see if I had heart failure, or whether it was collection trouble. He prescribed mountain air at once. He had a gold prospect at Delta, in the northern Sierras and three men had started a tunnel; why didn't I go up there for awhile; I could get in condition, and not be hounded for awhile; and when the mine poured out millions he would fix things up.

Delta—Oh, God! One saloon and general store, and a flag station.

It was Sunday noon, clear and sharp. Mike slouched out of the saloon and greeted me without introduction.

"Hello! Bill's brother, hey?"

We shook hands.

"Them thar hands is too soft, but after three or four weeks you'll be able to scratch matches on the palms."

He leered at my shining shoes, and ran his eye up the crease of my trousers to my vest.

"That's a grand watch chain. Anything on the end of it?"

It was a five-mile walk up the gulch. I was as soft as mush, and I sweated along with my two bags. He never suggested taking one, and I learned then and there that for the first time I was out on my own.

The cabin was up a canyon, next to a crystal and icy brook. There was a big mud and stone chimney at one end of the shanty. We entered. Two awful men said, "Hello," from their bunks, and subsided to nurse their heads. From the looks of things there had been a big time the night before, and the maid hadn't cleaned up yet.

"You get the top bunk on that side," Mike said, pointing to the right-hand corner. "Bill said to buy you some blankets—they're up there." They were the only clean thing in the cabin.

"Who cooks and cleans up?" I inquired.

"We do, and now you can take your turn."

There was a rickety table and some boxes. I sat down.

"What time is it by that gold chain of yours?" Mike sneered. I timidly drew out my watch and told him it was nearly two.

"Can you cook?"

"I don't know—I never tried."

The pots and pans were thick with grease, and everything was filthy. Mike stirred up the dying fire and started to warm over a pot of beans. I gathered up the dirty dishes in one of the boxes, found a cake of soap, and went to the stream. With the aid of some coarse sand I got some of the grime off things, and laid the table.

I was ravenously hungry, but things weren't very tempting.

I had worn all the polish off my nails; my shoes were filthy; and my trousers baggy.

After lunch I tried to clean up a bit. No one suggested helping. I brushed off the dirt floor and sprinkled it with water. But, what was the use, I was housed with three untamed animals.

In the afternoon a man came up with a couple of pack animals, with weekly supplies. I hung up the hams and bacon and stored things away as best I could.

For dinner I fried some ham, boiled some potatoes, and ate like a hog.

Next morning, stiff and cold, I got up and built a roaring fire. The three unwashed finally stirred and came to get warm. By seven we were at the mine. My first two or three days nearly killed me; but I stuck, and got used to it. I was young and as strong as an ox; and just as stupid—saved only by Mama Mizner's sense of humor.

We drilled, set our sticks of dynamite with fuses, set them off, and ran, counting the shots to see if they had all exploded, and then came back to clear out the debris, and wheel it to the dump.

We were on the vein, with solid rock formations on either side so we did not have to timber much. We were drifting a tunnel and, thank God, not sinking a shaft, where we would have had to hoist out our blastings.

Every day was like every other day, and I got used to it.

At night the arguments were so ignorant they were splendid.

Mike was born in Ireland; Otto in Sweden; and Herman in Germany; and I in the "lap of luxury."

We got on fine for three weeks, when someone imported a keg of whiskey. We had had a fog that hung in the pines like a Japanese print. With the other supplies, a box of dynamite had arrived. Mike thought it had better be stored in the cabin, as the trees were dripping so.

A few days before Herman had shot a deer (out of season), and we had a big haunch roasting in the pot.

It began to look like a nice Saturday night, until they tapped the keg. About midnight things were roaring. Otto was sitting on the edge of his lower bunk, and Herman on the upper one dangling his legs. Some new argument broke out and Herman brought down both heels on Otto's forehead, knocking him senseless. Mike called Herman some filthy names, and he leaped from his perch for Mike shouting, "I'll kill you!" Fortunately, he hit the table and together they crashed, giving Mike time enough to get out the door, grabbing the rifle, which had a belt of cartridges hanging to it, as he went.

Almost instantly he started shooting through the cabin. Once he struck the wall just an inch above the box of dynamite. Herman had crawled under the bunk. The shots were now coming from the end of the shack away from the door. There had been a moment's lull, showing that Mike had reloaded. I caught up a pick handle and opened the door a crack. It was pitch black. I stole to the corner and saw the spout of the rifle, and did a gigantic swing with my bludgeon, and brought down Mike cold. Then I sat down and cried. Not because I thought I had killed, but just out of nervous excitement. It has always been like that with me; I never get nervous going into battle—it's the coming out.

For the next few days I was nurse, surgeon, and drudge.

I was seeing the upper sediment of life—who the hell would think there would be so many dregs yet to come.

Draining the keg on the ground, I went in to Delta to get medicines and bandages, and found a letter from William. He wrote that Wilson had just returned from Alaska.

Wilson had gone into the Yukon during the summer with Edgar, who was the head of the Alaska Commercial Company for that district. Wilson had only stayed a few days there and sneaked out to get his girl. Edgar had sworn him to secrecy about a gold strike on Bonanza, as they were not sure, and they didn't want a rush until the company could open a store and supply food.

He also told me the assays on the Delta mine were not good enough to warrant going ahead with it at present.

I was to close it down and join Wilson and himself on the four o'clock train to Seattle on Saturday, and then on to the Klondike.

The old pioneer blood of the tribe rose in my brain, and I was panting to go. At least I'd get out of Delta.

CHAPTER XII
THE FIRST LAP

I HAD STARTED on my journey to the Klondike. Wilson was full of it. "Gold by the ton, mosquitoes by the billions, rapids, waterfalls, mountain passes"—my head buzzed. After an hour in the smoking compartment I asked for William and found he was to meet us in Seattle with the "outfit."

He and Wilson had worked out an ice boat. We were to cross Chilkoot Pass, cut down a couple of trees, and with the runners, were to make a boat that would sail into the Klondike over the frozen river, in three days at the longest.

"Go into the car, section six, and kiss the girl sitting there," instructed Wilson.

Lew Wyman was loitering over me, so I merely took a peep.

"Who is she?" I inquired.

"Just a friend. She's going as far as Seattle. She's a peach."

Seeing my timidity, he dragged me along and introduced me to Rena Fargo. She was a lot of fun, and we all laughed at Wilson's experiences together. The first call for dinner brought me to my feet. I hadn't had a decent "square" for a month.

I crawled into my berth early, and thought it the most comfortable thing in the world, although it was a couple of inches too short.

At Seattle we found a telegram from William, saying the skates for the ice boat hadn't come and for us to go on to Juneau, in Alaska, and he would meet us there.

It was late November, 1897. On the twenty-ninth we left on the *Topeka* for Juneau.

It was a miserable, rainy day, and utterly cheerless; no one to bid you God speed, or wave a hand. We were well away from the pier when the door to Wilson's cabin opened and Rena stepped on deck. I had not seen her in Seattle, and had forgotten her, in the excitement. Being a Mizner, I showed no surprise.

Only once were we in the open sea. The rest of the time was in calm water, behind beautiful islands. Mighty forests of huge trees marched down to the edge of the water on both sides. The trip was mild and lovely.

Juneau was a little town of three or four thousand, supported by the huge Treadwell mine, where several thousand men worked, coming to town to spend their wages. There were two or three gambling places, a dance hall—"Honky Tonk," a church, and plenty of saloons.

We stayed at the only place that called itself a hotel, and settled down to wait for William.

Rena went to work in the "Honky Tonk," and to save expenses, shared a room with Wilson. It began to leak out that they had known each other for a long time. It seems that when Wilson ran away, because Mama Mizner wouldn't send him the five hundred, he had sung in the same dump with Rena. Even then I didn't get it, being the prize sap of the world. Even now I thought she had come to Juneau to work and was going no further.

Juneau was wide open. It had snow streets, on which we used to coast. I had never seen snow at close range before, and when I started to steer the long sleds (we were to use on the trail) I was not a success. Once I lost control and ran right through a restaurant, piling up chairs, tables, and diners on top of us. As the service was tin enamel, and no one was hurt, I only had to pay for repairing the doors.

I was not unfamiliar with "honky tonks," for we used to make sallies on them in San Francisco, on what was known as the "Barbary Coast."

The Cremore was my favorite. Of course, you know that; the girls who sing, dance, or otherwise entertain on the stage (there are no men), later "rustle" the boxes, making the audience (of ninety-nine percent men) buy beer for them at one dollar per bottle—the girl getting a brass check for each bottle she sells, which she "cashes in" on her way home for fifty percent of the sale.

This particular night the announcer came out on the stage and in a very clear voice said, "Miss Nancy Lee will now sing 'Down in the Vale.'"

A drunken sailor parted the Nottingham lace curtains of his upper box and leaned far out. In quite as clear a voice, he shouted, "That dirty old — —. What I know about her." And he told in the most unchivalrous terms.

"Nevertheless, Miss Nancy Lee will sing 'Down in the Vale,'" said the announcer.

She did, with great success, for that was the day of sentimental ballads, and the sadder the better.

The first night I went to the Juneau Palace Rena sang "You would not dare insult me, sir, if Jack were only here." Jack turned out to be her brother and the best friend of the insulter, and everything turned out well in the song. The ballads were always virtuous; in fact, I have never heard a dirty word or even an innuendo from one of these girls.

Rena was little, slender, and very dark, probably of Spanish descent, as her temper showed later.

One night I was in a box with a girl named Myrtle. "See that big red-headed sap? He's from New York and thinks he is pretty good. He's one of the directors of the Treadwell, up here for a look around. Have you even seen the 'short change'? I'll show you; he is headed this way, and he is kind of stuck on me."

Sue leaned out of the box and beckoned him in, promptly sitting on his lap and encircling him with her arms. She made him buy her a bottle of champagne. He hauled out a bundle of green that would have choked a cow, and peeled off a hundred dollar note.

"Oh! What a pretty bundle the naughty big mans has dot," she said, in baby talk. It always made me sick at my stomach. "Let baby tount it for papa," she said, taking the wad caressingly away, as she pouted, "One, two, twee, four," et cetera. When she said, "One tousand," my eyes popped; but, she went on. Being perfectly sober, and with my eyes peeled in preparedness, I didn't see how it was done. I only knew that she tried to pass me about half the wad; but, being new at the game and not prepared to be an accomplice, I pushed it away, and it dropped to the floor.

The big sap was so engrossed in his "mauling" that he didn't notice anything, so Myrtle kicked the roll under his chair. In a minute or so she said, "Big man mustn't get too rough," and she slipped to the floor. When he picked her up, with apologies, the money was no longer there.

"How's that done?" I later asked Wilson. "I watched her like a hawk and she counted every note correctly, one by one. I saw the end of each one."

"No wonder the family always called you and Edgar the dubs of the tribe. Didn't she count them twice, and say that she thought she had made a mistake? Well, before she counted the second time she had doubled up enough to make up for what she had taken out, and that made each bill doubled count twice. She was just watering the stock, that's all. She is a great little banker. Why don't you hook up with her?"

I don't know whether it is cowardice or stupidity, or whether it has been watching those that have tried both, that has made me decide that "Honesty is the safest policy."

William had arrived with the outfit, and we were all a-buzz looking it over.

The snow was still rather wet and great avalanches boomed down the mountain sides from time to time. The older inhabitants advised us not to venture into the mountains until the thermometer had dropped below zero.

But we were all rearing to go, so we took the first boat for Dyea. The Linn Canal is an arm of the sea running seventy miles directly into the mountains. Great turquoise blue glaciers, high up between cliffs, urging their way to the sea, caught the slanting rays of the noonday sun. It was beautiful. The gorge of the canal lay in deep shadow even at twelve o'clock noon.

At three o'clock the engine slowed down, leaving only enough power to steer with. Even now we were speeding along faster and faster, for the overhanging cliffs were flashing by. The tide would be high at five-thirty. We would arrive at three-thirty, unload the ship, and go back on the tide at six-thirty. All this I did not understand, even when we dropped anchor three miles from the tiny village alongside a big flat boat.

There was feverish haste. We all had to help unload from the steamer to the barge, amid shouts of "Hurry, the tide is turning." Everyone was making a panicky finish. The steamer pulled up her anchor and swung down the canal.

We were standing still on the barge. Why? In an hour we were gently grating on the bottom. In twenty minutes we were high and dry, and wagons were coming out on the sandy bottom to get us.

The tide had dropped thirty feet, and as far as the eye could see the Linn Canal was empty.

We got ashore about ten o'clock that night, with the first relay; consisting of tent, stove, sleeping bags, and a little food. Although it was full moon, reflecting on the snow, giving twice its usual light, it was hard getting up a tent you had never met before, chopping wood, getting the stove together for the first time, and other things, that were to become a drill later. It was nearly three in the morning before we settled down in our sleeping bags and tried to sleep.

By now there were six in our party: Morie Nye, a man named Taylor, Rena, William, Wilson, and myself.

"Were Wilson and Rena married? Or was it better if they were not?" I tried to keep myself awake worrying about it; but I was so doggone tired I couldn't.

We were ashore, ready to attack an uncharted, unmapped country; and after all, that was really the thing that mattered.

CHAPTER XIII
DYEA

THE RUSH had begun; for the news of the "strike" on Bonanza had leaked out; at least to all the neighboring miners and roughnecks. At first there were not many from the outside, mostly miners from the Treadwell, old trappers and prospectors.

At first we were the only "Chee Charkers" (newcomers) and we were well named. I was more in training than the rest, and paid for it. Wilson was the leader, having been over the trail before; and that's all you can say about that. Rena, an ornament; and Nye "not all there in the hat," made the work that much more. William, who had spent several years in his office, could make us laugh but was no help. So the manual labor was graciously bestowed upon Taylor and me.

Like all Mizners, we could gather a crowd; and from the tent came peals of laughter all day and half the night. I could hear it while I chopped wood outside.

The thermometer had gone up and heavy rain had come down, which left no snow and we couldn't sled. So there we sat for three weeks.

I have before me a stack of letters from me to my mother. Perhaps I had better quote from them.

"Dyea, December 25, 1897.

"William is a little lazy yet, but that will soon be taken out of him. Wilson makes a good leader, now that he is on the trail. Taylor is a hard worker, and intelligent, never saying a word. Nye is the butt of all jokes, as he is positively feeble-minded. You cannot vex him in the slightest."

"December 27, 1897.

"Great guns! What an eye opener this trip has been. You know that I am not exactly 'green,' but if you could hear the schemes that your neighbor has for skinning you, you could not believe your ears. They all seem so palpable and stupid, and people discuss their schemes just as though they were honest.

"There is a black-haired man here who is cooking up a plan which will leave us tentless; but, as we are leading him on, I haven't the slightest doubt that we will come out on top. I hope we will 'do him good.' He has lent us his horses and done everything he could to get in with us, and when we leave he will be the possessor of one of the old trunks that William was going to cut up for kindling."

(I left out any references to Rena, of course, in my letters to Mama Mizner.)

The scheme referred to was one devised by Mr. Betterled (the black-haired man). He had got Wilson mixed up with Edgar, and had heard that Wilson had very rich claims on the Klondike. He had been on the coast a couple of years, doing freighting, and had several horses. It wasn't long until I got on to the fact that he was sneakingly making love to Rena.

Here was the proposition:

Rena was to get Wilson to put all his claims in her name; Betterled was to do everything to be friendly and helpful, to keep down any suspicions that otherwise might creep up. When Rena had the deeds nicely tucked away, then he and Rena would be secretly married, and "scram."

It was the one time in my experience of these girls that the word "marriage" did not hypnotize. Instead of falling for this, Rena told us all.

We put the works on Betterled and took all we could get, leaving him flat for Sheep Camp.

This was farewell to the law, and we left Ulysses S. Smith standing under his sign, which read:

"United States Commissioner."

He was a tall, slight man, with bushy, black whiskers. Although it was many years before I was to see him again, we heard from the law before we got over the border.

Betterled had taken our outfit to the mouth of the canyon ("for nothing but friendship"), and left us there, to struggle up the crack in the cliffs to Sheep Camp. The bitterness of that struggle through the gorge of seven miles was awful. Sometimes the cliffs rose five hundred feet, with a width of less than six feet at the bottom, through which had to pass a trail and a raging torrent.

We thought this was the worst that could happen, and struggled on; wet, freezing, and torn, to Sheep Camp. Had we known then that the thirty miles we had come was as nothing as to what was yet to come, we might have thought of turning back. But, we were all the sons of pioneers and didn't know the word "quit."

The greatest gift God has given me is to forget the horrible things, remembering only the funny ones. I have just made the mistake of looking over my old letters to Mama Mizner—and a shadow is across my vision—let me shove the letters aside, and wander on from memory.

We settled down at Sheep Camp. Six miles beyond was the Chilkoot Pass, which shut the end of the little canyon like a gate. We pitched our tent at the junction of the river and the trail.

The trail bowed out in a half circle to the "Big Tent Saloon." The creek ran straight like a string. Again the trail crossed the stream and ran up and up.

There were two or three shacks and a couple of hundred tents straggled along the floor of the gorge, and that was Sheep Camp. Nothing with more brains than a sheep would ever have camped there. There were no dance halls, gambling joints, and no "ladies" plying their ancient profession. It was just a beehive of energy, with everyone working to get their stuff to the top of the Pass.

After a few weeks at Sheep Camp, we ran into a man from San Francisco named Gamble. He had a partner named Louie Jonkie, whom we dubbed "Och Gott Louie." They wanted to join our party and as Louie was a good cook, we all voted for it, and they threw in with us.

After dragging your stuff on a sled up a mountain trail, you "cached" it at the foot of the pass and went back for more. One's stores were sacred, and woe unto him who laid a finger on them.

Back and forth for weeks. Day after day was the same, until it was all deposited. Then it had to be carried on one's back up the steps cut in the icy wall to the summit.

William and Wilson resented the strength, or rather the energy, of those that carried the big loads, and secretly hated Taylor and me for making four trips per day, with a fifty pound sack on our back, up two thousand feet in the air.

They would discuss for hours, ways and means of having made a huge papier-mâché stove, apparently weighing several thousand pounds, and filling it up with balloon bags and prancing up and down the pass, to spite the "dumb strength" of the persevering string of ants toiling up that forbidding wall.

But, finally, everything was on top of the pass, and we were arguing as to what part of our "home" could be best spared. It would take several days to get it all over the summit. Which part to move first was the question.

Finally, William and Wilson decided on a week's rest; though I never could find out what had made them tired, so they went out for a stroll.

At lunch time Nye came back with a huge hunk of calf's head cheese, which we all fell on at once. I had finished half of mine when William, pointing at my plate, said, "Look! What's looking up at Addison. It's the calf's eye—doesn't it look sad?"

I bolted out of the tent and snapped my lunch in the snow, and came back and threw myself down on the sleeping bag. I felt awful, so the joke had been a huge success.

They all fell to discussing the theft of a huge "cache" which had been left near the foot of the summit. Although its loss had been discovered ten days before, it was still the one absorbing topic; for if the thieves were discovered it meant death for them from the hands of a miners' meeting.

The "cache" had belonged to four men; one of them was a fellow by the name of Mead. They had all decided to wait a month or two, going back down the trail to make some money helping others through the canyon. With their earnings they had bought a few additions, and when they came to deposit them with the rest of the "cache," had found everything gone.

To rob a man was to deprive him of his food and, in theory, was the vilest kind of murder. The excitement was intense. Nobody's goods were safe. The law, in Ulysses S. Smith, was thirty miles away, and now everyone felt it was up to us all to ferret out the criminals.

Each thinking himself a sleuth, they all left me, intent on no clues whatsoever. About two P.M. (for it was getting dark), a man came to the tent flap and called, "We've got a clue."

I called for him to come in while I slipped on my fur "parkie."

They had seen two men pulling a sled with the name "Mead" badly scratched off; but, as there was a thin coating of ice over it, it made it legible again, like putting varnish over a faded picture.

Taylor and a couple of other men went up as sheriffs of the miners' meeting to arrest the suspects. They found three men: Wellington, Hansen, and Dean.

Taylor took Hansen, and each of the other sheriffs took his man, keeping them apart so they couldn't consult and make up a story together. Wellington was kept in one saloon, Hansen in another, and Dean brought at once to trial in the "Big Tent."

Wilson acted as one of the five judges. Among themselves they appointed a foreman, who had big square whiskers from the eyes down and a black fur cap from the eyes up. If you had turned him upside down, he would have looked the same.

Dean told a good straight story. He met Wellington in a saloon two weeks before. They had served together on the U.S.S. *Oregon*, and Wellington invited Dean to join them and share their big outfit. So they had started on what Dean thought was lawfully their outfit, and moved it all in one day only a mile. A few days later he had come into the tent suddenly and found Hansen emptying flour from their original sacks into ones he had just washed. He said he thought this was odd, but it had been explained away. Dean convinced us of his innocence and he was led away to be held as a witness.

Hansen was then brought in. His story was entirely different. Several people identified him as a man who had been tried some months before and turned back on the trail.

Wellington was then tried and again we heard a new story.

Dean was brought back to confront him. Before he had said ten words, Wellington had whipped out a pistol, and flourishing it, he broke from his captors and with a knife ripped a hole in the tent, and was gone.

I was next to the door and ran out to see him running down the trail, shooting twice over his shoulder to slow up his pursuers. Knowing that the frozen bed of the creek was a short cut to the intersection of the trail, I ran that way, thinking to head him off. More people were running on the trail now, and Wellington and I were coming together where our tent stood.

Whether he was shooting at the crowd behind, or at me, or intentionally shot his own head off, I don't know. I do know, however, that he lunged into my arms, and together we plowed into the tent, a smear of blood went all over the white canvas and froze instantly.

For months on the trail we were known as the crowd that lived in the bloody tent.

Quoting again from a letter to Mama Mizner:

"Lake Linderman, February 14, 1898.

"At about nine-thirty next morning I went up town to see what arrangements the people had made for the burial of Wellington. I found two men who helped me make a coffin. I painted in plain black letters on a head board:

William Wellington
Age 29 years
Died February 11, 1898.

"A gaping crowd filled the streets all morning. By noontime everyone for miles had come in, and pressed to see the corpse, which lay on a board in a little tent.

"The judges had voted a flogging for Hansen; but hardly anyone talked of anything but lynching. They also voted the committee appoint the number of lashes Hansen should get. Wilson resigned, as he did not wish to have this on his conscience. So the other four voted him fifty lashes.

"The next thing was to find anyone who would administer them. An hour or more was spent, when a little dark-eyed man, who was deaf and fifty-five years old, volunteered.

"Hansen (a man of thirty-two, and of the regular Swedish type) was led forth and tied to one of the posts to be used later by the Trolley Company. A great circle was formed, while Hansen was made to take off his clothes to the waist.

"Men climbed to the housetops with cameras, and one woman stood in the first row and laughed and talked as though she were at the play, and asked the prisoner to look her way while she snapped a kodak.

"All this time Hansen showed no concern whatsoever, smiling and eyeing the crowd as a dog might, without the least resentment. In a minute more the flogger stepped forward. A hush fell. He said, 'I do not do this because I like it, but because I like honesty and feel that it must be preserved in this community to save lives.'

"Cheers!

"Then with a gusto that resembled a relish, he grasped the scourge with both hands and let it drive with all his might full across the naked back. Two long purple stripes showing every twist of a rope the size of my finger followed each blow. I sickened and dug out, but stayed on the outside of the crowd.

"At each blow the flogged man crouched in a sort of writhe and leaped into the air three feet. One, two, three, they came until they reached fifteen. I could stand it no longer, and hollered out, "Enough," and pushed forward. The miserable, blood-thirsty crowd tried to shut me up; but, it did not work, and by the time the nineteenth was struck, Wilson and I had gotten conspicuous. William also told the doctor in charge it was enough, and the whipping was over. Dozens cried "More!" but the culprit was freed from his now crazed and exhausted executioner. His inhuman howls, or shrieks, and the whole scene will never leave my mind.

"Although I don't believe in flogging, and this sight made my heart sick; now, that the thing is over, I don't think that he got enough. It was his third offense, and in one case almost cost a man his life, and in this last case turned three men home, disgusted, tired, and without a cent, after saving up two years' money to buy the outfit that Hansen and partner stole in one day.

"Within ten minutes after Hansen's hands were untied he was eating the biggest meal you ever saw. A little later he was marched down the trail by a large posse, with 'THIEF! Pass him along' in large letters on his chest and back. He smoked a pipe quite contentedly, and carried some blankets on his scarred back.

"At three the body of Wellington was placed in the plain coffin and put on a sled. It was snowing heavily, and not more than a score of men trudged on behind.

"Near the trail as you enter Sheep Camp, someone had dug a grave; and there he was lowered. A minister (evidently a Congregationalist or Baptist) made a beautiful two-minute address. The prayer was not so good, but seemed to be meant:

"'But he that maketh haste to be rich shall not be unpunished.'

"As everyone on the trail, including himself, was on a 'gold rush,' I thought this odd."

CHAPTER XIV
FLIGHT

THE DAY AFTER the flogging we were all still in our terrific windstorm all night, and the stove had come down with a crash, early in the blow. I had been peeping out for an hour, and knew I would have to be the one to straighten things out all the time.

Finally, hunger got the better of my spite. I crawled out and gathered up the stove and put it together. It was twenty below and clear as a bell, with a twilight effect, for day did not actually break until nearly noon, and then we would not see the sun. The fire was as lazy as the rest of the expedition, so I made coffee in the frying pan, which had more heating surface.

The bread was frozen to flint, and I started to hack at it with a big East Indian knife, holding the bread in my left hand and whanging at it with my hatchet-like weapon. The knife skidded and I nearly took off my index finger. It hurt like hell, and I started jumping around, shaking my hand hither and yon, until I had the inside of the tent painted as red as the front had been the night before. By this time William came to the rescue, and after taking three stitches, said I wouldn't lose it.

By eleven-thirty we had all settled down again, with a good hot breakfast, when someone came to the tent flap.

Although Wilson was in the earliest stages of dressing; in fact, having nothing on but a very short undershirt, he yelled, "Come in!"

To our surprise, it was Betterled who stuck in his head.

"I serve you all with warrants to appear before Commissioner Ulysses S. Smith for taking part in the flogging, and—"

Wilson sprang to his feet, grabbing up the knife I had just cut myself with, and charged the intruder, chasing him half a mile down the trail.

Added to our other troubles, we felt that we would be charged with assaulting an officer of the law. I should say "attempted," for the erstwhile Lothario was very fleet of foot.

As the law had caught up with us, in the shape of an outraged deputy sheriff lover, whose vengeance would be a bitter pill, we decided to move.

That night we slept in the snow on Long Lake, over the border of the Northwest Territory. We had made eleven miles. Hungry, tired, and cold, we were far above the timber line. The thermometer registered forty-five below in the morning. It was a tedious trip down to timber line, where we might get a fire going. Everyone was cross, and worse, before we got a fire lighted. Each day we would say, "Thank God, the worst is over," and each day the worst was yet to come.

Quoting again from a letter to Mama Mizner:

"We landed on the Summit, in a dense fog and a south wind, at twelve-thirty. By one o'clock we were on Crater Lake. All one has to do in this distance (which is three-fourths of a mile) is to hang on to the back of one's sled by a piece of rope, and you are dragged on your stomach at lightning speed.

"The lake is covered with deep snow. All the way round huge mountains of powdered sugar rise into the clouds, and a heavy mist hangs on the surface of the lake. A half hour after the passing of a sled there is but little trace of the trail; so it was a mighty hard trip, where eight inches to one side or the other sent you up to your armpits in soft snow.

"Crater Lake is a mile; then comes a series of slight rises for three miles, and then two miles of the long lakes. All this was like pulling through sand.

"William, Taylor, and Nye gave out completely. Gamble and I, who were way ahead on the first sled, had to go back and help bring them up. The next mile was a tedious one. We 'cached' our sleds at the first tent, where we cooked some cans of soup on their hospitable stove.

"All this way from Stone House there is a decided line above which not even a tree four inches high, nor any sort of shrub, grows, just as there is a line of high tide.

"It was too dark and no poles to pitch tents with, so Fritz and I spread it out and put the beds upon it. Our clothes were all damp and we had no change. Everyone but Taylor and myself slept well; but, I never closed my eyes. My feet were wet and cold, and by no hook or crook could I get them warm. The thermometer registered thirty degrees below, and by five o'clock I was driven to the strangers' tent and fire.

"In the afternoon we moved on here—a quarter of a mile from the lake. I dug out a hole for the tent, five feet deep, and still we are three feet from the ground, which we will be down to in a couple of days, by the melting process.

"We had a good dinner of rice and bacon, tea, pickles, and soup last night and got thoroughly thawed out.

"This entire letter has been written from three A. M., as I was awakened suddenly with an old fashioned belly-ache, so I got up and lit the fire. I am going to get the breakfast and then I will go back to bed, after my things dry out. The rest will get boughs and wood and make the camp comfortable, as we will be here at least ten days.

"Nine o'clock—thermometer thirty-six degrees below. Tent warm and comfortable.

"With lots of love from us all.

"ADDISON.

"P.S. Enclosed you will find a comic valentine, and as there is no paper lace you will have to consider this letter the real valentine. More love."

Back-tracking to bring up the food, moving on, is a long story within itself, so we will leave that out.

I was check-mated with seven of the laziest idiots ever got together. They were always going off at tangents, and would never "stay put."

Having dragged the paraphernalia for the ice boat, weighing almost half a ton, over the damned pass, it proved an utter failure, as the lakes were covered with snow, and the bloody thing wouldn't budge. William and Wilson insisted on fooling with it an extra week, and then we abandoned it.

Frozen noses, frozen hands, sprains, and fatigue, were the order of the day. For the first time I got busy with both "seam squirrels" and "pants' rabbits," and an argument commenced as to who had them first. The louse prize was never awarded.

One day someone came in to say there had been a strike twenty miles down the river, so they all rushed out, leaving Rena and me to keep house. We decided to get drunk. "How?" was the next question. We had twelve bottles of Jamaica ginger and six of lemon extract, so we made a "punch." We cemented our friendship, but did not commit incest.

I have never been much of a drinker, and I quit on the border line, but Rena kept her word.

I almost died the next day; so I would hate to think how Rena felt.

January ran into February—February slid into March —and now it was April.

We were camped at Sixty Mile river, and months ahead of the mob, even with all our delays; so we settled down to build a boat. The first thing to do was to find four trees properly placed, saw them off about seven feet from the ground, and then place two beams across to hold the log, which was to be whipsawed. A whipsaw is a big-toothed animal about seven feet long with a handle at each end. When you have tugged your log up two skids, and got it in place on top, then you snap a chalk line, top and bottom, so as to get your boards straight, and the same thickness. Then you start, one on top, and one below. The man on top has to be almost a tight rope walker with new back muscles to pull it through. The one below gets just as dizzy looking up and trying to follow the line, while he gets his eyes and mouth full of sawdust. There is little choice between the two, and I changed forty times with Wilson the first day. Each time he argued that I had all the best of it. In fact, we spent most of the time climbing up and scrambling down.

At the end of two hours we had half a board sawed, and he asked me if I was tired. Of course, I wouldn't acknowledge that I was nearly dead. He called me a "big stupid dumb brute," which started a slight unpleasantness.

By the time we had sawed up our first log I could stand off the rest of the camp, taking them one after another. The work had to be done, and why haggle about it?

It came to the felling of our next tree. Wilson had the axe, and I made some suggestions.

"Don't chop so much on that side. We want to fell it towards the sawhorse. You're going to drop it the other way, and then we will have to carry it twice as far."

"Good God Almighty! You know it all, don't you? I'll drop it right alongside the horses."

It dropped, however, in the opposite direction. He picked up a calking iron and hit me over the head. This started an unpleasantness between us that lasted nearly a year.

After I had "come to" enough to get on my feet, I had my say, which was more or less fulsome. William separated us, and from that time on we did not speak.

There is something in Alaska, where work is not equally divided, and people are jammed together, without outside contacts, that breeds dissension. I have known lifelong friends ask for a miners' meeting to help them divide their outfit.

One that comes to my mind, were two fellows who had gone to school together, worked in the same bank, and married sisters, because they couldn't bear to be separated. When it came to dividing the outfit they had twenty sacks of flour. Do you think each took ten? Not at all; they sawed each sack in two and each took twenty halves, which left them without anything to carry the flour in.

We were finishing the boat, gathering pitch from the trees, and soaking our old winter underwear in it, caulking the seams. We were all fighting like mad by this time; and we had plenty of time to do it, for the days were over eighteen hours of sunshine now. The rivers were going out between the lakes. William and Wilson; in fact, the whole bunch were impatient.

I had painted the name "San Francis Company" on the bow and stern, and we launched the boat. Bag and baggage, we embarked, and in three miles we turned a bend and were nearly sucked under a jam of ice, which made a dam across the river. How we ever saved the boat I will never know, but we finally got ashore and made camp.

Each day we did something more foolish than the day before; but, as we all hated each other, anything was better than sitting there scowling and thinking of new things to fight about. "Och

Gott Louie," William and I were still on good terms, but no one else spoke.

Several days later we heard a roar and I made myself very unpleasant by insisting on stopping on the bank and going ahead to see what it was. It was just as well I did. A half mile ahead the river turned abruptly to the right and shot between cliffs fifty feet high and running at such speed that it formed a comber in the middle several feet higher than the sides.

We decked the boat over with canvas, leaving just room enough for William and Wilson and me to stand; and manning the oars, and a sweep, we drifted to the entrance and were picked up by the current and flung onto the crest.

The others walked along the cliffs, hoping to see us go to pieces, but luck was with us. The only incident was when some ducks flew up from a backwater and William yelled for the gun. As we couldn't hear him, we got through. Before we knew it we were out of the canyon and through the Squaw Rapids, bumping several times, and then into the White Horse and dropped about six feet into calmer waters. For the first time in seven miles and fifteen minutes we caught our breath.

Just below was more ice. We waited a few days, helping other boats through and trying to save lives. Many were lost, however, and their bodies never found.

By the time we reached Lake LeBarge the ties had become so strained that William and Taylor bought a canoe from some Indians and loading it on a sled they made off across the lake, which was still frozen, and disappeared.

Wilson and Rena followed soon after. As Nye and Gamble had disappeared earlier, it left "Och Gott Louie," and me to bring on the huge boat with the provisions. At that it was a relief.

There was a tent next to us occupied by a man and his wife. The man seemed a decent sort but I thought the wife a fat, lazy sort.

On the third day of our camp I heard shrieks and groans. The husband rushed out yelling. "She's having it!" and ran wildly down the trail. Being of a curious disposition, I had to see whether she was having a drink or just a spasm, so I stuck my head in the tent. Right then and there I became a wet nurse.

It's lucky I had spent so much time on a farm and had learned that cats couldn't be hatched out.

CHAPTER XV
ON TO DAWSON

THE BABY next door cried so much and besides, after a week's changing and washing, didn't appeal to me. Louie and I decided to move. There was a stretch of water along the shore about fifty feet wide. We cut a couple of green logs and set the stove on them in the bow of the San Francis, piled in our camp, and left "Addison Mizner Olsen," and his parents, behind.

"Och Gott Louie" had been a waiter at the Waldorf in New York and had a fund of waiters' experiences, but his chief attraction was his dried apricot pie.

After harrowing experiences, we got through the lake into the open water.

The Yukon was a great river now. We had passed hundreds of big and little tributaries, each adding to its torrent.

The sun was never out of sight, just skimming around the tops of the saw-toothed mountains, dipping a little closer at midnight, and on again, without ever hiding its red and bloated face.

Whether it was night or day I don't remember; but, we were floating along quietly, with the smoke pouring from our stack. Louie had just baked a pie, brown on all sides, even without a "pie lifter." The coffee pot was steaming and everything was lovely. Even Louie looked picturesque, silhouetted against the sun, with a big hunk of pie in one hand and a tin cup of coffee in the other.

I was in the stern with the sweep under my arm and well "heeled" with food. Nothing could have been lovelier.

The river was broad and sluggish, when we were suddenly caught in a current and whipped around a corner. Right ahead were five enormous rocks sticking up seventy-five feet in the air and a horrible roar. There was no time to choose between which we would go. Throwing my viands into the air, I grabbed the sweep as we rushed sideways for what I thought might be Niagara. Struggle as I might, the best I could do was head for it stern first, for we had been caught in a whirlpool. There was an awful crash. We righted and sped ahead.

We had come through the Five Finger Rapids and I didn't even know it was there. In the great noise I had not heard Louie's screams when the coffee pot had hurtled against his leg. We were in calm water now. I peeled Louie's leg and dressed it like a boiled potato with butter; but, never for an instant did he let go of his pie.

The boat had sprung some bad leaks; besides, the twenty-four hour sun had dried out the boards, so that we had to get to shore for a day or so and make repairs.

No one passed us, which meant the ice must be holding on LeBarge.

So little is known of the Yukon River, even yet, that it may be a surprise to you to hear that some think it is bigger than the Amazon.

Have I impressed you with the fact that there were no maps of this vast inside country or its streams? Few had ever come down the upper waters of the Yukon and none of those ever came up again to report on its terrors.

On the third day a boat came by with five men in her. The craft was called "The Hattie G." Having seen so many rows, I couldn't help wondering how five men all agreed to one woman's name. I wonder if they agreed on anything else?

On we drifted on the bosom of an ever greater river, without much incident, except running on a few rocks and hitting driftwood.

One day we grabbed a man from a rock in the middle of the river. He said he had been hanging to it for days. It may have seemed like it to him, but it was probably only hours. He had lost his partner, outfit, and boat. We searched and called for a bit, but couldn't find any of them, so we went on. The man (Hewett) insisted he had pneumonia, but some of Mama Mizner's cough medicine brought him about in a day or so.

The river by now was winding in more open country and was from a mile to three miles wide, with the current sometimes fast and sometimes so slow you hardly knew you were moving. The trick was to keep out of the backwaters.

On the third day of June we sighted the big landslide back of Dawson, which was visible for many miles. In the late afternoon we drifted past Louse Town, which was then the Indian village on the upper point, formed by the Klondike coming into the Yukon, and there two miles beyond was Dawson.

Our pneumonia patient, completely cured by now, was the most excited. Even Louie came out of his apathy and laid down a huge slice of caffie cooken.

We had arrived in Dawson, after having been on the trip over six months, most of it being from Dyea to Dawson, which is less than six hundred miles.

As I had arrived at Juneau in 1897, I was eligible to join the Pioneer Association, which was called the "Sour Dough Stiffs." The name meant you could bake bread without yeast and were stiff from rheumatism. As it was the only swell club, I joined.

Dawson was afloat with the Spring freshets and a three-day rain. I waded up to the Alaska Commercial Company and inquired for Edgar. He had gone to one of his claims for a day or two with William, but had left me a letter and some money.

It seemed so funny to handle a "poke." It looked like a "moker eclair," made out of moose hide, and was full of small yellow gravel. The letter explained that the sack held thirty ounces of gold dust at thirteen dollars an ounce—three hundred ninety dollars. It was a fortune. After I had bought dinner, consisting of corned beef hash, a hunk of sour dough bread, and a wedge of soggy pie, and found it cost half an ounce, I changed my mind.

Only about fifty people had beat us in that spring and the rest of the fifteen hundred inhabitants were old timers on the river, who had gathered in the last eight months, coming from other camps in the vicinity.

It was Sunday. All the saloons, dance halls, and gambling dumps had closed Saturday night at twelve. It was rather drear. I had hoped to make spritely for one night at least.

Louie had found Gamble and I was alone. I found Edgar's cabin; but, as that was flooded, I dragged my sleeping bag onto the roof and slept there in the rain.

It was a week before the "rush" struck town. In three days Dawson grew to forty thousand, a city of dirty white tents.

As I didn't want to live off Edgar, I started looking for something to do. Through Edgar, who returned on Monday, I got the job of laying out Dawson. I had a crew of men cutting big stakes and trying to drive them into the frozen tundra. As no one had a tape measure, I waded off the blocks and laid off the streets by eye.

We were hardly finished when the first of the flotilla appeared around the bend up river. The Northwest Mounted Police were wonderful in the way they handled the crowds.

The city was quite impressive, from my lot, which I had at once staked out, near the spring on the hillside. The crowd had set up their tents, leaving their outfits in their boats. At once they started running about to stake claims. Most of them expected to find nuggets the size of buns in the streets.

After a few days they settled down and went back to get their provisions. The river had dropped forty feet, and they found their boats hanging like cherries to trees to which they had tied them. Everything had spilled out.

With the bitter cold on the trip we had all grown whiskers to keep our throats from freezing; so when William spoke to me on the street, I did not know him. He was shaved and looked so thin.

"What do you think of it?" I asked him.

"Think of it? It's rotten. I'm for beating it. Stay?" he answered with his queer grin. "Stay until I get strength enough to get out. This is a country for the young, strong, and stupid."

He left on the first boat out, but I stayed.

The Alaska Commercial Company was not only a fur trader, a general store, carrying groceries, hardware, dresses, perfumes, and notions, but it was also the bank. The Company was getting ready to ship four or five millions in dust, so I went to work, alternately, checking and weighing, with Harry Davis. The weighers in the gambling houses and saloons got three ounces per day; but, being one of the family, I was put to work for one.

After the shipment was ready, the first boat up the river arrived. There was great excitement. Everyone gathered on the bank and waited for hours for the *May West* to come in. Her smoke was in view for three hours before she docked.

Friends I had left behind in San Francisco came down the gangplank in store clothes. They had left four months later than we, and travelled with every comfort—hell!

But when you thought it out, the answer was simple. It was less than six hundred miles from salt water over the pass and down to the Klondike. It was fifteen hundred miles from the mouth of the river on the Bering Sea to Dawson. All winter there was twenty feet of ice either way. Besides, no steamer had ever crossed the American border into the Northwest Territory; in fact, no steamer had ever gone further up the Yukon than Circle City, which was four hundred miles west.

The entire white population of the territory was hardly a hundred souls, and these were fur traders, buying their "Russian" sables, ermine, and silver tip, from the Indians, who brought them by dog sled or canoe to the trading station, which was Dalton's post near the coast. There was virtually no one in this vast waste.

Remember, there were no maps, no travelogues, or any data whatsoever on this land that God and man had forgotten. All that anyone knew in civilization was that no steamer had ever reached Circle City before the middle of August. By going over the pass we all thought six hundred miles was an easy jaunt and that we would be well established with rich claims before anyone could get up the river.

Imagine Captain Scott starting out for the South Pole, and you can picture this Yukon desolation more clearly.

Dance halls, gambling places, and every conceivable sort of amusement places were being built. A flood of girls were pouring in, both for the dance halls and for more sordid entertainment.

In a month the place had changed from a struggling little village to a metropolis.

Someone had floated in a sawmill, which hummed twenty-four hours per day. Everything was noise and bustle.

The streets were four feet lower than the wooden sidewalk, to take care of the snow, and now they formed benches from which a continuous fringe of dangling legs hung. The streets had been churned deep in mud and watching the floundering horses was one of the sports.

Every old timer had a team of huskies. To every "Chee Charker" there was an outside dog, anything from a chewawa to a St. Bernard; so the crowd had a dog fight to watch nearly all the time.

I had not seen Wilson as yet; but I knew he was not teaching Sunday school, for the new Catholic Mission burned down the second week after I arrived.

The Alaska Commercial Company had such trade now that I was turned over to the grocery department, and stood behind the counter twelve hours a day.

The hardest customers to deal with were the Indians. A big squaw would get her eye on a certain label on a tomato can and you had to get the right one the first time or she would point it out accurately with tobacco spit, which made tongs necessary.

There was one young square squaw who used to play the harmonica. She would get one hundred pounds of flour on her shoulder, something in both hands, and then swallow the instrument and spit up "Nearer My God to Thee" in static. It was wonderful.

One day I sold her three cases of vanilla extract. That night she and several of her lady friends serenaded me. I had to protect my honor with the toasting fork—Gawd, they were tight.

CHAPTER XVI
STAKING IN SOCIETY

THINGS HAD settled down to some sort of system by August. The "Chee Charkers" had learned that all the gold-bearing claims had been staked before they even heard of the Klondike.

Any chance of a new strike was prospecting in creek beds, drifting down to bedrock, and panning out the last gravel for signs of gold dust. Ninety percent didn't know where to look or how to work, even if they happened to find the right place. There was another way, however, and this I will try to explain.

The gold commissioner's office was in Dawson. When a prospector struck "pay" he drove his stakes (as nearly as he could judge, by stepping it off) one thousand feet apart, up and down the creek. He wrote his name on a clear blaze he had made with his hatchet on a stake and started for the commissioner's office to register a new discovery. The discoverer was allowed two claims. Any new staker who adjoined him was only allowed one claim, or five hundred feet.

Sitting around the commissioner's office, or as near it as they could get, one could always find a huge crowd waiting for someone to come in and register a "strike." Then the stampede. Everybody had a "pack" containing blankets, grub for three or four days, a hatchet, and above all a pencil. The minute the discovery was announced everyone slipped into their pack straps and started to run. It was a marathon that might be twenty miles, or a hundred, and it wasn't the tortoise that won. It was the strong and fleet. The going was awful, for the ground was a foot thick with moss, like you stuff funeral wreaths with to make the flowers last, and this was springy like walking on a mattress. It tired you no end. Up streams, over mountains, and down dales.

Little by little out of two or three thousand men (who had started out on a sprint), you saw them thin out to a fourth the number in the first ten miles. Little by little after that it thinned out more and more.

Being in the grub department of the Alaska Commercial Company, I had made a lot of friends, so I got a tip four hours early about the Dominion Creek discovery.

A fifty-five mile jaunt brought me to the gorge. I found there had been two discoveries about four miles apart on the same gulch the same day. Thirty-six men had already staked down stream from upper discovery, and twelve had staked up stream from lower. This left me only two hundred and two feet, which I staked as "Thirteen above Lower."

I was so tired after my long walk that I didn't light a fire to cook anything; but, after munching some bread and dried beef, I fell down and went to sleep.

I had started from Dawson at five o'clock in the morning, in the blazing sun and a cloud of mosquitos and now it was ten o'clock at night. The sun was beginning to set, for it had gotten tired of just circling. The air was soft and still warm, so I went to sleep in an instant. In half an hour I was nearly frozen to death and was awakened by a crackling sound on all sides. It had dropped fifty degrees and now was about twenty. All the little pools about me were freezing tight. Stiff and chafed I crawled around and gathered up some wood and huddled over the fire until two A.M., when the sun came up. I was able to get a few hours of sleep and then hobble back to Dawson to register my claim.

Being a "mine owner," I resigned as "tin can counter skipper to spitting squaws," and started to work getting an outfit.

All the stuff we had dragged down the river had gone sour from the different drenchings they had got and I had to start from the beginning. Of course, this was only ordering, as I couldn't freight stuff to the mine until the snow came.

When we had crossed the Chilkoot Pass, months before, we found that the Canadian Customs had moved sixteen miles west over the old American border. This created a great deal of talk and we all bragged that Uncle Sam would put them back in their place (which he never has done).

With the Northwest Mounted Police we found nothing but fairness, help, and justice; but the minute you ran into any other official you got nothing but pomposity, ignorance, and impertinence. People said it was all graft. I do not know. Perhaps the government at Ottawa got it all; but, I have my doubts.

We were taxed for everything and when they finally slipped in the one-fifth royalty on the net cleanup of your mine, it was the last straw.

The feeling against the Canadian was growing in leaps and bounds.

It was strange how politicians could be so rotten and hated while an organization like the Northwest Mounted Police could be so splendid, loved, and respected.

In our own country I had heard whispers of, "Do you suppose he might take a bribe?" Here it was different, for they yelled, "How much does he want?"

Less than two percent of the inhabitants were Canadians; excepting, of course, the government and Northwest Mounted Police. The great flood of pioneers that had come in stood ready to develop the country, but the tax of twenty percent gross of all dust to go to "Her Majesty, the Queen" was unbearable, for a man couldn't take a chance on a mine and hire help for fear that the labor, et cetera, would cost more than he took out and he be left in debt, with the old debtor's prison staring him in the face. This the government threatened; although no one knew whether such a law really existed.

You couldn't work a mine alone for you had to have one man down the hole and another on top to hoist out the dirt.

Trying to make a more friendly feeling, a big banquet was given at the Regina Café by the government officials. All the prominent people were invited to pay a huge cover charge. Barney Shagroo was called upon for a speech. He was a clever young Irishman and an English subject.

"I have been asked to represent the mining industry. It seems unnecessary to discuss it, for it is now on the downward course and it is never charitable to kick a thing when it's down. The Canadian government reminds me of the thief—"

There was a yell of "Sit down! Call him to order!" et cetera, from some of the most notorious grafters, while the crowd cheered and applauded. Shagroo, who was still on his feet, continued:

"The gentlemen who interrupted me put a full stop to my sentence where I only meant a comma to be; although that might be a finished sentence in the minds of many citizens, that is not where I was going to end."

The chairman called him to order, and then the riot started. The police dragged out many battered Canadians and a few others.

Barney told us afterwards that the speech was to have been:

"The Canadian Government reminds me of the thief who stole a penny and left a pound, for they are now driving people from this great territory by their exorbitant royalties. These people who had risked their lives and their all to develop the country and finally bring in a much larger income."

There was great excitement throughout the country and much talking. Some wanted to take the government by force, put them on a raft and ship them down the river. Everyone, to a man, was with Shagroo, but no one dared take the leadership.

And with mumbling and grumbling, we went on. Crowds were leaving with every boat. We got up a petition to the Canadian government and another to the people of Ottawa; but, of course, nothing came of it.

Edgar, who had more at stake than anyone else in the country, made me promise to keep out of it. He, like Papa Mizner, was always on the side of law and order. Though I saw him lick sixteen men (with the aid of the bartender) one night in the "Oatmeal Sister's Dance Hall."

It doesn't matter how the row started, but it happened at the bar. The first four or five went down almost instantly. The others rushing Edgar, who by now had his back against the bar. As they rushed at him they tripped over the fallen ones. As they came he would grab one in each hand and throw them over the bar, where the bartender whacked them on the head with a bottle just to keep them quiet. It was over before I could get to his aid (from the dance floor where I was dancing with "Nellie the Pig"). It was very evident he did not need help.

The "tribe" used to grade the family saying, "The stronger the body, the weaker the brain." Edgar, William, and I were the strongest.

Speaking of "Nellie the Pig," she was an awfully nice girl. She got her name on the first night she was in town. She had a couple of suckers in a box at the Dominion who were buying her champagne (which she called wine). As it cost twenty dollars per pint she insisted the waiter address her as "madam." He made some crack as to what the title implied, which she resented, so she bit his ear off as they clinched and fell down the steps to the dance floor. Seeing her wallowing in the sawdust with the waiter, some of us dubbed her there and then. She had a little turned up nose, so that she had to wear a broad-brimmed hat in the rain to keep the water off the roof of her mouth. But she was kindness itself, when she wasn't drunk, and I saw a good deal of her. In a nice way, of course. She had three sisters, who each in turn married Swift Water Bill. Nellie, herself, being the first bride.

That reminds me of the shipments of things sent in by the Alaska Commercial Company. One was a hundred wedding dresses. As far as I could find out, there never had been, nor ever would be a "decency band" slipped on anyone's finger. You had to get your man into civilization and tip a hotel manager to throw you out of the dump, before anyone thought of a certificate for merely living together.

Glass-eyed Annie sang beautifully; Myrtle Drummond had charm; diamond-toothed Gertie was tough, but attractive; over-flowing Flora, who looked like mud squeezing up from between your toes, had lovely eyes; but, most of the rest—my Gawd—what sights!

I remember once asking an invalid friend of mine, who had a cook named Jennie, aged seventy-five, with one tooth, and cock-eyes, "How long do you stay in this lonely spot?"

"Until Jennie begins to look good to me," he replied. In the couple of years I stayed on the "inside" none of 'em looked good to me.

Wonders will never cease. The brave souls that helped them "go wrong" must have been blind and have lost the sense of touch.

The social lines were very strictly drawn. The "kept" ladies never spoke to the dance hall girls; although the performers rustled the boxes and danced with "friends," they were very snooty to those who merely danced. There was another strata far below, mostly foreigners, who lived in a district all their own. These were snubbed by the others.

There were a couple of girls named Pickering who did a sister act. They put on airs with everybody. One afternoon they drew aside to pass "Nellie the Pig" on the street, with their heads in the air and sniffing. Nellie stopped them on the narrow sidewalk and said, "Do you smell anything bad?" They both sniffed some more, in earnest this time, and answered, "No, we don't smell anything." "Then there isn't anything bad in the world," she said, letting them go and in imitation of the Pickerings she started on up the street.

One of the girls grabbed her by the dress and the other one slapped Nellie. They had better have slapped a wildcat, for what "our Nell" did to the Pickering sisters was lightning, winding up with rolling them in the mud.

Of course, a man couldn't interfere in ladies' quarrels, so I just leaned up against the side of the saloon and laughed until it hurt.

It didn't take a letter from the Pope to get into Dawson society and so I was admitted.

I forgot two more who arrived later. Cad Wilson had been younger, some fifteen years earlier, and Muckluck Maude was all right. They were both stars at the Dominion; but a rich boob grabbed Cad, without orange blossoms. Muckluck fell into the arms of Harry Davis on sight, so both their stage careers were short.

The social itinerary was simple, for you dined (either in a restaurant or at home); went to the "play"; perhaps gambled while they were taking the boards off the boxes (which formed the orchestra seats), and then danced and made merry for the rest of the night.

Hootch was a dollar a swig and the girl got half of the "weigh out."

Wilson lived over the Dominion, which was the swellest hotel in town. Needless to say, he was not alone.

Poor kid got the mumps, and they weren't all in his neck. My heart and sympathy went out to him. I called and we buried the hatchet, but not in the mumps.

Wilson was always crazy about prize fights. Nettie, the negro maid who helped take care of him, had a nephew named Sunny Barber, who Wilson thought was a comer. He hired the Dominion for the night and they put on some bouts. It was a big social affair and everybody bought seats for their girls and themselves. All the sheiks and "jeunes doré" of Dawson formed a brilliant audience and the betting was lively. Wilson had touted Sunny to the skies and he was favorite ten to one.

The preliminaries were over and Sunny entered the ring. He threw out his chest and did some shadow boxing to show himself off to his admirers. A great big Swede crawled through the ropes at the opposite side. It was evident that Sunny had never seen his opponent before. One had a feeling that Sunny was beginning to look for a trap door, or any other hurried means of exit.

Nettie was on the stairs, full of pride, and telling her neighbors what Sunny was going to do to that big white man, when the bell rang and the race started; but, the big Swede couldn't catch the fleet-footed negro. It brought down the house, with all kinds of insults for the brunette. The bell rang for the second round and the Swede burst across the ring and socked Sunny before he could get out of his corner.

We all foregathered in Wilson's room to condole, or abuse, according to our bets. Nettie, who had lost four ounces, was in the corner pouting and fixing drinks.

"What did you think of it, Nettie?" I asked.

"Think of it?" she pouted, her eyes bulging like a frog. "Why, I told Mr. Wilson never to have no dealings with that negro.

Why, Sunny Barber ain't neber ben no good. He always were have worms."

As I stepped out onto the street the snow was flying and it had turned bitterly cold. I knew my vacation was over, and I would start at once for Dominion Creek with my men and start building a cabin. So, I bid farewell to society.

CHAPTER XVII
THIRTEEN ABOVE LOWER

ON THE TENTH of September, 1898, the snow was flying when I woke up, and the feeling of loneliness assailed me. Edgar had taken the last boat out to spend the winter, leaving Captain Hansen to take care of the Alaska Commercial Company, and me to take care of his personal business and "Mama's Angel Birdie."

I knew very little of placer mining in this frozen land. In California I had seen them working the "rockers" on small claims and the enormous, hydraulic workings, with a mammoth fire hose playing against a bank and washing the "pay" through huge sluice boxes.

I had learned here, of course, that you could not work until the freeze came to keep the water from flooding you out; that you had to thaw your hole out with big fires every night; and that you spent the day at a windlass hoisting out of the hole what had been thawed during the night. Other than this it was rather hazy.

The family had owned quartz mines and my Delta experience had been quartz; but, in this land no one had ever discovered a ledge and it was all "placa." Placa means that some great disturbance had torn a ledge to pieces and millions of years of glaciers had ground the gold from the quartz and then more millions of years of rain had washed it down to the creek bottoms.

Gold, being the heaviest substance in the world, had gradually settled at the bottom, and had caught in crevices in the bed rock or stopped where the flood had struck a dam and the stream had not enough force to carry it on. Therefore, one claim might be very rich and the next almost barren. Bedrock on Dominion was forty-five feet below the surface and on Thirteen above Lower the bottom of the valley was eight hundred feet wide. Which way the stream had run several millions of years before was a question.

I started out early one morning a little befuddled and very vague as to what the future would bring forth. I had gotten a little soft in my three months of social whirl and my dancing muscles were not the ones that one uses on a hike, with a forty-pound pack on one's back.

Andy, Axle, and Hall, whom I had hired, had been at work for a week, packing camp outfit and tools to the claim. They were to also start cutting down logs and above all scraping up moss for chinking and roofing. Everything was to be ready so that I could pick out a cabin site and we could start at once building the shack.

I have always been a fellow that likes being busy, and I had become rather fed up with Dawson's frivolities. It was with no regrets that I turned my back on the "Big City." But I did feel qualms of conscience in leaving my baby brother behind in this den of iniquity, for after all I had been a mother to him all my life. He seldom wrote a letter home and for years I had lied for him in mine. At heart, I expected him any minute to turn to the dullness of righteousness and become a God-fearing, outstanding character. He has always been his own worst enemy, thinking it smart to know the doings of the lowest characters and, generally, getting the blame for their indiscretions, where generally he was absolutely innocent. So, it was with this delusion that I always wrote to mother.

I had a long talk with Wilson in which he had promised to come out to the creek and spend the winter with me, so with that solace I trudged on.

We spent three weeks getting logs down and building a cabin. We also started our shafts, thawing out eighteen inches per day. As far as anyone knows the ground is frozen for several hundred feet and is just like flint, until you thaw it out.

The struggle building a cabin is rather a bore, so I will skip that; although the luck and pull I had exerted in getting two windows with four panes of glass in them made the cabin an outstanding and architectural triumph. The pole cage to the left of the front door was for the "cache." The cabin was sixteen by fourteen feet. Across the back there were four bunks, double deck, and behind the door was one apart for me.

Things were quite shipshape and I sent the boys in to get the grub and other necessities. They took the dog team with them, as there had been a good freeze and snowfall.

I had named the dogs after a menu that I most craved; Scramble Eggs was a little yellow fellow, who was the leader; Oysters, grey, and my pal; Salad was white with black tips; Mushroom was pink and brown; and Cake, chocolate. It made the fellows you passed furious to hear one call them by name and, incidentally, led to several battles.

For the last two days we had been getting gravel with tiny specks of gold. The day before the boys started for Dawson we had struck bedrock. The last foot above hardpan, and it averaged three dollars per pan (which means a shovelful). This was good, and I was delighted.

Perhaps a letter I wrote to Mama Mizner will give you an idea of life on the creek. Of course, it was exaggerated and makes me out so pure, when in reality I was as pure as a sewer; but, here goes—

"Dominion, October 25, 1898.

"My dearest Mother,

"I am tired, for today I have done a good day's work. One hundred is the number of buckets an average man brings up per day. My score for the day was one hundred thirty-five, not counting a dozen buckets of water and bringing up the man from below three times.

"Jimminy, I wish they would begin to sled, but the rivers won't freeze and tonight is another warm one.

"They killed a beef at the store on Twenty-Nine yesterday and we had a variation from the festive beans in the way of very tough steak at one dollar and twenty-five cents per pound.

"Dominion, October 28, 1898.

"Snow lies thick on every inch of ground that can be found and bends the limbs of all the feathered trees to almost breaking. Even on the leafless skeletons the snow stands several inches deep, for there is no wind, not a breath of air. And still it snows, and has been snowing for more than a week.

"It is hardly cold enough to wear mitts and every evening we sit in the cabin with the door open while the cooking goes on.

"The Iowan has been sitting on the edge of his bed puking tobacco juice 'til one needs rubbers. He is a queer combination of Mefisto and Yankee in appearance, with a weird, light mahogany skin, black hair and whiskers. He is a regular cyclone in his movements and thoughts. I am sure it has been an hour since he began to convey an idea to Andy and he has not given birth to it yet.

"I had to stop reading because of the hammering that was going on. All three are now sharpening a pick, and each stroke of the hammers shuts my eyes with a bang, so that I have nearly blinked my eyelids off.

"They are discussing a trip into town for tomorrow, but it would take a good deal to get me to take it.

"Dominion, October 29, 1898.

"They left early this morning. I cooked their breakfast at five.

"Milton Latham and Shorty Fitzgerald came down the creek this morning, bound for Four below Lower with a big load and a good dog team. Later they came back and had lunch with me and took me for a ride up the creek on the ice. You have no idea what fun it is to be whisked along behind six fine malamutes with jingling bells and shouts. The trail is like ice and swings in graceful curves in the bed of the narrow creek. Talk of Santa Claus—he couldn't be one-half as picturesque with his deer as the dogs are. It's different lying in a sleigh wrapped up in bear robes and having someone else running in the handle bars behind than mushing a team yourself.

"It's full moon tonight and almost as light as day. The dear old moon circles around above the horizon, never going out of sight save for the twenty-eight hours when she is changing her quarters. She seems so much bigger than she ever did before, even when we were kids and thought her green cheese; and then all the light she gives is glared back over the sky again from the glistening snow. The sky is clear and the stars stand crisply out in the pale blue.

"October 30th.

"It is more than a year since I left San Francisco now and longer still since I saw you. Well, we will all be together again soon now and if things turn out as they promise, we will come out all 'honky dorey.'

"Fritz Gamble came in last night. He is going to be on Twenty-Seven A, which is a mile above.

"Over two-thirds of the good fellows in the country are going to be between the discovery on this creek.

"Fritz said that he crossed the Louse Town bridge and was gone an hour, to come back and find that one of the cables had parted, letting down a dog team of twelve drawing one thousand pounds.

"The dog team fell through the thin ice and was instantly swept out of sight, never to be heard of again. The two men that were 'punching' the team were found clinging to the ice and frozen to the waist. They died in a few moments.

"I put in yesterday morning fixing and making another bunk and expect Wilson over every day with the grub, though he won't start 'til the Klondike freezes. I left him in town to attend to the freighting arrangements, as I could not come to any definite terms when I was in town.

"November First.

"Well, winter has come, for it is just as cold as it can be. Dozens of sleds pass down the creek every day; still, my stuff has not shown up, so I am sojourning on bacon and beans.

"Gamble and 'Och Gott Louie' arrived on Twenty-Seven below Upper three days ago.

"Gamble has a lay of one hundred feet and is working several men.

"Tell William that I went there to lunch today and that Louie ate steadily the entire time. Also, tell him that Taylor went out of here in rags, having to work part of his way out. Everything he got went to the dealer of the 'stud' game. He worked the entire time he was in here and should at least have had something at fifteen dollars per day.

"November Third.

"Wilson is expected here every day now, as I have heard that the Klondike is frozen so that sledding is good to the mouth of Hunker. He was merely waiting to get the ball rolling; in other words, to start the dog teams to work on some provisions.

"Each day the scene changes. This morning it was all in gray and white with faintest touches of blue and pink. From three holes in the foreground long columns of amber smoke twisted to several hundred feet, spreading out into capital-like clouds, which supported the palest gray-blue sky, where the moon hung as a dainty lantern, not afraid to face the excuse we have for day. The only living thing was one big black raven that croaked its lonely sovereignty to the stillness and was gone. Snow, snow, snow, everywhere, even on your whisker ends.

"November Tenth.

"This morning Douglas Waterman and Vernon Gray came out to take a look at things. They had a fellow named Ed Mayor, who was assayer at the Alaska Commercial Company, are going to take the hundred feet that Crawford was to work out. They will make it fine for company's sake.

"Did I say that one hundred twenty-five buckets was a good day's work? Well, yesterday I hoisted over two hundred and every day it averages one hundred and seventy-five. I am afraid they will work me to a 'frazzle.'

"Tell Edgar that the policy and heads of the Alaska Commercial Company are more unpopular this year than Healey's was last. Hope, Haron, Walters, and several others, are heartily disliked and the miners swear they won't purchase anything that they can possibly get anywhere else. Captain Hansen has been on a spree for more than two months and doesn't see how things are going.

"We have had a cold spell of a couple of weeks. Fifty-two degrees below was the coldest. It was fine; no wet or snow. When you open the door a cloud of steam condenses to your waist, and a great rush of steam rushes out the upper half of the door. From the ventilator in the roof steam issues like smoke, even when there is no fire. Every nail that is driven through shows a frost-covered head and thick glaciers flow down over the window sills.

"November Sixteenth.

"We have had a week of sloppy warm weather. Springs have broken out and overflow the creek, making it as a trail impossible. The thaw in the hole has been tremendous also.

"Today I hoisted two hundred and fifty-six buckets and am just alive to tell the tale.

"This morning the thermometer had fallen from thirty degrees above to thirty-three below (I don't mean above and below 'discovery').

"I don't think I ever explained how the mining here is done and I am sure that I would never have guessed the method had I not seen it.

"The fires are built against the angle of the floor and wall so that each burns down enough waste gravel from above to cover up and smother in the heat.

"One strikes bedrock with a straight shaft. It is only the last or bottom four or five feet that contains the gold. With the fires against the walls, your shaft gradually looks like a creme de menthe bottle and then it spreads out more like those old squatty Dutch decanters at home, but always the slender neck remains the same. Kindling about three feet long is split and a couple of large armfuls are let down in each hole, then twice as much larger wood. These are stacked upon shavings (made with a draw-knife from a small dry tree). The entire is covered with green poles the size of your arm. One has to be pretty quick to get six or seven fires lit and make connections (in the smoke) with the rope and be hoisted out before you smother. Then, and not until then, is the day's work done.

"I am beginning to get tired of the Swedes and Iowan. They are dirty things. You have never read or seen pictures that in any way illustrate this New York tenement.

"At the present writing Andy is lying on his back on a long bench, warming a pair of distorted feet—fine examples of corns and bunions. Axle is buried deep in 'The Crime of the Century,' spelling out the words and whispering them to himself. He is rather the attractive part of the picture, for he is young and his certain sort of fair Swedish features seem rather fine in the light of the candle, which is stuck in a bottle just before him. The rich brown bark of the logs lend a beautiful background for the blue shirt. The 'chomping' and chewing punctuated with the occasional sound of a 'spit' as it strikes the floor, anywhere in the radius of possibility, comes from the darkest corner, where Hall sits, swinging his legs, on the edge of his bunk and stares out into space, with an owl-like stubbornness that is unique. Kindling is piled up against the sugar barrel, which now holds water. A long line sags low with the weight of dirty washed underclothes, and the smell of stewing socks comes fragrantly from their bean pot.

"Three candles throw most contrary shadows from stool to shelf and leave much in somber uncertainty, for which we may thank heaven, for a light would show a heterogeneous mass of stiff stockings, old moccasins, rope, cans, half filled sacks, and any old thing you might find on a respectable dump.

"Well, this letter will be my only possible present for Christmas, as there is no way to get anything to you. Drink a great big 'nog' and think of us in here. You can bet we will have an excuse for 'eggnog' ourselves, and one of the finest dinners on record. The cake and candy you sent will play an ending part with the pudding. I haven't quite decided whether we will have dinner here or in Dawson. If we have it here, you can picture about a dozen fellows in a nice warm cabin enjoying life much more than those who are having what they think is a 'snap.' Billy Fairbanks and I were preparing a possible menu for the occasion, as follows:

Caviar and Anchovy on Toast

Frozen Oysters
(Everything is frozen in a can)

Bouillon
(Out of Capsules)

Grilled Sardines   Roast of Moose

Asparagus
(Straight from the Can)

Plum Pudding   Cheese   Coffee
(From Home)

"What do you think of that? And as turkey is only two dollars and a half per pound we may have one. Nay, probably will have one. When you wake up on Christmas morning say 'Merry Christmas' to me, for that is the first thing I will do.

"Wow! 'Them' registers fifty-six degrees below now and it is not yet eight o'clock. I have just been out to lower wood to Axle and you cannot imagine how fine the weather is. Not warm exactly, but every star shining and as still as death. With plenty of clothes on one does not mind it as much as a San Francisco fog.

"Wrank and Whitney were here this afternoon. Wrank tells me that Hope has gotten the G.B.

"Well, my dearest Mother, I hope this will reach you by holiday times, just to let you know how happy I am here.

"Merry Christmas!

"ADDISON MIZNER."

I must say the letter is refined and guarded, and down in my heart I knew Wilson had no idea of leaving the bright kerosene of Dawson. Also, I wasn't as happy as I made out; for, fundamentally, I am rather a neat and orderly person, who likes creature comforts.

The Christmas dinner was a great success. I had soaked desiccated eggs for twelve hours and although they wouldn't whip they would stir into the condensed milk and by adding plenty of whiskey we could call it eggnog, on account of the grated nutmeg.

Waterman, Gray, and Mayhon had taken a "lay" of one hundred feet of my claim, which means they worked it on a fifty-fifty basis, I getting one-half of the "clean-up."

As they were all invited for Christmas dinner, we decided in order to get away from the Swedes we would entertain in their cabin. There were twelve in all. Milton had brought Irene and her friend, so this made enough leaven in the pie to start any kind of fight you liked.

God had planted a Christmas tree right in front of the door and we studded it with candle butts set in the snow.

The party started off most formally, with place cards and a grand manner. Then gaiety crept in, drifting more and more towards heated arguments until someone pulled the door off the hinges because the cabin had gotten too hot. The last thing I remember was helping tie the girls onto the sled—they were just so much meat. As the dogs leaped into their harness Irene fell sideways and Milton plowed up the trail with her to twice its width.

It was in the early part of January that I noticed a change of atmosphere in my household. I had been in the hills Sunday and had killed two caribou and had returned to get the Swedes to help me drag them in before the wolves got them. As I stopped at the door to look at the thermometer I heard them talking, and listened.

"Andy is right," said Hall. "We can stall around 'til they go to bed. Tell him the fires won't light, or something."

Andy broke in, "If you don't knock him out the first wham, he will holler and bring the bunch next door out, and then what?"

There was a moment of deliberation and then Axle's voice. "If I was on top, I know I could knock him down the hole with one sock. That's the way you'd have to work, cause the big bastard will yell like hell. You know that, don't you?"

It suddenly dawned on me that they were discussing me.

Then Hall's voice. "I told you the gang next door are all going into town on Friday, then there won't be anyone within a mile. Why not wait and then just belt him over the head with a log of wood and shove him down. By the time he has fallen forty-five feet you can't tell one wollop from another."

There was a long pause, then they agreed on waiting until Friday to kill me, and everything was decided. I began backing away from the door, when they began arguing as to who would re-stake the claim.

I went down the trail several hundred feet, and began whistling as I turned back to the cabin.

"Got some meat up here about a mile," I called. "Come along and help get it in. You'd better bring the dogs and the sled."

We worked hard for a couple of hours, skinning and butchering and loading the sled. Then we beat trail back to the cabin.

I cooked my dinner and then they got theirs. Everything was full of conversation, and we went to bed.

How stupid and ignorant they were. They didn't seem to know that the mere fact that they were trying to stake the claim would sound funny. It would take a year, for I had done a lot of work; more than enough to cover "representation" for that time. Why didn't they wait until the "clean-up" and get the gold dust? I couldn't figure it out, so I went to sleep.

Monday, Tuesday, Wednesday, and Thursday, we worked like dogs. Friday morning Gray, Waterman, and Mayon, left for town.

After lunch I lowered Axle back into the hole and waited an hour. I knew this would get on his nerves and also on Hall's nerves, seeing that I wasn't hoisting buckets. Finally, I heard Axle yelling to be hauled out. I paid no attention. Then, from a corner of the window, I saw Hall come to the door. "Axle wants to know if you are sick or something. He's got a lot of dirt ready."

"You'd better haul up those two Swedish 'summer squashes' out of their rat holes and tell them to come here, and make it on the run too, for I want to talk with you fellows."

Hall's face fell and he stumbled out. He hauled Axle out first and then Andy. I didn't give them a chance to talk, but ordered them into the cabin. I was standing in the door as they passed in.

"Sit down, you lice!"

My voice was a studied calm. "So you are fixing to murder me tonight. That's a joke. I have always been fair with you and I'm going to be fair with you now. I just want you to know that I sent in to Dawson a letter, describing my murder. It is sealed and to be opened only in case of my death. I did not tell the boys next door anything about your plans, because I want you to be friends."

They all tried to interrupt with protestations of innocence.

"Shut up! You stupid clowns—don't you know I'm a mind reader? Everyone else does. What you're each thinking now is how you can throw the blame on each other, and if you say anything it will only lead to fighting among yourselves. As to killing me—none of you have got guts enough for that."

I threw my hunting knife into the middle of the floor.

"The rifle is next to you, Andy; but you are thinking how far you could get with the Northwest Mounted Police on your tail; Axle is thinking that he'd like to have me on the American side of the line; and that other big bladder-head isn't thinking at all. Now, get out, and do some work."

I stood up and opened the door and they all filed out in silence.

The bluff had worked. You can do the same thing with a dog. Don't ever let one think you are afraid of them.

"Hall, lower Axle down in the hole. I'll be out in a minute."

I slammed the door and fell down on the bunk, for my knees had gone queer all of a sudden. It took ten minutes and two big shots of hootch to get any strength in them, and then I was like the mouse who licked up some whiskey, for I was "looking for that damned cat."

I rode them like a slave driver, for the next few months, and kept them cowed.

CHAPTER XVIII
UP AND DOWN AGAIN

THE WINTER was wearing away and day by day the piles of dirt averaged one-tenth the pannings, it would be a fortune. I began dreaming of a trip around the world and a ranch where I could have all the dogs, horses, and an incubator, I wanted; a place where I could send curious things I gathered back to.

I rode my gang morning, noon, and night. They were like sheep; although I surprised a sullen look in Axle's eyes occasionally, he would spring to life and ask me what he could do for me.

Odd days we would get in logs so that we could whipsaw them later for flumes and sluice boxes. I even got the riffles made, which were to go in the bottom of the sluices to catch the gold as the sand and gravel were washed off and carried away. I was so busy at this time that I did not have time to "read" Axle's mind, as we went on piling up the dumps.

Any day now a thaw might come that would flood us out of our diggings.

Then we had to think of building a dam to raise our water high enough to sluice with. I had one thought only, and that was of the "clean-up" and the thousands of dollars to spend on fresh vegetables and thick beefsteak, beds with springs, and a bath tub.

There was no question that Thirteen Above was a very rich digging.

Waterman, Gray, and Mayon had got out a big dump too and half of that would be mine. I had paid off two-thirds of the "Swedes'" salaries from the pannings alone, and owed very little else. It looked rosy, for Dominion gold had much less alloy than any other in the Klondike. It assayed seventeen dollars and thirty cents to the ounce against twelve dollars and ten cents on El Dorado.

From time to time I had been keeping an eye on my laymans' diggings for fear they might drift into the "Queen's Fraction" next to them.

Let me explain more fully what the "Queen's Fraction" is. When the stampede to a creek took place, no one had a tape or any other surveying instrument, so from the discovery stakes the man who was staking out, no one wanting to make sure that he got his full five hundred feet, generally stepped off five hundred and fifty or even six hundred feet. When they all were registered the gold commissioner's office sent out a surveyor, who accurately measured off five hundred feet, from your upstream stake, and then jumped to the next man's upper stake and did the same. This, with hardly an exception, left a fraction between claims, which became the property of the Crown and was called the "Queen's Fraction." Of course, everyone cursed the queen, but I doubt if the poor old girl ever heard of them.

Although no one on the creek had a tape, or even a twelve-inch rule, I had a watch chain, which in an idle moment one day I had measured and found to be ten and one-half inches long. With this to go by I made a six-foot rule. Every two weeks I would drop a plumb line down the hole nearest the "fraction" and measure off below ground how far they had gone; finally, leaving the queen a couple of feet extra, for fear my measure was not quite accurate. I was very fussy about this detail and Waterman and his partners laughed about it.

One morning we awoke to find the whole world melting and the holes filling up. A few days later a deputy gold commissioner arrived on the creek and opened up an office, so he could keep an eye on the huge and outrageous taxes.

By this time all the diggings were flooded and we had not been able to get down the holes for a week, when the commissioner came in to call on me. He was a slimy, shifty-eyed "summer squash," and a little over-polite. I returned his courtesy in kind, walking over the dumps and talked about the possibilities of the "clean-up."

He asked me how near I had gone to "Her Majesty's Fraction," and I described exactly how I had measured, and being an architect, I knew something of engineering and surveying. He then measured my six-foot rule and found it nearly three inches short. We laughed about it. I cooked lunch for him and bade him goodbye.

In the next two weeks we all turned to and built a dam and got our boxes ready.

During the winter I had at odd times built a rocker and as I had kept the richest scraping off bed rock in a separate pile, I began to clean up this. In the last month or so I had noticed that the three men would go off for walks in the evening and when they came back they would never look at me. I felt there was something phony going on, so I scraped a hole under the rocker and buried more than half the dust beneath a stone. When the men went for their stroll, I would dig it up again and hide it in a rubber boot under my bunk, amid a lot of other trash. It was such an open place that I felt they wouldn't think of it.

In this way, at the end of the month I had approximately twenty-seven thousand dollars in the boot and over twenty thousand in tin cans on the shelf. On the first of June I would have to make my report to the commissioner; but, there was no use letting Axle and Andy know how rich the claim was.

On the twenty-ninth of May the deputy gold commissioner arrived with two mounted police and took possession of "Thirteen" in the name of "Her Majesty the Queen," asserting that we had drifted in on the "Fraction."

You could have knocked me over with a feather.

"How much have you rocked out?"

"I don't know exactly—I haven't any scales."

After the first shock I began to get boiling mad. All my life I had had to control myself and besides, my brain had begun to work again. I knew they couldn't prove it and even if they could, they couldn't get down the hole again for six months, until the freeze came. It was highway robbery—taking bird seed from a cuckoo clock. What was I to do? It meant years of litigation. Was this just a little private graft, or were the higher ups in it too?

"Is this your 'clean-up'?" said the commissioner, as he took down one of the cans from the shelf.

I nodded my head.

He called in a man from the outside, who was carrying a bag which contained scales. Together they sat down on the bench at the table and began weighing up the dust. "Twenty-one thousand three hundred and ten dollars, figuring it at twelve dollars and ten cents per ounce." It was really worth seventeen dollars and thirty cents.

"This is a very rich claim, Mr. Mizner, if you could rock this much out in less than thirty days."

How did he know I had only been thirty days? He did not ask if it were all I had taken out and my mind flashed to the rubber boot beneath the bunk, on which I was sitting.

By now I felt I had a hold on my voice and ventured, "Just what does this action mean, Mr. Commissioner?"

"Well," he answered, in a very pompous way, "we can't say at present. It may mean a complete confiscation or it may only mean a heavy fine. It is a very serious matter which will have to be taken up at Ottawa. In the meantime, we will take this dust to my office and you will go on with your 'clean-up.' Of course, I will leave this gentleman (pointing to the man who had brought in the scales) in charge. He will watch the 'clean-up' and take care of the dust."

They poured up pretty golden sand into a couple of leather sacks and started out with it.

"Don't I get a receipt?"

"How dare you, sir! Are you questioning my integrity?" With a hideous glare he strode out.

As the police had been dismissed when the man with the scales had come in, I realized that I had had no witnesses, and that I was in the hands of the "philopenas." I was swamped.

When Axle, Andy, and Hall came in to get their lunch they pretended they had known nothing of the raid, and all the way through, looked a little too innocent. But, even then, I wasn't sure.

By mid afternoon I had decided to go into Dawson and see a lawyer. There was nothing I could do with the boot, but take a chance with it as it was. Everyone in the cabin knew that it leaked and I felt sure no one would want to borrow it; besides, it looked very natural where it was.

When I reached Dawson I found that my predicament was not an unusual one, and there was nothing I could do at present, so I decided to throw myself into the pleasures of the great City.

I had been in Dawson early in April and had been at the Phoenix dance hall the night that our American Consul had got so "boiled" that he had disgraced us all, but "Nellie the Pig," and I had left before the actual "kicking" began.

He had sued the *Klondike Nugget*, which was our great newspaper, for libel, for some articles which appeared soon after. As the case was set for June Second I got myself a front seat.

I took Nellie with me, as her sister, Florence Lamar, was going to be one of the leading witnesses.

I will let the *Nugget* tell the story of the trial:

The trial of the criminal libel action brought by James Church McCook, the American Consul to Dawson, against Eugene C. Allen and A. F. George, manager and city editor, respectively, of the Klondike Nugget, took place before Judge Dugas, of the Territorial court, and a large audience of interested—even excited—people on Thursday last.

The result was an acquittal of the defendants, a complete vindication of the course of the Nugget in its expose of the official's misconduct, and a rebuke to Consul McCook that would have been stunning to a man of fairly sensitive perception.

The trial also proved a testimonial of the highest nature to the thoroughness, accuracy and reliability of the Nugget's news service; for the evidence showed that every one of the hundreds of statements contained in the principal article constituting the alleged libel was absolutely true—so much so that the presiding judge was impelled, in his summing up of the evidence, to tell the jurors that they might consider all the allegations as proven beyond question.

The objectionable articles were read aloud by the clerk, and the audience was convulsed with mirth. The prosecutor,

Consul McCook, was present at the time, but his bowed head showed plainly that he appreciated his position at last, and he disappeared entirely after the charges had been so fully verified by the first witness.

PROSECUTION SURPRISINGLY WEAK.

Eugene C. Allen on his oath says as follows: "My occupation is printer by trade. I am the manager of the Klondike Nugget. It is sometimes customary and sometimes not to insert the names of the paper's management on the head of the paper. That name on Exhibit One was inserted with my approval as manager, and the accused is the A. F. George mentioned on the paper. I take the responsibility of the editorial myself."

Q. Do you know who was the writer of this editorial (Exhibit 1)?

A. I do not know who was the writer of the article referred to.

Q. To whom would you have to refer to ascertain that?

A. Would have to refer back to the copy. That copy has been used, to the best of my knowledge and belief, to light the fires. I place no one in charge. I do not delegate the writing of the editorials to any particular one. I do not look to anyone in particular for the editorial.

Witness Clifford was shown a cartoon consisting of a figure dancing on a flag-draped coffin and labeled "Here Lies American Dignity," which he said showed some resemblance to Consul McCook.

AND HE HAD A GLORIOUS TIME.

The defense then took the helm and proceeded with the evidence that was to establish the triumph of the Nugget. The first witness called to the stand was Pearl Hall, one of the girls at the Phoenix dance hall, where Consul McCook had indulged in the drunken and disgraceful revelry which called out the objectionable articles. She spoke clearly, pointedly and intelligently. "I saw Consul McCook enter the Phoenix on the occasion in question," she testified. "It was about 3:30 o'clock in the morning. He was accompanied by Gertie Lovejoy, known as 'Diamond Tooth Gertie.' They went to the bar and drank a bottle of wine, after which the consul danced with me and we had a bottle of wine. He was intoxicated and very jolly. The next I remember of him was when everyone was dancing; I spoke to him about being Consul McCook. He invited me to take another drink and then the other girls, coming up and saying they were Americans, were all invited to drink. A young man came in as the consul was asking 'Who is not an American?' The young man said he was not, but that he was a Canadian. The consul said he would rectify the mistake at once and make him one. They began to scuffle in a friendly way, I supposed, but the consul finally got angry over something that was said, forced the young man into the corner occupied by the Nugget Express, and they would have gone through the window had it not been for Mr. McDonald. The two then had several rounds of drinks, but the trouble continued all night. Later on I saw the two men and Peter Burke, the porter, in a bunch on the floor of the dance hall. Several other men took hold of them and dragged them into the bar-room. Soon after that the consul was again drinking at the bar with the girls and gave them some quarters and other pieces of money he had about him. When they were all gone he gave them a lot of nuggets and one of them his watch. Presently he threw up both hands and exclaimed 'Take the whole works.' (Titters and laughter.) They did it, too, turning all his pockets inside out—but they were empty. (More laughter.) The consul was laughing all the time. Soon after that he and Peter, the porter, got mixed up and were scuffling and rolling about on the floor as drunken men will. The next thing I noticed was that the consul had a small American flag, the Stars and Stripes, pinned to his back. He was then placing his hands on the bar telling Pete to kick him and leaning over so that he would have a good square show. Peter then ran from the other side of the room and kicked the consul. Both were nearly knocked over the bar. The consul laughed and encouraged Pete to continue kicking him. Mr. McDonald tried to get them to stop, but they wouldn't. There was a big crowd present and everybody was laughing. The last time I saw the consul he was at the bar drinking and still cutting up. That was about 6:30 a.m." Witness then told of the girls being summoned to Col. Steele's office for the inquiry into the whereabouts of the consul's watch-chain.

This testimony confirmed nearly every statement made by the Nugget relative to the consul's revelry at the Phoenix, and its effect was sensational in the extreme. The prosecution hadn't a word to say in the way of cross-examination, while a buzz of noises told of the excitement under which a large number of spectators were laboring.

THE EVIDENCE ACCUMULATES.

Florence Lamar, another of the Phoenix girls, told of the consul falling to the floor while he was dancing and of her assisting in helping him to his feet. Witness did not share in the distribution of the nuggets, but saw the consul turn his back to the bar and throw up both hands, with the remark, "Take the whole works," or "Take the whole cheese." Witness described graphically the picture of the consul being kicked by Pete, the porter. The consul had his hands on the bar and was bent over with his head half turned to Pete, who was running across the floor. Miss Lamar's happy style of description was too much for her hearers, and it was necessary for the police to suppress the tumult of mirth that followed.

Nellie James and Edward Cowley substantiated all of the testimony given. Concerning the consul's condition, the last-named witness said he was not awfully drunk when he came in, but that after he had drank the wine he got pretty drunk.

P. J. Britt was in the Phoenix on the occasion in question. He did not know the man who was making all the fun, but a friend said who he was and asked: "What do you think of our American consul?" (This was objected to.) He heard Pete, the porter, say to the consul. "I am an American; you and I come from the same part of the country and you have got to be kicked." The kicking followed, and witness was so convulsed with mirth over the affair that he sat down on a bench and laughed so much he couldn't keep track of subsequent events.

Hattie Lee saw the scuffling, drinking and kicking, but not the other happenings.

P. A. McDonald met the consul at the door as the latter entered with Gertie. He appeared to be under the influence of liquor. Witness asked him if he knew where he was, and the consul replied, "Yes; I am having a good time tonight." Witness then told of the consul drinking, of his demanding who was not an American, of the trouble with the young man, etc. The consul had his hat and coat off and a small American flag was pinned to his back. Witness didn't know whether it was pinned on him there or somewhere else. Witness was finally holding the young Canadian down while two of the consul's friends took him away by the rear door.

George Pudges testified that he was one of the men who picked up the consul and carried him from the dance hall.

John A. Glover testified that on the morning in question he was a bartender at the Rochester bar and saw Consul McCook emerge from the alley some time between 7 and 8 o'clock. The consul attempted to walk across the street, but couldn't do it, fell down and finally made his way clear across the street on his hands and knees. He went into the saloon where witness was, asked for whisky, but was refused. The consul then sat down, bowed his head and said: "Kick me if you want to." After being there about half an hour the consul started up the stairs to his room, but fell down en route.

THE SUMMING UP.

Attorney Pattullo took the floor and presented a recapitulation to the jury.

He then presented citations to show that newspaper statements are not libelous when shown that they were published for the benefit of the public and that the plea of justification on those grounds shall constitute a defense. On that point he alluded to the fact that the majority of residents of the territory are Americans, and that it was their right to know through the public press that the representative of their country was bringing disgrace upon it and upon them.

THE CHARGE TO THE JURY.

At the conclusion of the judge's instructions the jury retired to deliberate. At the end of an hour the foreman appeared and announced that a verdict had been reached. Judge Dugas ascended the bench, and the jury was brought in. On inquiring of the clerk of the court, the foreman rose and stated that a verdict of "not guilty" had been found. The crowd which had been in attendance all day remained to hear the verdict, which, from the faces and expressions of all, was eminently satisfactory. The case of McCook vs. A. F. George was then called. The same jury was retained, and, without hearing further evidence or argument, found the defendant not guilty.

There was much testimony that wasn't printable, and much that was struck out; but the account is carefully accurate.

When I got back to the creek I wrote my first and last whining letter to Mama Mizner.

> "Thirteen above Lower.
> "Dominion, June 16, 1899.

"Mother dear.

"It's more than doubtful whether I can get out this summer. I have tried not to kick much, but when one sums up all the squabbles, law suits, and general troubles, it makes a beautiful hard luck story.

"About a week ago, at lunch, I happened to say that there was absolutely nothing else that could happen, and that things would go better now.

"Mayon broke in with, 'Wasn't that thunder? It's the first I have heard in years.'

"Ten minutes later the rain came down in sheets, soaking through the roof and soaking everything. For three hours it was a deluge. The creek soon rose and swept over the tops of our dumps, half were gone. For a little it looked as though we would have to move out of the cabins.

"But, Oh! How sad a sight was the top of Mt. Arrarat when the waters subsided. The dam was quite half gone. Flumes washed away, and wreckage strewn in every direction.

"I told you that the mining inspector would not let us close our dam for three weeks and back water up on our neighbor, instead of letting us have it every alternate week.

"Well, now it just makes me ill to look toward the remaining dumps and hear the continual splashing of the dirt as it caves in. Great hunks drop back into the drifts.

"It's my sincere prayer that I will be able to pay off all I owe and make enough this next winter to get out of this infernal 'hell hole.'

"June Seventeenth.

"We have been trifling with the dam for days and have finally given it up as a bad job, and now get our water through half a mile of sluice boxes.

"From my vantage point on the hill I can see its snaky curves, wriggling among the emerald patches of new marsh, clear into the blue distance.

"At home, summer is almost over, and here the cottons and poplars are just showing their freshest shrieking green in great long belts, alternating with the darker green of the firs, in a striped watermelon fashion. Little blotches of blue lupines, and others of a queer, brown, yellow daisy, freckle the hills with color, and the wild roses promise to be out in a few weeks.

"The radishes and lettuce I planted on the roof are up in long rows, though not fit to eat yet.

"Enclosed you will find a sheet of the *Nugget*, which goes to show how a foreign representative can make himself famous without being exactly a diplomat. I wish I could get you the articles referred to; they were tremendously funny.

"Going down the river is much the cheapest; so if I happen to get out, it will be that way; though I won't leave here with less than a thousand.

"For two nights the mosquitoes were annoying but I have not seen a half dozen since.

"June Nineteenth.

"Three or four more days will see us through and I will not be sorry to get away from here.

"I wish I could get a hundred dollar engagement outside. Dawson could not see me for steam, getting out of here.

"Yours lovingly,

"ADDISON MIZNER."

It was several months later that Hall came to me, in a destitute condition, and wanted to borrow the price of a ticket out of the country, saying that they had all been gypped out of their part of the "spoils."

He claimed that Andy, Axle, and he had given affidavits, swearing that we had drifted far into the "Queen's Fraction." He acknowledged that none of them had ever been down the upper holes; but that Axle had met a clerk from the commissioner's office who had told him that if they would swear to such a statement that they would split the "clean-up," giving them one-half and distributing the other half where it would do the most good.

When it came to a showdown, the clerk laughed at them and asked them if they wanted to go before the judge, and now acknowledge that their sworn affidavits were perjury.

I did not give him confidence for confidence and tell him that I had taken a boot from under my bed and buried it up on the hillside.

CHAPTER XIX
CALIFORNIA HERE I COME

I WAS NEVER able to find out exactly what my "cleanup" was, but I knew it was nearly nine thousand ounces.

The thing that impressed me was that they always gave me the weighings in dollars at the general store over the bar price of twelve dollars and ten cents an ounce, when I knew that if it were properly sold in a large quantity like this it would bring five dollars and twenty cents more per ounce. This difference might be their only graft, and two could play at that game.

Little by little I began milking the boot and making a "cache" more easily accessible. Two hundred pounds of gold isn't easy to move, all at once, and it was dangerous; but, I finally got it out and ran it up to seventy-five thousand dollars in a couple of months. But, I will let that matter drop.

I arrived in Dawson late one night after a two-day trip through muck, mud, and mosquitoes, and was dead tired.

A friend of mine ran a rooming house over the Dominion and I staggered up the stairs from the dance hall, hoping to get a room.

I found "Georgie the Moose" (the proprietress) sobbing in the hall. "I want a bed, Georgie. I'm dog tired."

"There ain't one," she sniffled, "'cept the one Jack Evans and Millie got and God knows when they are going to get them out."

There was a shuffling of feet on the stairs and five police-men appeared at the end of the hall. The door of number two opened and a sergeant stuck his head out. "This way, boys," he commanded, "let's get them out as quickly as you can." There was the sound of a tin pan piano from below and a strident voice singing a ballad.

"What the hell's the matter?" I inquired.

"Matter!" Georgie stopped her nervous sniffling. "It just goes to show you it doesn't pay to be nice to anyone. I was always nice to Jack and just look what he has done to me. Just a case of no consideration at all. He could have done it outside just as well. Do you know, I never had this happen before in all my life. The more you do for them the less they think of you."

I saw that she was full of self-pity, and tried to comfort her.

The door of number two opened again and two men were carrying something heavy out, followed by two more doing the same thing. The first load was Jack Evans with half of his head blown off, and the second was Millie. It had been murder and suicide—just a lover's quarrel.

I stopped the sergeant and asked him if the room was vacant, and moved in. I had been asleep two or three hours when I was

awakened by an angry voice from the other side of the thin
board partition. Georgie was getting drunk with some friends.

The burthen of her complaint was that she had stood for
everything else in this dump, but she'd be damned if she was
going to have a lot of bums messing up her rooms.

The next morning I started out to look up Wilson and found
there had been a new strike reported at a place called Nome, out
on the Bering Sea, and Wilson had taken the first boat down the
river. So Edgar, who had gotten back over the ice early in the
spring, was the only other Mizner left in the Northwest Territory.

It was the end of June. The fine, lovely, sweet, innocent
commissioner had allowed me days' labor wages for eight
months' time. This was to keep me quiet. I knew full well that I
would never get another cent, so I made a long face, and swallowed it.

The "clean-up" had been enormous all over the creeks.
Money was being flung to the winds. There were more rich
unmarried girls in a dance hall than you could find in any ball-
room today.

I took Milton Latham's cabin and settled down for the rest
of the summer. By now I realized that however it was done one
could never prove that they were grafters, for they had made it
seem legal, and my only thought was to get out of the country,
having the authorities think I was flat broke.

There was a rich old Colonel Brady who kept a woman
named Bessie. I had known Bessie in San Francisco when she
had worked in a riding academy. But now she was the leader of
society and lived in the only two-story house, with a porch, and
a kitchen. She also had a cook, who used to be a tattooed man
in a circus.

The Colonel was a mining engineer, and was buying up prop-
erties for a big "outside" syndicate. Therefore, he had to make
trips that would take him away a great deal. We arranged a
series of signals and used the place as a club during his absence.

There were about a dozen of us: Linn, Ralph, Hansen, and
a lot of boys whose names I have forgotten. Bessie was about
thirty-five or forty and liked young boys, which is more than I

can say for the Colonel. The cook used to tattoo us and feed us so we liked him better than we did the Colonel.

The old man had an office down town, which you could see from the kitchen window. His secretary was stuck on the tattooed man, and used to like to turn him over to look at the pictures. They had a series of signals and we added a red rag, hung at the office window, to let us know when the old boy was coming home.

One day we saw the Colonel start off with his horse and packer, and the cook told us he would be away ten days. Several of us moved in for a house party. We were making a great success of it, when the signal went up at the office. There was instantly a snowstorm of clothes from the side windows, and we had to spend an hour on the roof of the porch and another hour gathering up our clothes. I never did find my cuff buttons.

A new saloon and dance hall had gone up that spring which was very fashionable. It had made such an instantaneous hit that they had not time to finish it, so that the walls were merely two by fours covered with blue denim.

Behind the bar was the biggest safe in town. It was shiny black with a big oval painting of a tropic sunset, with Swiftwater Bill's name painted in an ellipse over it.

Skiff Mitchell had come down from El Dorado with a heavy "poke" and had asked me to dinner. "Let's stop at Swiftwater Bill's and leave this 'poke.' It's too heavy to lug around all night. I've got a small one on my hip, and when that runs out we can fill up again."

When we got to Swiftwater's he was behind the bar, and with a great show he turned several keys and splitting the tropic scene in the middle threw open the safe. He tagged the bag and threw it on top of a big heap of others and closed the big doors.

Skiff and I dined and "made merry." Skiff gambled enough to empty his small "poke," and we went back to fill up. There was a small alley running up behind the bar, so that ladies could dart into the boxes at the back without being seen in the saloon; but, we took the main entrance and bellied up to the bar, ordering drinks and asking for the big "poke."

This time Swiftwater swung open the doors without going through the unlocking process. To our horror there was an arm without a body, just dragging out the last sack of dust. With an oath Bill dove into the safe and grabbed the arm. While a terrible struggle was going on inside the safe we rushed to the alley and fell over a wheelbarrow full of "pokes" and jumped on the miscreant from the outside.

When we got him into the saloon Swiftwater recognized him as the cabinet maker who had built the safe out of packing cases. He had just slit the denim and pried off a loose board. It was considered enough to celebrate for, so everyone got drunk and staggered around, acting as their own bankers.

A few nights later I decided to cross the Yukon and dine with a friend who lived a solitary life on the opposite bank. I kept my canoe under a store which was built out over the river and was just across the street from the gold commissioner's office. I paddled over and enjoyed talking and spinning yarns for three or four hours. About twelve I started home.

We were having a couple of hours of black night now, but I could tell by the lights of Dawson just where to land. As the nose of the *Peterboro* slid up on the mud someone caught it and said in a whisper, "Is that you, Ad?"

"Oh, hello, Tommie," I replied, recognizing the voice out of the dark, "what are you doing here?"

"I didn't know you were out, so I just came down to borrow the boat. I've got to take a message across the river. I only want it half an hour."

"Get in—I'll take you over. It's early yet, and I haven't anything to do."

He hesitated an instant and then said, "All right—just wait a minute till I put in a package or two."

We shoved off and reached the opposite bank in a few moments.

"Will you wait a few minutes and take me back? I've just got to 'cache' these supplies so a pal can get them in the morning. I'll be right back."

It was nearly one when we got back to town.

"Where are you going?" Tommie queried.

"Home, I guess; though I may drop in at the Phoenix and have a whirl for a bit."

"Gee!" he gasped. "If you run into my 'popover' don't tell her you saw me. I told her I was going up to the Forks this afternoon and wouldn't be back for a couple of days, and if you tell her you saw me she'll think I've been out with Bessie; she's a wildcat when she gets jealous and, besides, she hates Bessie—says she's old enough to be my grandmother. You'd better not tell anybody you saw me; it might get back. I think I had better 'screw' now before it gets light again; somebody might see me and there would be hell to pay. I'll be at the Forks before morning." So we parted.

At the Phoenix I saw the "popover" in a box with a couple of live ones drinking champagne. She didn't seem to be missing Tommie much.

I didn't wake up until late and when I got down town the excitement was intense. Someone had broken into the gold commissioner's office the night before and stolen thirty-six thousand dollars in dust.

Three days later I stepped into my cabin and found a big bunch of the finest sables I ever saw lying on my bed. To the thong that bound them together was tied a piece of paper, and on it was written: "To a good sport." There was no signature and I have never found out who left them; and neither has the gold commissioner found out who robbed him.

Have you ever tried minding your own business? Sometimes it keeps you out of trouble.

In the middle of August I got a letter from Andy Martin. He had gotten a spot on his lung he said and would have to live at Palm Springs, on the Southern California desert, for a year. He had asked Genevieve Goad if she "would," and she had said "yes," and he wanted me to be his best man.

I had my bib full of Alaska and any excuse would do; besides, I loved Andy and Genevieve.

I had shipped my "dough" out in small shipments and was all set. So when the *Susie* drifted away from the bank I was on her.

You couldn't leave the country if you were in debt. I was cleared up, but Eddie Mayon had been hauled off a steamer a couple of weeks before for not having his bills marked paid. I got in cahoots with a couple of stevedores at the Alaska Commercial Company and we rigged up a box with some holes in the bottom and put Eddie in it.

I should have learned something from "Georgie the Moose," but I hadn't. Mayon had taken as his only baggage a bottle of hootch. He had no sooner been set down on the deck until he began moaning that he was a corpse, and it didn't matter where they buried him. I kicked the coffin and was uneasy until we steamed over the American line. Then I opened the casket, dragged out the remains and socked him a good one. Gee! It was a relief.

There was a Mr. & Mrs. Herbert Brown on board. He had been a hoofer at the Oatmeal Sisters, and she had been conducting her own business. I happened to ask her how they weighed out an ounce when they were owed (there were only three scales in Dawson in ninety-eight), and she said that the girls had all gotten together and decided that a tablespoonful would be about right. Brown got excited and began to wonder if they hadn't been cheated, so we took a tablespoon and went to the purser's room. A tablespoonful weighed nearly four ounces, so the Browns made up and were as happy as turtle doves for the rest of the trip.

It is nearly fifteen hundred miles to St. Michaels, and once on my way this seemed tedious and uninteresting.

I had to wait at St. Michaels for three days for a rotten little boat to take me another two hundred miles across the Bering Sea to Nome. I knew if I went home without a recent report on Wilson that I would think I had neglected my brotherly duty. It was a rotten trip, over a choppy sea, and I nearly turned inside out doing it. We dropped anchor off shore and were landed on the beach in small boats from shore.

I found Wilson in his glory. As I remember, he was running the "McQuestion," and it was a hot joint. His own cabin was out on the tundra. You walked a single plank over the swamp to get to it. I nearly fell off the walk when I saw it. He would never have made an architect. It seems that in trying to cut the ridge joints he had gotten them so sharp that the thing was all gable and two-thirds attic. It looked like the steeple of a church, looking at it from the end.

The town was agog with Wilson's prowess. Everyone said he was "the bravest man in Alaska," a title that he modestly cherished.

It was years later that I got at the bottom of the story, which was as follows:

About three o'clock one morning there had been a tap at Wilson's door and my friend Tommie had stepped in. He was white and scared and whispered to Wilson not to light the light. It seemed that he and the "Mit" and a "half kid" together with "Two-Tooth Mike" had tried to rob one of the richest claims on Anvil Creek, and they had been embarrassed by a load of buck-shot. Tommie said that the kid and Mike had been killed and that he had just made his escape by the skin of his teeth, and could Wilson hide him out for a bit.

"Mama's Angel Birdie" would rather be hanged than thought inhospitable, so he slid back a board in the ceiling and boosted Tommie up. He hadn't gotten the board back when someone else sneaked in the door. It was Mike, with a buckshot in his hip. Again there was pushing and pulling, while they got Mike safely stowed away. It was only a few minutes until the kid stumbled in with his arm badly torn and fainting from loss of blood. It was getting gray outside and gave enough light to make first aid possible. Then, by throwing the corners of a blanket to those above, they were able to get the invalid into the attic.

Wilson was washing up, when he saw through the window the sheriff coming along the planks. He flopped into bed and made a great show of being asleep. When the sheriff came in, Wilson rolled over and yawned laboriously. "What the hell's the matter?" he gaped.

"Hell's a popping up on Anvil; a band of a dozen men tried to rob a claim and were driving off after a big gun battle. We have got 'em all cornered in that deserted cabin on the hill, about a mile up—you know where the trail turns to the right. A trail of blood leads right to the door. It's the most desperate bunch I ever heard of. You got guts enough to be a deputy, Bill?"

"Sure," said Wilson, slipping into his pants and jerking on his boot, "let's go."

There were about sixty men, all laying on their bellies, with guns cocked, watching the cabin from every angle. Already the sheriff had dropped to his hands and knees and was crawling along.

"Drop, you big idiot," said one of the men lying on the moss, "that hut is a hornet's nest, I tell you. There must be about twenty of them, sheriff." "I saw at least a dozen rifle barrels," said another. "What are you fellows going to do? Lie here like a lot of snakes until you starve 'em out?" said Wilson, as he rolled a cigarette and lit it. "What do you think we're going to do, rush it and all get shot in the gizzards?" said the bouncer from one of the saloons.

"I'm for going in and having a parley." Wilson pulled out his cannon and held it by his side, holding up his hand, like a flag of truce.

The crowd was breathless.

He strode on to within a few paces of the cabin and taking a pose, he shouted, "Come out, you rats, or I will shoot you out." There was no answer and after a moment's dramatic waiting he stalked on inside. In two or three minutes he came out again smoking a fresh cigarette. "There isn't anybody here, sheriff. Just some blood, that's all."

It went over big, and that's how he got his title.

I only stayed in Nome a few days, playing around with Wilson and Tex Rickard and a few old friends.

I met Cherry Melott for the first time. She was the one that Rex Beach used for his heroine in "The Spoilers." I have known her ever since, and she is one of the wittiest and most delightful women I have ever met.

The trip home on the steamer *Portland* was without event, until we reached the Golden Gate. Then such a racket. The constant booming of cannons; the shrieking of whistles, as we joined a huge flotilla steaming by the forts. No one knew what was the matter. At first, I thought it must be for me, until a saucy little tug slipped up alongside and shouted for us to get out of line.

It was the return of the troops from the Philippines, and no one knew that I was coming back to my native heath.

CHAPTER XX
IN A ROYAL PALACE

SAN FRANCISCO had gone mad with joy; everywhere there were signs with "Welcome our Philippine heroes"; triumphal arches spanned the streets; bunting flew from every pole or lamp post and draped every window; garlands of flowers were everywhere; the streets were crowded with cheering, excited people, and I was lost.

It had been nearly seven in the evening when we had docked and I went from hotel to hotel trying to get a room; finally landing at the Occidental. They apologized for the fact that the room was small and in an annex; but, it had a bath, which had been an unknown luxury for nearly three years.

My wardrobe was nil: except what I stood in, I had nothing; a Stetson hat, Northwest Mounted Police, straight brimmed affair, an old coat and knickerbockers.

Mama Mizner had come to town with Min to see the welcome parade, and after an hour's telephoning I finally located them. As my retreat from Dawson had been unexpected, they were much surprised to see me walk in.

I hired a victoria and we three took in the sights until twelve, when things got too gay and I took the family home.

We met the next morning and went to some windows on Market Street to view the parade. Being a highly temperamental soul, I cried all over the place as the regiments marched up the street, with the wide open spaces showing the missing. Here was some boy smothered in garlands of flowers, and there some stranger without any. All my Yukon hard-boiledness melted into a cup custard of tears and gulps.

I spent a few days with the family while my tailor ran me up some clothes. He almost dropped dead when I paid him what I owed him, with interest. From a cold and harsh greeting he flopped to groveling bustle, and within a week I was arrayed like a movie star; in fact, I had an orgy of clothes, fresh food, and civilization.

Spick-and-span I boarded the train on my way to see Andy at Palm Springs.

He looked a little thinner perhaps, but better than I had expected. We spent a few days going over the job of fixing up his house for the honeymoon.

He left me behind to carry out the work, while he went a-courting and trousseauing.

Palm Springs was sizzling in the desert's sparkling clearness. The thermometer registered one hundred twenty-eight degrees in the shade, and only a few months before on the Klondike it had been sixty-two degrees below zero—nearly two hundred degrees difference in temperature. Would you think that the human machinery could stand and adjust itself to such a change?

In a month's time I joined Andy for the wedding and for the first time met all my old friends, and had a grand time, for I could walk right down the middle of the street, now that I had paid all my bills.

I promised the honeymooners that I would join them in a few weeks, as Andy wanted to do more alterations.

When I returned to Palm Springs, everything was lovely. The "love birds" were so happy that it made your heart ache to think that they were banished to such a desolate place.

There were a half dozen little houses and a ten-room hotel, at which I stayed. It was several miles to the station, over a road so deep in sand that a horse could hardly pull a buggy through, but I was happy in dining each night with Genevieve and Andy and laughing over old times. I was busy all day and two months flashed by before I knew it.

One Sunday we had taken a picnic lunch up the Canyon, where the only Washingtonian palms had been discovered. It had been a bright, clear morning; but, suddenly, out of nowhere, a cold drizzle caught us, and before we could get home we were all sopping. Poor old Andy had caught cold, and died three days later.

It was a harrowing few days, with a heartbroken widow, and over a hundred miles from the nearest town. Finally, all arrangements were made and we left for Los Angeles, where Andy's family were to meet us. Of course, the Martins being Catholics, I had to have a priest draped around my neck, and went through three funeral services; one at Palm Springs; one in Los Angeles; with the final "send-off" at the cathedral in San Francisco. The only bright spot was the size and sparkle of the diamond cross that Mrs. Martin wore at the funeral. I never have liked funerals anyway.

The old century was dying and the new one not yet born, when I realized my bank roll was dwindling. I had made two or three investments, given presents to everybody, and paid my bills.

I met a man from Honolulu, who said he was important in his home town. He was a doctor, but should have been an artist, for he painted a most alluring picture of an architectural future for me in Hawaii, and I still being the gullible sucker, accepted his offer. He said he headed a syndicate which was going to build a big hotel. He wanted me to design a new house for him, and had a list of things that were going to keep me busy for at least two years.

I hadn't been in Honolulu a week when I found he had about as much influence as a Protestant in the Vatican.

I had only taken enough money to last me a couple of months. All I had left I had put into a trust fund at a savings bank, not to be touched for two years. I couldn't squeal that I had been licked and write home for dough. Although I moved at once from the hotel to the California rooming house and took my meals at Licurgise's Beanery, I was soon broke again.

It was in my second week in the islands, which had just had a revolution, and the rich missionary families, whose ancestors had swapped religion for acreage, had set up a republic, that I wandered into the Royal Palace. The building had been turned into the capitol.

I was standing in the upper hall, with the trade winds sweeping through. On either side of this great gallery hung canvases, flapping on their shrunken stretchers. There was a full-length portrait of Napoleon III by Winterhalter; two excellent portraits of a Hawaiian king and queen, signed "Vergine Le Brun"; and many others of great historic value. One of Louis Philippe had a jagged tear, and a portrait of Queen Lilioukalani had a gob of tobacco spit in one eye.

A door opened at my left and an old gentleman with a long white beard came out. I was standing in front of a fine portrait of a British Admiral, who turned out to be Marshal Blucher.

"I beg your pardon, sir, but can you tell me of whom this portrait is?"

"I am sure I have no idea. I never noticed it before," he said.

"Well, perhaps you can tell me what 'summer squash' is responsible for the way these pictures are being neglected?"

"I don't know; unless I am; I'm President Dole."

Apology seemed impossible, so I laughed and said, "It is too bad they can't be restored and taken care of, for in time to come they will be priceless."

He asked me back into his office and we had a chat. The outcome was that he gave me his personal order on King's Art Store for one hundred dollars worth of supplies and I moved into the throne room as my studio. I had offered my services gratis.

The impertinence and assurance of youth! The family had gathered up a lot of old pictures in Guatemala and I had tinkered with them; but I learned a lot now, and I really think that I saved the collection. When I started I thought it would take a couple of weeks, but it turned out to be nearly a year.

No one knew who any of the portraits were, and they gave me the run of the archives, attics, basement, and out houses. I found pictures thrown in among lumber here and there and brought them all together. I patched them up and soaked them and varnished them. I covered the walls of the throne room with them, and still over half of them were unidentified. Finally, through a lady in waiting to the ex-Queen Lilioukalani, I gained an audience with Her Majesty.

I got a most cold and formal reception, as I was an American. She classed us all as her enemies and the dispoilers of her nation. Of course, in a way, she was right, for the coup was made so that the United States could take it over as a territory, killing duty on Hawaiian sugar.

But, personally, I have never been very proud of this rape of a happy little island kingdom, and often have had a mental smile when Americans criticize high-handed England in India.

Being sincere in this belief, I finally convinced Her Majesty that the records of her dynasty should be kept as a monument. She finally softened and we became fast friends, with simple, honest directness. It was through her that I was able to accurately name and date all the portraits.

One late afternoon we were having tea on the lawn and were discussing the lack of common courtesy she had received when she was taken from the palace.

"I was not allowed to even pack a bag," she said, "nor was I allowed any of my jewels or decorations. Later I was allowed a few things, but to this day I haven't even one decoration."

In my ransacking of one of the attics I had found a trunk full of decorations that had been forgotten, so the next day I sneaked in under the eaves and dragged it out near a ventilator and laid them all out on the floor.

In many cases there were duplicates, and it took some time picking out one of each. Late in the afternoon I appeared at her house, with bursting suspenders. My pockets were bulging and I was covered with dirt and spider webs. I must have been a sight, but Her Majesty received me on the lanai.

When I began unpinning and disgorging, tears ran down the old lady's cheeks. She caressingly laid them out on a table, as she named them, the star of this, or the cross of that. It was one of the most pathetic scenes I think I ever witnessed. At the end of the interview she picked up a great star with a pin on the back and a cross with a long blue ribbon with two white lines on it. She had made no effort to thank me (for which I was duly thankful).

"Were there duplicates of these?" she finally said. I looked at them carefully and said I thought there were.

"Could you bring me one of each tomorrow at five o'clock?"

I told her I would if I could find them, and so I was dismissed.

At five the next afternoon I slipped in through the royal gates. Before I was able to ring a bell the door opened and I was confronted by a tall native man with a feather cape carrying a staff in one hand and a tray in the other. In a clear voice, he said, "Did you fulfill the royal command of Her Majesty?"

I looked at him to see if he had a frog face, for I felt just like Alice in Wonderland. His dignity was unshaken, and I felt that I had done the very wrong thing by grinning. He thrust out the tray and I managed to lay the decorations on it without laughing.

As he turned to leave me, another man, dressed like the first, appeared and bowed me into a small reception room.

"You will await your summons here." He again bowed and left me.

After a wait of five or ten minutes they both returned. I had been served with so many summons that I wasn't much frightened; but, I thought it a dirty trick if they had tipped the police off to the fact of my robbing an attic. The first man spoke again. "As Her Majesty is at present without a chamberlain I will have to instruct you. You will approach the throne and kneel before Her Majesty, the Queen, with lowered head."

I pinched myself to see if I were asleep, and wondered if she was going to hit me with a meat axe.

With the two staff bearers marching just ahead, I crossed the hall and entered the long drawing room. At the far end sat Lilioukalani on a big armchair, which was up three shallow steps. On either side of her, standing on the middle step, stood two women in long feather coats over their mother hubbards, and holding three great yellow feathered kahilis, which I recognized as the royal insignias.

What the hell this was all about had never dawned upon me, and for the moment I didn't know whether to laugh, cry, or run.

I knelt and she struck me three gentle taps on the shoulder with a feather duster made of the same yellow feathers as her own cape, and said, in the most serious tone, "Arise, Sir Addison."

She then pinned the star of Kalakau on my left mamric and tied the blue ribbon about my neck.

I don't think I have ever felt sillier in my life—not even when William caught me trying to shave my downy chin for the first time.

Until this instant, I have kept my restoration of the decorations, and this scene, as my deepest secret.

Chapter XXI
ART AND LITERATURE

I WAS TRYING to keep the wolf in the hallway and out of sight; but, the damn thing began to growl and snarl a bit.

Through getting my art supplies at King's, I knew every article they had. One day I found several thin sheets of ivory, so I decided to be a miniature painter. I could get a laborious likeness for seventy-five dollars, and probably left a trail of atrocities for future generations to wonder at. But it kept the wolf more or less dormant.

In nineteen hundred Honolulu was a small, gossipy, little city, with one steamer a week and no cable. Everyone knew everyone else's business, and embroidered it. The acetylene lamp had just reached the town, and the chief sport was driving about in a covered buggy and flashing your light into people's porches to see who was there and what they were doing.

At a picnic given by the ladies of the Presbyterian Church I met Mazie Wood. She was very sweet and pretty and asked me to call. She lived on a corner near the center of town. The next evening by appointment I called. In a half hour I discovered she was very dull and insisted on talking in a semi-whisper. I tried to get away, but each time I made a start she would show me the family album, or some other detainer.

At five minutes after twelve I heard a door open and close. The portières at the end of the room parted. From the dark room beyond a voice said, "All right, Mazie, you can go to bed now."

She turned to me and said goodnight without any further urging. I was frankly puzzled over the whole evening. The next day at lunch I met a friend and asked him if he knew Mazie. "Sure, she's the undertaker's daughter,"—I hadn't realized that I had been sitting "company" with two dead ones.

Feuds were much in vogue and before you knew it you were drawn into one, and once in they would make up and leave you out in the cold from both sides.

I started one that rocked the island. I was very fond of a girl whom Tarn McGrew criticized. I made some snappy remark about some friend of his and he said his friend was more virtuous than mine. I had always thought that you were or weren't virtuous, and being a little unvirtuous was like having a slight touch of leprosy; you either had it or you hadn't.

Unfortunately, I have been given to ridicule all my life, and it has split me up more than once. Tarn and I had been roommates at Boon's. I was very fond of him, but we didn't speak for two or three years over this silly quarrel, and people took sides, as usual.

Steamer day was the bright spot in the week, and one forgot his feuds in seeing new faces and getting news from the mainland. Hardly a steamer landed that did not bring people with letters of introduction and although they paid for carriages one had to do something for them, and this shaved my purse to a splinter.

One steamer day a most lovely young woman arrived. She had the usual letter, introducing Mrs. Ethel Watts Mumford to me. She had with her, her aunt, Mrs. Morrow, and cousin Ethel, and last but not least the "hell child," her son of about seven. He was a terrible brat, but Ethel Mumford was so gay and attractive that even this handicap did not fend me off. She had just been divorced and wanted to be an author and was looking for local color. It was not long before she had the islands by the tail, for she thought the natives more interesting than the missionaries' offspring.

She took a house at Waikiki, on the beach, and any moonlight night you could hear native music and see dimly the hula under the coconut trees, with a long cloth laid under the hoawa trees for a luau.

All this so scandalized respectability that at any odd time the acetylene lights would flash on the scene, and finding nothing worse than a native feast, would blink out in disappointment. Curiosity became so keen that, finally, the more advanced came to call. At first they warned politely that one did not mix with the "Kanaka" as a social equal, but many stayed to do a little mixing themselves.

At the end of a few months Ethel had gathered together all the amusing and witty ones, so that it became the first outdoor salon the island had ever known.

Every word or deed was repeated each time with a little more lace and trimmings until one hardly moved or spoke.

I might as well have moved in, for I spent most of my time with them.

With aunt Annie, cousin Ethel, and the "hell child" on your hip, nothing could have been more circumspect.

Ethel had too much sense of humor to be considered sentimental. We swam all day, feasted, and learned the hula, and Honolulu was split in twain with those that were shocked and those that were curious and defended the cause.

One day I twisted an old adage to fit the time, and Ethel came back with a quotation from Oliver Herford. We began twisting all the old saws and bringing them up-to-date.

It was nearing Christmas time, and Ethel suggested that we get out a calender like the Shakespeare ones of the period, where you tore off a quotation each day, only we were to use our twisted aphorisms instead.

We got three hundred and sixty-five together and sent them to Elder and Shepard in San Francisco to be printed for our Christmas presents. Elder wrote back and asked us if he could publish it for sale, with a few cuts. The cuts brought our one a day down to one a week, for this was the beginning of the nineteen hundreds and the things the editors cut out would be sewing circle stuff today. But, we thought it would be fun and we got up a design, with a gingham cover, and illustrations and sent back the dummy of the "Cynics' Calendar" by

ETHEL WATTS MUMFORD

OLIVER HERFORD

and

ADDISON MIZNER

The very first "crack" in the damn thing cost me plenty, for I had said:

> *"God gives us our relatives; thank God, we can choose our friends."*

I moulted a couple of rich old aunts on the instant.

Oliver Herford had never heard of me and got fussy and resented our using his name and thought he should get ninety percent of the royalties. As Ethel and I didn't expect any return, we didn't pay much attention to his squawks; besides, we had only used two or three of his jolts, and had done all the work, both as to designs and contracts. We thought a third was fair enough for him. Imagine our shock when the first royalty checks came in and we found that we had made over fifteen hundred dollars apiece!

This made some of my back accounts look more healthy, but it didn't put me in affluence, for I have always liked the fattening things of life.

By this time seventy-five dollar suckers on ivory were giving out and things looked bleak again.

Over King's Art Store, Melville Vanaman held forth as a photographer. I had known him for some time, as he had always developed and printed my kodak snaps. I had been spending a week with the Swanzies at Kualoa, and had taken some pictures. As I was lunching with them in town, I wanted to take the prints along. Early in the morning I dropped in to get Vanaman to do them for me. He was sitting at a table touching up an enlargement. He said he was too busy as he had to get the picture out by one o'clock for a newly bereaved family, who might not want it in a week's time. I told him I was an expert at that work, but didn't know how to develop; so I pushed him into the dark room and took his place.

I soon found that it wasn't as easy as it looked, for he was doing it with a sharp, lusterless pencil, in a sort of herringbone stitch to cover up the spots.

Lying on the table were a few sticks of charcoal; so, thinking I would be funny, I made a charcoal drawing out of it, like one used to see in the nineties in a gilt frame with a red plush passe-partout.

I had hardly completed my crime when Vanaman came out. I crouched to receive the expected clout on the ear, for I knew I had ruined several hours of his work. He came up behind me and stood still. I was afraid to look at him.

"Gemini, did you do that in half an hour?" His voice was one of admiration, and I turned timidly to look at him.

"Gee! We could make a lot of money with those. Will you go into partnership with me?"

"What do you mean?" I said.

"What do I mean; I mean about ten years ago a man went through the islands with a wagon, doing those portraits, and he cleaned up on them. King told me he used to buy twenty-five to thirty frames per week from him, so King imported five hundred more frames and before the man could use any of them a sailor murdered the artist for his 'roll.'"

The thought of being murdered for my wealth so intrigued me that at once we got out pencil and paper and started figuring.

> "Cost of photographs..... $1.00
> Salt paper for enlargement..... .40
> Other supplies..... .40
> $1.80"

We dashed down to King and started negotiating for the frames, which he hauled out of a shed and started dusting off. We finally struck a bargain of one dollar and ninety cents each, in lots of twenty-five—and then the stumbling block. He wanted payment in advance. Vanaman and I looked at each other, so I went to hock with my watch.

The portrait firm of Vanaman & Mizner started business.

The first stipulation I made was that I was not to be known in the business. I even got the privilege of sneaking through King's backyard and up the back stairs, for at first I thought I was prostituting "my art," and then Honolulu gossiped so.

For a dollar a week we made arrangement with King. We got the privilege of hanging two pictures in his window.

Including the exhibition, it would cost four dollars and seventy cents to turn out a picture. "Would we get customers?"

I did one of the late King Kalakana, and one of the Princess Kaulani, who had died only a couple of years before. I was afraid to tackle the Queen, for she was alive and might sue me.

We had a violent argument as to the price. I was all for asking twenty dollars, for I knew that a profit of anything over fifteen dollars and thirty cents would be highway robbery, but Vanaman held out for fifty dollars, and I felt sure that this would kill the whole thing.

The first day the atrocities appeared in the window I passed on the opposite side of the street several times to find a jabbering crowd of natives and Chinamen admiring.

The first week we did ten, and then the business came pouring in, leaving me with a tired arm, to wallow in riches. At the end of about two months the charcoal gave out. It would take at least two weeks to get more from San Francisco, so I snooped about the Art Store and found a couple of boxes of pastels, and we raised our price to seventy-five dollars.

It took us six months to hook every mullet-headed moron in the vicinity, and then little by little they gave out.

Vanaman was a character. He had started out by being a barn-storming ham, who played the trombone in the orchestra and any part on the boards. While counting railroad ties between engagements, he had hit on an improvement to the camera. He took parts out of an abandoned alarm clock and made the nozzle of the camera move evenly in a half circle. In this way he could take a panorama.

The Inter-Island Steamship Company was putting on an advertising campaign, and Vanaman had made a huge camera that would take a picture six feet long; so he got the contract to tour the islands and take the most interesting and beautiful spots. As the camera was nearly the size of a coffin, he needed a husky to help carry it, and he chose me.

Our first jump was to be Hilo, on the island of Hawaii, and the volcano of Kilauea.

Some idiots had placed a lot of flower leis and garlands on top of the camera as we carried it aboard the little ship. It looked just like a baby funeral.

Jack Ames, Freddy Sears, and some other Harvard boys were on board. We sat on deck, talking and "throwing up."

At Hilo we stayed at the hotel. The first morning we took views of the harbor from the top of a hill. Vanaman stepped into a hornet's nest and had to lay up for a day or two, so I went in to dinner alone.

There was one long table. I sat down near the end. There was no one else in the dining room at first. Then two men came in. One was tall and slender, with a fine, smooth-shaven face. His linen suit was fresh and his whole appearance was one that knew and liked the tropics. They sat opposite, and nodded a formal greeting.

They resumed their talk, which was about Alaska. The tall man had spent a couple of years along the cost and although I listened, I was not much interested, until he began talking of the "gold rush" through Dyea in '97 and '98. Then I pricked up my ears and, being always a gabby gussie, I joined the conversation. We began swapping experiences. Finally, he asked my name and like a jackass I told him.

"Really? That's interesting. Mine is Ulysses S. Smith. I remember your name very well. I came across it only a few days ago on an old warrant for your arrest, for contempt of court, for failing to answer a summons."

I suppose I had turned ashen, for he added, "That's a long time ago and a long way off. Come over to my office—we're going to have a drink and you might like to have one. Also, I would like to give you that paper just as a cado. You know I'm not an official any longer."

I drew a great sigh of relief and went for the drink, and until I had torn up the paper he handed me, I was not quite comfortable.

Vanaman and I moved up mountain a few days later and stayed at the Volcano House, on the edge of the largest crater in the world. It was the most appalling and beautiful thing I had ever seen.

President Dole, now governor of the territory of Hawaii, was there with Mrs. Dole, and we spent a couple of weeks together, exploring and enjoying the cold nights, at this great elevation.

We visited a couple of other islands and got back to Honolulu to show our wares. But, misfortune was all ready to bite me in the seat of my pants, and here it was again. Freddy Sears had told someone, who had repeated it to one of the heads of the Inter-Island Steamship Company, that I had re-named their fleet the "Inter-Island Pukers."

I lost my job.

CHAPTER XXII
HISTORY

BY THIS TIME very few people were speaking to me. I was out of a job and, besides, the wanderlust was gnawing at my vitals.

At the end of two years I was to receive dividends from one of the investments I had made in San Francisco. As the two years were up, I wrote to the Company to send two thousand dollars to Apia, Samoa.

There was a trading steamer in port and I booked passage to the South Seas. This left me little residue, but with two thousand coming in every three months I was elated.

It was a calm and beautiful trip; but, the Captain said that it could be a treacherous one at a moment's notice. I couldn't help wondering at the seamanship of these South Sea Columbuses, who put out into the open sea with a couple of dugouts lashed together for a long voyage of two or three thousand miles or even more. They steered by the stars and invoked the elements with the calabash of the winds. They had never heard of a compass, or any other instrument. They made these trips many times and, to me, have taken some of the glamour from our great explorers. They carried their princesses to Samoa for a royal wedding and brought one back to marry and keep up their own royal mystery. If they would take these long and perilous trips, why was the line of inheritance always vested in the female line?

I had left a few very dear friends behind; some enemies; and a lot that didn't care a damn one way or another. I had grown to love the natives as well. They were just big children, who lived by the sea and cultivated their taro patches in the valleys. They laughed, danced, and sang, and through it all, had great dignity and simplicity.

They had always had the dirty end of the stick, from the time that Captain Cook discovered the islands. He had landed one beautiful afternoon and being out of firewood put ashore to demand some. The king had been most courteous and tried to explain that they had none on hand, but would bring them a good supply in the morning, as this day was a feast day and too sacred to be disregarded. Cook flew into a rage and ordered his men to tear down the temple and chop up their gods.

Through all times, men have fought for their deities, and one can hardly blame them for splitting Captain Cook's head open as he was making for the boats. This, and many other things, I had dug out of the archives.

A few decades later the Capitals of Europe were vying with each other for a naval base, and loading these simple people with presents. Great Britain sent their biggest battleship to Honolulu to take Kamehameha II and his consort, with a suite of thirty persons, to England as guests of the Crown. They were received at Windsor with the greatest ceremony.

From an old London paper I found a description of Kame-hameha and his queen at the opera at Covent Garden.

"The Sandwich Island Royalties entered the royal box just before the curtain rose. The audience stood and cheered. Their Majesties then bowed and took their seats. The king wore a uniform of dark green cloth with gold epaulets and his star and cross, so lately bestowed upon him by our Crown.

"Her Majesty was dressed in blue satin, with a bandeau of blue and silver gauze, with a large brooch of aquamarines, which held in place several ostrich plumes.

"The poise and dignity of the entire suite has never been outdone by any other visiting potentates, and we cannot believe the report of casual visitors to these far away islands, who come home to tell us that these people are half-naked savages."

What a calamity was to be theirs, for they and their entire suite died in Paris in 1824. Like all diseases that reach a new people, who have no inheritant resistance, it cut them all down, but the worst was yet to come.

The same British battleship that had taken them away, amid the booming of guns and the blare of the band, sailed into the harbor of Honolulu a year later with thirty-two leaden coffins in her hold. The people went wild with mourning, and the rumor went around that their beloved king and queen were held as prisoners and that there were only stones in the caskets. With great fury they attacked the funeral cortège and tore open the coffins.

The disease spread like wildfire. There were no doctors, and when the fever came on they plunged into the sea to get cool. It is variously estimated, but somewhere between two hundred thousand and a half million died within six months.

No foreign power ever got a naval base, for which several had been angling, and this was the answer; their great bereavement made them ever after distrustful of all nations.

The trading ships brought new diseases, mosquitoes, and rum, and the psalm-singing settlers distributed them, while the missionaries harangued the natives and let the settlers build a church. Portuguese settlers began to inter-breed. A stray negro would desert his ship for this tropic paradise, and the result was the hophouli, who inherited the worst of both.

No one knows where leprosy came from, or what its cause, but by 1880 there were a few cases. King Kalakaua set aside part of the island of Molokai as a leper settlement. But the natives resisted this living death for their beloved ones. A cousin of the king's, a young prince of wealth, discovered he had the first symptoms, and instead of taking a steamer to Japan, where it was a common thing, he stayed to lead a thousand of the stricken to the settlement.

At about this time smallpox broke out and the king appointed a certain doctor to buy a vaccine point for every soul on the islands, and made vaccination compulsory. The doctor saw a way to make some easy money, and charged the government for the full amount, but bought only one-tenth the points necessary. He inoculated fifteen hundred new cases with leprosy for Molokai.

One can't help hoping the doctor's soul is sizzling in hell, for he has been dead for twenty years.

Dr. Walters, who was in charge of the leper colony, took me to see the settlement on one of his official trips. The horror of it lingers with me yet, so I would rather change the subject.

The language is very simple and can be written down with twelve letters. The construction is so simple that I learned to read and speak it within six months. This helped me no end, in that hot and dusty attic, when I delved into the past.

As far as I know I have the only complete English-Hawaiian dictionary in existence.

Although I had told my friends that I was sailing, they thought it was for home, and I stood on the wharf alone, surveying my little tramp steamer. I have always hated "goodbyes" and dodged them, where possible.

There were three old native flower vendors; I had bought many a garland and wreath from them and when they saw my trunk go on board they hung the lei alima about my neck, with a long one made from the fragrant white ginger flowers.

As we steamed out of the harbor, I went to the stern and gently dropped the wreaths into the water, and there were tears in my eyes as I said "Aloha nui."

CHAPTER XXIII
KILLING TIME

APIA WAS hot and still; with its fringe of coconut trees hanging over the beach. There was a general store with rooms over it; a boarding house, also of frame construction; and most of the rest was palm-thatched houses.

I had been here a week and was waiting for the steamer to bring my money from San Francisco.

The long walk out to see Mrs. Robert Louis Stevenson had been hot and tiring and I stayed nearer the village after that.

Samoa was what Hawaii must have been in 1830. It was little spoiled by civilization. The king wore a small "lava cloth" about his hips, with hibiscus flowers behind his ears, and nothing else.

The seva dance was done sitting down, instead of like the hula. There weren't clothes enough on the entire royal household to flag a waffle wagon; otherwise, it was much like Hawaii, for the missionaries hadn't yet inflicted their mother hubbards and other pruderies.

Another week slipped by and the steamer came in.

I was reading my sad letter under a tree by the beach, when I heard an argument going on beyond some bushes, between a second-rate Englishman and a Jap, both passengers from the ship. The Jap was demanding two dollars more per slide than he was getting and the Englishman was as strenuously refusing. Out of the jumble I gleaned that the white man was gathering up material and lantern slides for a lecture tour, and that his advertisement was that the slides were colored accurately by a great artist on the spot where they were taken, and this was the whip hand the Jap was using in threatening to leave the Englishman here to take his pictures while he, the Jap, went on by the same steamer.

My letter had been a disaster. The investment had been more or less a failure and there was no money forthcoming. I turned my pockets inside out; four dollars and eighty cents. It looked like a banana patch and a few coconuts for life. I had whetted my wits on the world for years now, but this one stumped me, for there were no whetstones in sight.

I wandered back to the general store, trying to work things out as I went. Sitting disconsolately on the porch, I saw the Englishman and an idea occurred to me. I went upstairs and got my sketch block and water colors and bringing them back, I started a sketch of the sea through some coconut trees. You can get ninety-nine dubs out of a hundred into a conversation with a sketch block, even an Englishman, so I worked in silence. In ten minutes he was peering over my shoulder, introducing himself as Professor Collins. In another five minutes I was discussing Japanese art glibly and told him I had studied their method of coloring photographs and lantern slides. I kept my innocent blue eyes on my work, for I felt he would see in my face what a liar I was. But the case was desperate. I was too big to be a stowaway and too easily made seasick to be a deck hand. At last I led him around to it and he popped the question. "How much do you ask for coloring slides."

I had been working on him so fast that I hadn't thought of the price so I began to stall. All I knew was that the Jap wanted two dollars more, but what he was already getting I had no idea. I heard the professor say that with his travelling expenses paid he couldn't afford to pay him any more. Going on with the sketch, I said I did not know exactly as I had had no practice for a couple of years and that I would have to try two or three out to see how long it took. I thought it would be. about a dollar and a half or a dollar and seventy-five cents—I couldn't say offhand, it might be less. I stole a sly glance, and he hadn't fallen down. On the contrary I saw he was interested.

He told me that the man he had brought with him was very impertinent and he was thinking of letting him go. He could return on the steamer, which was coaling, and waiting two days for passengers from the other islands. We came to a tentative arrangement. I was to get a half dozen plates, that had been discarded, and he loaned me his lantern to try them out with.

I had a whitewashed wall in my room, which would do for a screen. I dashed for my room and started in. The water color dried so fast that it made humps, and when I threw it on the wall the colors were opaque and in places made the film look as though it had rocks scattered over it. I hurriedly tried to wash the colors off in my basin; although it was better, it was far from good.

Under the corrugated iron roof the room was boiling and I thought I might think better if I got some air. Down on the porch I found a cooling breeze and flopped in the nearest chair, to despair. After a few moments I discovered that the wind was coming from one end of the porch so I dragged my chair over to the edge and tilted it back against a post. In my new position I was half facing the display window and there staring right at me was a big piece of fly-specked cardboard with little packages pasted all over it. At the top was printed "Darling Dyes." In an instant I was in the store.

"What do you want for that card in the window?" pointing at the dye sign.

"They ain't no good," said the energetic storekeeper, who I had wakened from a nap. "They don't hold their color down here in this sun. They tell me it's too damp for 'em."

"Where I'm going to use them there won't be any sun or damp." I got twenty packages for twenty-five cents.

I combed a dozen jelly glasses from the dump heap and made a set of colors. By wetting the plates first the colors flowed easily. In an hour I had four very creditable pictures.

That night the professor told the Jap to go to hell.

The through steamer to Melbourne, Australia, was due in ten days and the professor was busy snapping everything in sight. I could color them much faster than he could take them and develop them. I did fifteen in a morning easily. That meant that I had to hide out like a church cat so he wouldn't think it too easy. It again didn't make much difference where I went, as long as I went; so we sailed for Australia.

Collins was a dowdy old pedantic of the typical school teacher type, and day by day I grew to hate him worse, and more of it.

After ten days in Melbourne, we got into an argument as to whether something was yellow-green or green-yellow and we busted up.

I had only been with the professor a little over a month and had not made a fortune. To conserve "eat money" I moved into a rooming house which was next to a ham and egg dump named "Murphey's Place."

Melbourne was a hell of a place to be in, even if you had enough dough to get out with; but broke, it was awful. One couldn't find anything to do; especially an American.

"Murphey's Place" was the hangout for all the prize fighters and toughs in the town, for there was a gymnasium above where the "Pride of Australia" was training to meet the "Brisbane Kid." I got to know most of them and used to sit around the training quarters with them. Occasionally I would put on the gloves and go a few rounds, just for fun. I was better than a raw hand at the game, having started my career in the tank house at home. It didn't take me long to see that the "Pride of Australia" was something of a dub, and I began to wish that I had some cash to bet against him, although I had never seen the "Brisbane Kid."

It was Tuesday night and the big battle was set for Thursday, a twenty-round go, and the main event of the year. On Thursday afternoon the flashy promoter came to me at the lunch counter and beckoned me upstairs and into a private office. "Look here," he said, "you ever done much fighting?"

I thought over my turbulent past and acknowledged that I had; though I did not tell him that my career had not been a professional one. He looked at me keenly for a moment and, seeing I was stupidly honest, he said, "Things are a little messed up. The 'Brisbane Kid' has turned yellow. He got a slant of 'The Pride' last night and is running out on us. Says he's got a sprained wrist. Now, this is the set-up: The house is sold out, over eight thousand seats. I can't disappoint them and it came into my mind that you are the only one around here about the same weight so I thought you would do. You're an American I take it. And you probably know that your countrymen are not popular. I'm sorry, I mean no offense, but it has occurred to me that the audience wouldn't mind giving up their money to see 'The Pride' wallop an American."

"Just what is your proposition?" I asked. "There isn't any use beating around the bush; I'm listening." This seemed to relieve him of any embarrassment, for he went on.

"It's just this—you go in and box six rounds with 'The Pride'; he won't hurt you much; and in the first part of the seventh round he steps up and knocks you out. You see we will announce you as the bloody American (I beg your pardon), I don't know your name."

I couldn't think of any name but Grandfather Watson, so I said, "Watson—Whirlwind Watson, from Frisco."

He smiled sardonically, "Then it's all fixed."

He started to rise. I laid my hand on his arm and forced him back in the chair. "There are two things that aren't fixed at all. The first one is how much do I get?"

"Fifty dollars."

"Make it one hundred and fifty dollars and I might."

"All right; we'll make it one hundred and fifty."

"Now, the second thing is just this—if 'The Pride' can knock me out in the first round, okeh; but if I can stay the twenty rounds, I stay. Do you get that?"

He laughed tolerantly and said that was fine. I could borrow some tights, and I had some old sneakers, so I was set.

I had seen "The Pride" box but not fight and I knew he was slow and that I was fast, so at a little after ten that night I took my corner and kept it the twenty rounds. "The Pride" was crazy and the crowd yelled for a return bout. The promoter hopped into the ring and came over to me. "How about a return for next Thursday?"

I had heard that the winner was getting two-sixths and the loser one-sixth of the gate, so I told the old bone-head that I would do it if the winner got one-third of the gate and the loser one hundred and fifty dollars. He finally agreed and held up his hand for silence and made the announcement. There were yells of "'The Pride' will kill that blighter!" and much worse, for there were no ladies in the audience.

I had no friends, no training quarters, or no second, but I did have one hundred and fifty dollars, which would buy more muscle-building grub that I had been getting. I spent the week walking and doing some shadow boxing and sleeping a lot.

I had gotten "The Pride's" number in the last bout and knew that if I got him mad he would open up like a fan. I hadn't tried to lick him the last fight—all I wanted was just to keep him off me. Unless something went wrong, I had a good thing and besides I was fighting for a ticket home.

Looking up the sailings, I found that there was a steamer leaving at one o'clock Thursday night and I had made up my mind that if I was still alive, I'd be on my way home to Mama Mizner. I packed a bag with my best stuff and left the trunk in the room. I put the bag under the rubbing table in the dressing room at the arena.

The preliminaries had been long, each going the limit, and there had been no knock-outs. Was this an omen or were they waiting for me to get the big slam? I was getting nervous; it was ten forty-five before I got in the ring and I was thinking of missing the steamer.

I looked over my opponent's bandages to see he did not have an anvil strapped to them. The gong clanged and I stepped out. I realized that I was a little shaky and that I had a slight nausea of nerves—not so good, hey? I kept away from "The Pride" for the first three rounds, while the crowd called me a yellow-bellied bastard and cheered "Australia's darling."

The gong rang for the fourth. What was the matter with me? I was thinking how hungry I was and my mind wasn't on my business. Suddenly, "The Pride" clipped me on the end of my nose. It had always annoyed me to be hit on the nose that way, so I reached out and picked one up off the floor and slammed him one on the chin.

He dropped like a felled ox and lay still. There was a terrible hush; save for the slow droning count there wasn't a sound. "Ten." He still lay on his back with glassy eyes looking up at the rafters. The referee lifted my arm, and I scurried for the dressing room. I had my pants on over my tights and my coat over my bare and sweating shoulders when they carried "The Pride" in, still as limp as a wash rag.

I was at the door when someone grabbed my arm. "Don't go that way. They will mob you." It was the promoter speaking. "I just came from the box office and here's your bit; get out through the back alley as quickly as you can. I think you've killed him. The crowd is in a rage. It ain't no spoof for a bloody American to knock one of us out like that. I don't want another murder. They would stop fighting in the whole country of Hedies. You'd better make a run for it, I tell you."

I needed no further urging, for the crowd was howling and pressing for the dressing room door. Everyone was working over "The Pride," and no one noticed me slip out the back door and run down the long alley with my bag.

The streets were nearly empty at this hour but the few I passed looked at me strangely, for I had no hat or shirt on and my nose was bleeding. I hailed an old hansom and told him "the pier." It was after twelve and I had no idea how long it took to get there. I shrank back in the shadow as much as possible, trying to keep out of sight.

Had I killed him? Perhaps I better go to the police and give myself up. I hadn't meant to hit that hard. No; panic and flight was uppermost and we finally clattered down the wharf.

They were just pulling in the gangplank and I made them pull me with it. I was out of breath, very tired, and scared to death, but we were under power now and going down the harbor.

A man in uniform stepped up and said, "First or second," and I said, "First," looking dazedly at his cap while I spelled out "purser" on its label. "Ticket, please."

"I haven't one; I want to buy one," I stammered.

"Manila, Hong Kong, Shanghai, or Yokohama?"

I had had too much excitement for one evening already, and told him I didn't want to clown around at this hour. "I want a ticket to San Francisco."

"Well, you can change to the Pacific Mail at Shanghai," he suggested, smiling in a nice and friendly way. "You are on the wrong boat. The Vancouver San Francisco Line is just pulling out over there," he said pointing to a ship half a mile away.

I was too tired and too frightened to care whether I was going to Tierra del Fuego or Helgoland, so I bought a ticket, registered my right name, to Shanghai, and turned in.

The next day we touched at Sydney and I locked myself in my cabin, saying I was sick. I had the steward get me the papers and found that "The Pride" had been out three hours and that "Whirlwind Watson" had escaped on the San Francisco boat.

I may have nicked most of the other Commandments, but I don't think I have ever committed a murder, although I have wanted to often.

In a few days I was on deck again and chumming with the purser. I found that the steamer touched at Merauke, in Dutch New Guinea, and at Manila. I arranged with him for an indefinite stop-over in Manila. I only stayed a couple of days there, and headed off for Siam and India.

I had time to count up my blood money and I found that after paying my fare I still had nearly two thousand dollars and I felt it would be a shame not to spend it. I wrote to the bank in San Francisco, where I had left the savings account, to forward me a checking account to a bank in Shanghai. So I travelled about until I just had enough to reach there.

The Geographic can give you a better description than I, so that's that!

When I reached Shanghai I made straight for my bank and found a letter saying that they would forward two thousand dollars in a letter of credit as directed and honor my drafts to the full amount of my account. But, I had not figured in the twenty-one day trip from San Francisco to Shanghai and was temporarily embarrassed.

There was a funny looking little man hanging around the hotel, named Einstein; if I was embarrassed, he was mortified to death. One morning I found him in the lobby reading a discarded newspaper.

"There's going to be 'an unclaimed sale' down on the Bund this afternoon," he whispered.

"And what the hell might that be?" I asked.

"Why the steamship lines have them every year. The stuff that people don't call for is auctioned off to pay for the storage after they have held it a year."

"I don't see how we can stop it," I answered.

"That ain't the idea. There is lots of money to be made that way. You buy it blind and maybe it's something good and maybe it ain't, but business is always a gamble like that."

He looked so wistful that my heart melted, and I began mentally taking stock.

I had shown the hotel man my letter from the bank and he had given me credit for board and lodging for three weeks. I had about thirty dollars, which I was saving for rickshaws, et cetera.

"How much would it take?" I asked.

"Not much," he answered; "let's go down and see."

At two-thirty that afternoon we gathered on the Bund with a lot of other nitwits and gaped. The bidding was not spirited, so when a very large case was tilted out, it had struck me as being very heavy, so I bid one dollar.

"It's too big to be any good," my friend nudged me; but I bid up to four dollars and ninety cents and got it.

"Now, you pick one."

In a few minutes a case rolled out and someone bid a dollar and Einstein raised him fifty cents and finally got it for three dollars and a half.

It was evidently not a new game to Einstein, for he knew just what to do.

Within a half hour we were in a shed down a side alley opening our prizes. His was a gross of celluloid spectacles with plain glass, and mine was a dozen sets of coffin handles, with six to a set.

It was easy enough to sell a Chinaman spectacles, for they loved them and thought it made them look scholarly; but what to do with eighty-two coffin handles was another matter.

I knew a little Chinese, which I had learned from Ying, and with some pigeon English to fill up the wide open spaces, I started out. I got many a laugh. I showed Shanghai how beautiful they looked as door pulls and towel racks, and demonstrated them in every conceivable way and before my steamer arrived I had sold them all at a dollar Mexican apiece, which was worth fifty, so my first mercantile adventure was a success. Perhaps my luck was changing.

I sailed back home, thinking I might become a Merchant Prince, like Wanamaker.

CHAPTER XXIV
ICEMAN, SAVE MY CHILD

ON ARRIVING in San Francisco I found Mama Mizner in despair. Her "Angel Birdie" was lost.

He had come out from Nome on the last boat, to sell part of his holdings, so he could work the rest to better advantage. On the old *Portland* he had left again so as to be the first one back in the spring. That was over three months ago and the steamer had not been heard of since.

Mother was getting out her mourning and pinning her last hopes on prayer. It was not a cheerful home coming, for she clasped me to her bosom and cried. I couldn't remind her that "A bad penny always turns up," or anything else cheerful, for they all seemed to have a twist I thought she might not appreciate.

I went down to the Steamship Company and had a long talk with the manager, which wasn't exactly encouraging. There was one chance he said, and that was that the ship might have been caught in an ice floe and if she had not been crushed to pieces long before this, there was a slight possibility still of a change of winds that would break up the floe and open up a way out.

The *Portland* had a cargo of food and supplies, but the drinking water couldn't hold out much longer and, of course, they might have run out of fuel, had engine trouble, or a broken propeller; he could only speculate like the rest of us. The manager had been a captain and sailed these treacherous seas for many years and knew what he was talking about. There had been no bad storms reported up to the time the ship was long overdue. He threw up his hands and added that they couldn't put in an insurance claim for total loss for another week, for the severe freeze would come then, and there would be no hope left.

We all got together at Min's for a family conclave. As mother did not come downstairs for it, we sat around telling one another what a fine fellow Wilson was; how he had done this generous act, or that thoughtful thing; reminding each other of the time he had jumped off the Oakland boat in midwinter to save Desmond Cosgrave's life; what a wonderful fighter he was; and describing all his fine qualities. From a "hell raiser" we elevated him to the misunderstood angel. It was a glorious gathering of sorrow and regrets. All his little foibles were excused and painted out.

Another week dragged by on leaden wheels. None of us had accepted any invitations or gone anywhere, except to Min's house on Pacific Avenue, where every afternoon we gathered to tell one another how we loved our baby brother.

The telephone rang. "Just another inquiry of sympathy," someone said, and I was pushed toward the phone. It was the captain from the Steamship Company.

"Just received the following telegram from Seattle, from the captain of the *Julia*, just docked from Nome," he said. "I knew your family would like to hear it first."

He read the telegram.

"Steamship *Portland* arrived an hour before we sailed. She had been caught in an ice floe and carried through the Bering Straits far into the Arctic Ocean, locked tight for one hundred and three days. All on board well."

I dashed in and told the family.

William said, "Oh, hell!"

Lan said, "Wouldn't you know he'd do something like that?" And Mama Mizner and Min cried.

During the days of worry and sorrow I had been summing up myself. I made up my mind that I was growing old and I should settle down. Of course, love had a great deal to do with my retrospective mood, but all the things that had happened to me in the last year or so came to my mind.

Selling coffin handles in China had taught me something of trade and the value of money. I had worked three or four hours at a time selling one handle, and after two weeks having finally sold my goods, all but one, I happened by an undertaking parlor in the foreign quarter. Just out of curiosity, I went in to price his stock and found that the proprietor would have bought all mine at ten times the price I had worked so hard for.

My escape from a mob in Melbourne; the feeling that one might be a murderer; and a few other trifles had shocked me into the realization that life was a more or less serious thing.

I had arrived in San Francisco a much more thoughtful fellow than when I had left there nearly two years before.

I had also been fancy free (except for a few "flashes in the pan"), and now I fell desperately in love with Bertha Dolber. I had known her for several years, even before I had gone to the Klondike, and watched her grow from a gawky kid into grace and girlhood. She was a new type for me; tall, straight, and dark, with a great deal of dignity, and a quiet humor, and a certain "hands off" attitude.

The first barrier was money, for she was an orphan with several millions in her hip pocket. Her mother had died when she was a baby, and Miss Warren had come to take care of her and had lived on as one of the family. She became more like a mother than a companion, and now that Mr. Dolber was dead, Bertha clung closer to Miss Warren.

I looked over my own cash register. Ten or twelve thousand was the best I could do, so I began looking for a job, or some way to make money. You couldn't ask a girl to knock about the world on an off chance of painting lantern slides or selling nickel-plated casket fittings.

I was always a timid lover and afraid that I was making myself ridiculous. I would turn a situation into a joke just when I should have been serious, but I felt that she liked me, but it wasn't much encouragement to be told that you were "the funniest man in town." I tried a lot of things financial, but like "Portia" they didn't hatch out well, though I kept my nest egg intact.

The Mizner blood, being three-fourths Irish, was naturally full of sentiment. Also, it was full of teasing and ridicule. I was always between the devil and the deep sea when it came to love, and it certainly was not my most attractive side. I was insanely jealous and if Bertha looked at anyone else, I would slink away and cry and sulk and indulge myself in self-pity, to its fullest. It was a bumpy sea; one minute I was on the crest of the wave and the next in the trough of despond.

Bertha had gone to the Hotel Del Monte, Monterey, for a week or so, and my great pal and only confidant, Jack Baird, suggested that we motor down and take a rest, which neither of us needed.

Automobiles were very rare at this time and fifteen miles an hour was breakneck speed, then too the damn thing wouldn't run uphill.

The first day we made over sixty miles in eight hours, on the level floor of the Santa Clara Valley, without horses or other aid. The second day was awful; pushing and pulling, we ran out of gas and had to telegraph back to San José to send it on by train to the nearest town, for there were no gas stations by the roadsides. After hiring a team of horses to pull us ten miles to the top of the San José grade, we coasted down to Del Monte on the third day.

I spent two heavenly days with my beloved—just watching her—for I didn't dare lay a hand on her, except when we waltzed. That was nearly thirty years ago and "necking" was an unknown dish.

On the third day Milton Latham came down by train and I had a rival. He was a couple of years older, much better looking, and "had a way with him," and no timidity.

I was "beside myself" and told Jack I was going home. Jack, though younger than I, said, "You haven't got the brains of a Welsh rabbit. Don't let her see that you care. I tell you what let's do; let's make her jealous; let's motor down to Santa Barbara. The Finlay girls are down there and Bertha told me the other day that 'although they were pretty in a way' she didn't see what we saw in them."

Jack had a way of making everything look alluring. No one had ever made the trip from San Francisco to Santa Barbara in an automobile and it would be wonderful to be the first.

It *was* wonderful that we got there, after ten days, over the San Luis Obispo Pass and the San Marcus.

We were hailed like Lindbergh and enjoyed "the freedom of the city," and made very free with it.

Jack had a semi-trainer and rubber who sometimes acted as valet. He telegraphed to the "Saginaw Kid" to pack up some things for us and bring them to Santa Barbara.

We stayed at the Hotel Potter, and were very stylish, with a suite of rooms. Entertainments were given for us and we were rather splurging. We kept the "Saginaw Kid" in the background and referred to him as our "man."

Joe Weston, who was staying at another hotel, met us at the pool one day and suggested a picnic. Jack thought that would be fine and said, "I'll have my man bring out the lunch."

"You keeping a man, Jack? Hell! I can't even keep a woman."

A few nights later a party was breaking up and we asked several of the young bloods to have breakfast with us in our rooms at twelve. There were several New York boys that were rather giving themselves airs, and Jack thought he would impress them.

We woke up about eleven and sent for Saginaw. Jack began to instruct him as to the behavior of a valet.

"You can't roam around here in that dirty sweater, joining in the conversation, and sitting down with us. I'll give you that black suit of mine and you wear a black tie. Speak as little as possible, but when you do, say 'sir,' not 'redhead' to me."

We showed him his manners, after he had dressed up. He didn't look so bad, though his cauliflower ears stuck straight out and his nose was plastered flat on his face.

Our guests arrived; breakfast was served and everything was going great. Charlie Fernald was saying that he had found a "lightweight" up at the livery stable who could lick anything his weight in the state and he was thinking of backing him for a fight in Reno.

This was too much for Saginaw and he stepped out of character with, "I seen that son-of-a—; he couldn't lick a postage stamp. Say, Red, give me a wallop at him and I'll fold him up like a sheet."

There was no use pretending further and I began a quick description of the "Kid's" prowess. It wound up with a match between the two at the livery stable for Monday night.

Fernald was a Californian and enjoyed the situation, but the Easterners thought us pretty common.

Arrangements had to be made with caution, for there had been a strict law passed about prize fighting in California and Santa Barbara in particular was old-fashioned. By devious routes and with great stealth we gathered in the carriage house at the livery stable.

Charlie had obtained some gloves somewhere and the proprietor of the stable had hung a single electric light from the ceiling. Everything was set and the opponents faced each other. There were only about twenty of us.

Jack was the "Kid's" second, with a pail, a towel to flap, and a sponge.

It hadn't gone half a round when I saw that the sponge was the only important thing in the paraphernalia. The other man whanged one to the "Saginaw's" belly and knocked him under the hearse, which was parked in the corner. Jack and I rushed over to try to get him out, but he wouldn't come.

Crash! The police had broken in. The audience started hopping around like rabbits. Very quietly I opened the back doors of the hearse and crawled in. I was the only one not arrested, but the rest were merely taken to the station and sent home to have a good night's rest, while I spent a most uncomfortable night.

The "Saginaw Kid" had not been a good bet, and we had to wire to San Francisco for fares home. The car went by boat.

The papers were full of "The society prize fight," but my name did not appear. Bertha congratulated me for not going to anything so vulgar and vile. We soon came to a better understanding.

For the next few months I saw her every day. She chided me about not having anything definite to do and said she would never marry anyone who expected to go through life without a purpose. Working as a draftsman didn't seem to be getting me anywhere and every successful architect I knew was a doddering old man. So I set out to work up a scheme that had been in the back of my head for years.

Coffee! That was the thing. A good brand of coffee. Mocha and Java, or your grocer's best, were all lousy. There was no one putting out brands in those days; why not get a good brand and advertise? The automobile companies were the few that advertised. Of course, there was Lydia Pinkham, and Carter with his little liver pills—why not get coffee on the market the same way? Guatemala shipped all her good coffee to Vienna and Russia because no one in America knew good coffee.

I wrote to New York to friends of mine in the importing business and finally got some capital interested and tentatively sketched out a program. The first thing I would have to do was to go to Guatemala and see if I could get contracts signed up. This would take at least six months.

Bertha was going to Europe anyway, so I asked her if there was a chance for me if I made good with a salary of ten thousand dollars per year and a part of the business. We talked it over for days and she finally thought there might be a slight chance. We left it that way—just a chance—but that was something to work for.

Jack was mixed up with a girl that was doing him good and he thought he would like to go along. Joe Weston, whom I had known from infancy, wanted to go too, but his case was the reverse. He had been living in sin with Mae for two years and wanted to marry her. His family was very prominent in California and he knew that if he committed matrimony in San Francisco the papers would spill all the girl's past, so he begged me to take them down with us and they could be quietly married at the legation.

Jack, who was never very strong, had attached another bodyguard at the last minute; one Jack Otts.

So, Joe, Mae, Jack Baird, Otts, and myself were ready to go.

Bertha was to go East a week before I sailed and I went as far as Benicia, saying goodbye.

Joe, Otts, and Jack had gathered up an arsenal and were planning a jaguar hunt. Everything was set and we shoved off early in the year 1904.

CHAPTER XXV
MY TRAGEDY

THE TROUBLE began at San José de Guatemala. The preparations for the hunting trip had been so advertised in San Francisco that the custom officers waited on us with a regiment of soldiers and confiscated all the firearms. A complete search of our luggage, divulging no compromising papers, further convinced the authorities that we were revolutionists importing munitions of war.

Cabrillo, who was now dictator, had not eaten anything for two years but soft-boiled eggs, which were cooked by his aged mother for fear of assassination. He was not taking any chances. He never left the palace and was guarded night and day, while spies were everywhere. People were afraid to speak to me and I could do no business, so I thought the best thing to do was to make character by minding my own business and showing the country to my friends.

After a day's rest we all got dressed up in our best and descended on the legation for the wedding.

The plenipotentiary was away, but the charge d'affaires was there and could act in his place. I made an appointment and things looked bright for the nuptials.

We were shown into a long drawing room and after a moment's wait the charge d'affaires came in with his wife. He didn't give me time to introduce my party, but, after shaking hands with me, bolted over to Mae and said, "How do you do, Mrs. Weston—I want to introduce my wife."

This confused us all so completely that we talked of everything in the world but the blessed bonds of wedlock. After a most uncomfortable half hour, we all filed out as unmarried as when we went in.

As the San Juan doors closed behind us, we started wrangling as to who should have taken a stand—and there it ended, for no wedding bells rang out.

A description of the cast is necessary. Jack Baird was tall and very slight, without being scrawny. He had yellow-red hair, and a slightly bulbous nose, and was the most considerate, thoughtful person imaginable, with Old World manners; but he was not flint in the hands of a pretty woman, and he had asthma.

Jack Otts was way above the average pug, with an ambition to advance in the world. His one thought was physical well being for others.

Mae was just a blonde with matrimonial ambitions.

Joe Weston was a character. He was half an inch too short to get into the naval academy, which had broken his heart. He knew the rating of every ship that had ever floated, with the exact armament and the range of every gun. A half inch had robbed the navy of a great officer. He was nearly as broad as he was long and looked like a cross between a polliwog and a baked potato. A man of one love, and a periodical desire for liquor. If you kept him off the subject of the navy, he was very amusing, with a keen sense of humor and a cutting wit. He inhaled his conversation instead of exhaling as most people do and could be most annoying in his cups. Our families had been intimate for half a century and his mother sort of bequeathed him to me at her death.

If you had gone through hell with a sulky rake, you could not have gathered up a more mis-mated quintet. There was but one bond that held us together, and that was the ridiculous, and a good laugh, for we all could roar at nothing.

Twenty years before, the older Barrios had expelled the religious orders and confiscated everything but the actual churches themselves. There was only one priest to every two churches, and they were very poor. So, waiting for politics to cool off, I turned to the church.

They had vast treasures in old velvet, damask, and embroideries, together with silver and furniture. All these things were going to rack and ruin, as they were out of use. So in the interim I decided on a looting expedition.

Thirty miles from the capital there was the beautiful old city of Antigua, which had been the original capital. It had been so damaged by an earthquake early in the seventeen hundreds that the capital had been removed to its present site.

Antigua lay in a little basin a mile above the sea, with five volcanoes surrounding it. Agua rises eight or nine thousand feet directly out of the plane, in a perfect cone, and Fuego and the others stand as sentinels to the south. Acatenango is the only one in eruption, and this burns with a sullen light. Great clouds of smoke rise from it, giving a most mysterious touch, as though the gods of the Mayas were keeping their altar fires going.

In an hour's ride up the mountain you are above the timber line, in snow, and in the same time you can descend into impenetrable jungle. In all my peregrinations, I think this is the loveliest and most inspiring place I know. It's true it had an earthquake, but after all what is an earthquake among friends?

From my window one looks out over a deserted city and can count fifty-three churches, one dating as early as 1521. When the Pilgrim Fathers landed in Massachusetts this was a city of one hundred and fifty thousand souls, and now only rates about ten thousand.

On one side of the enormous plaza the arcades of the vice-regal palace run the whole length; at the far end the arcades of private palaces; and nearest us are those of the barracks; all in good order and in use; across the end stands the front of the old cathedral, with only part of it in use, for the back is a huge ruin, although over thirty of its flat domes form a terrace to which we climb to see the sunset.

Three evenings a week the military band gives a concert in the plaza and the town is in bed and asleep by nine.

After showing my gang my favorite spot on earth for a few days, I began palling up the priesthood.

I mean no disrespect to the church, and it should be understood that it was legitimate at this time for the priests to sell, and that they were near starvation.

One beautiful morning I found the priest of the cathedral waiting for me in the sacristy and we immediately began haggling over prices. I knew that if I offered him over one per cent of their value he would become suspicious, and he knew that no matter what price he would ask he would have to come down ten times before we traded. I had gathered up eight or ten large bundles, weighing one hundred pounds apiece, and after three hours, we both being exhausted, I paid him his pittance.

I was about to call a gang of mosves or carriers, when the priest grabbed me by the arm.

"I have never sold so much to one customer before," he said, "and I've been thinking it might annoy some of my parish to see so much go out all at once. I think the best thing to do would be to come to the far end of the ruins tonight at nine-thirty and I will deliver these things to you then and there."

So we agreed on his plan. I was to whistle a bar of "La Paloma," and he would deliver the goods.

At a little after nine I started out from the hotel. Joe had insisted upon coming with me. I had ten mosves stationed in the side street and found them all sprawled out asleep. Quietly we slunk along to the rear of the cathedral looking for a door. Nothing but sheer walls seventy-five feet high. I went to the corner and still no door. I was bewildered. Surely a starving old priest wouldn't gyp me.

Everything was as silent as the grave, so I started whistling my song of the dove—bang! From the roof he had tilted off the first bundle. It came within an inch of killing Joe. We all fled to the middle of the narrow street while the other bundles were being delivered. The phlegmatic Indian carriers thought it was an earthquake; but, without question, picked up their loads and followed us home.

That was one of the many hauls I made. Another, but very different one, was the purchase of an old monastery on the edge of town. The reason I wanted it was that eight of the side chapels of the church were intact and in each stood, thirty feet high, carved wood altars with heavy gilding. I could see in my mind's eye a beautiful panelled room made from them.

This property belonged to a grandee with a profligate son. We bickered about the price for ten days and I finally got it for six hundred dollars, the price I would have paid for one altar had he known what I wanted. There were three big patios and eighteen acres of coffee.

I finally sold the altars for six thousand dollars. My client didn't like the gilding and I scraped off all the gold and sent it to a smelter. There was a little over eleven thousand dollars worth of the precious metal when I called to see the result. Fortunately, the client bought the woodwork, if I would deliver it scraped.

As a by-product, I got fourteen hundred pounds of the best coffee in the world every year for fifteen years, after all expenses were paid.

If you don't want to know the difference between good coffee and coffee, skip this paragraph.

Coffee grown down on the lowlands is very coarse and rank. Each tree produces several times as much as a tree which grows at an elevation of five thousand feet, which is about the greatest elevation at which it will grow. The higher the elevation, the finer the coffee. The tree is about the size of an orange tree and has bright, shiny leaves. Growing close to the limb are bright little cherries with a sweet, pithy meat, enclosing two beans. Every year the tree sends out new shoots and on this growth the cherries are smaller and have only one little bean. This is called the caracole and is gathered separately. To an expert, this is as different as grape juice is from a fine French wine. Coffee should be hung for two years at least before use and then browned and ground every few days.

It was my idea to have two brands; one for the real lovers of coffee, with nothing but caracole, at a high price; and another of very fine high elevation growth, which I could put on the market to compete with any fairly good coffee.

My expeditionary forces were beginning to rub edges and get restless, so I was not sorry when they announced they were leaving for the World's Fair in St. Louis, via the Gulf of Mexico.

I went back to the capital with them and saw them off. They would have to travel by stage and horse one hundred and fifty miles to the head of the little jerk water banana trains, which would take them to Puerto Barrios and the steamer to New Orleans. With mixed sentiments of regret and joy I watched their dusty departure.

In a few days I went back to Antigua, where I spent a month closing up some coffee contracts and getting more familiar with the treasures of the church.

I had been alone about six weeks and had arranged to feed a couple of ravenous old Fathers at dinner when the telegraph operator came in and handed me a cablegram. He told me over and over that was the first one he had ever received and said it must be from the government, for they were the only ones, he heard, who ever sent cables. I finally got rid of him with a second and larger tip and opened the telegram.

"New York.

"Bertha dead writing.

"Jack."

How long I stood with that sheet of blue paper in my hand I will never know. Things had gone numb. My guests arrived and I wondered how they could tuck away so much of that awful food, and whether they really believed in God, and why they didn't re-whitewash the walls where the dirty hands had been near the door.

My guests stayed for hours, sipping old sherry and reminiscing, but it all seemed vague to me. I had no desire to cry, which

was the thing that most impressed me, for I was highly sentimental, dramatic, and emotional. I just sat.

The wife of the proprietor came over to complain that her
food no longer pleased me and the old boys got onto their second
bottle. I looked at my watch and was sure that it had stopped.
That was the way I felt; things had just stopped; everything had
stopped. Oh, hell! What was the use?

For the next three weeks I got a long letter from Bertha by
each steamer. She had returned to New York. Had had a wonderful time and had missed me very much. If I was coming to New
York soon, she would wait for me there.

I went about my business and got my contracts all signed.
What an absurd sense of duty I had. Why couldn't my financial
backers all go to hell?

Ever since I had received the cable I had noticed vaguely that
I was being followed, but what was the difference?

One morning, coming back from a long walk, two army officers joined me and we walked along toward the barracks. At the
great entrance we stopped, still chatting, and they invited me
in to see some old Spanish documents. I fell for it like an over-
ripe plum and was ushered into a far room, with heavily grilled
windows. What of it?—every window in the country was barred.
It was the clanging of locks and bolts behind me I didn't like,
and besides there was too much effort at entertainment going
on. They insisted that I stay to lunch and food was served. At
about two in the afternoon the jefe politico (the highest official
in the district) arrived, and then I began to get more uneasy, for
outside the door I got a glimpse of two men on guard with rifles,
and every time anyone came or went there was that ominous
clanking of bolts.

I was sure by now that I was being held prisoner and that it
must be some political offense or I would be in the police hoose-
gow. So I came bluntly to the point, for I had seen too many men
shot on mere suspicion.

A two-hour cross-examination boiled down to this:

I had entered the country with armed troops; I was the
nephew and agent of Roosevelt, who had been sent into Guate-

mala to stir up a row so that he could grab the country as he was doing with Panama.

I was in a jam. These people were utterly uneducated and would just as lief shoot me as not and throw my big carcass to the buzzards. Who would ever know what had happened to me? The hotel proprietor would say I had left; everyone was terrified of the dictator. A few hours before I thought I wanted to die, but now things looked so different. My mind was working clearly and racing at top speed.

It was the cablegram which had cinched the case against me.

"How do you explain those three code words?" the jefe asked me over and over again.

The more I tried, the more balled up the situation became.

My inquisitors had dropped all ideas of entertainment. As the hours wore on they became very nasty. At about six I was left alone. At eight P.M. a soldier brought in some filthy cold beans and a few tortillas.

I had been moved into a cell now with some straw in one corner. You could see the bedbugs crawling through it. The dungeon though above ground was all of stone and very high, with no air. Hanging on some rings in the ceiling were two big vampires with shining red eyes, which shone in the candle light. One short candle; how long would it last? I felt in my pockets and found I had matches and blew out the candle. Then I began thinking of my cell mates and lit it again.

Ten, eleven, twelve, one o'clock. We three kept perfectly still. At two I heard the sliding of a bolt and the jefe came in and greeted me like a long lost brother.

"You must come over to the palace at once. I have a nice supper all ready and some excellent sherry."

His manner was as though nothing had happened.

"By the way, I must apologize for keeping you waiting so long; I was on the telephone."

He kept up a running conversation as we crossed the plaza and climbed the great staircase to his drawing room.

"You're no relation of the Roosevelts, are you?"

It was not a question, but a statement, and I had known it for years.

I stayed an hour, not knowing whether I was at liberty or not. Finally, I got up my courage and said good night. We both bowed and bowed 'til I reached the staircase. My first impulse was to bolt for it, but I kept my dignity and sauntered home.

And that was that, for I never heard of it again.

I had gathered up tons of loot and had my contracts. I bade farewell to Antigua and Guatemala in haste.

A letter from Jack had told me the mere facts. Bertha had fallen out of a window at the Waldorf-Astoria and had been instantly killed.

I wrote a long letter to Miss Warren expressing my deepest sympathy and told her that I had had a long talk with Bertha about her will and that I had promised her to see that she (Miss Warren) got the money, and not her mother's relatives, who her father despised.

I took the steamer from San Jose and went down the Pacific to Panama, which then was just a dirty, sleepy Spanish colonial town. One crossed the Isthmus on a rickety old railroad. On all sides there were millions of dollars worth of machinery going to decay. Most of it outlined with tropical vines.

I saw no evidence of Mr. Roosevelt's grasping until I got to Colon. There all was bustle. Barracks, officers' quarters, and warehouses were going up in every direction.

The steamer was ready to sail the following day and once on board I found several decent men and a couple of disappointed women, who found that their profession was either disapproved of or over-stocked; I have forgotten which.

The first two or three days were delightful, but the captain said it wouldn't last, as September was a bad month in these waters. He was right, for coming through the Florida Straits we were overtaken by a hurricane.

My cabin was far aft, for the boat carried quantities of freight and that got the precedence.

By four o'clock in the afternoon there was a thick brown atmosphere, which obscured the sun. The sea was deadly calm and one thought of the "Ancient Mariner," but there was no albatross or any other bird in sight.

By morning the ship was like a lump of ice in a cocktail shaker and I hoped she would sink once and for all. At dawn came the first crash, which nearly threw me on the ceiling, and then at regular intervals of about a minute again and again.

Men were running back and forth in the passage yelling above the roar of the wind and sea. There I lay too sick to care what it was all about. Finally, a petty officer came into my cabin, which by now was ankle deep in water, and ordered me out, but I didn't move. He yelled at a man who was passing and together they dragged me out to a bulkhead and slammed it against rushing water.

"The rudder's broken loose at the bottom and is beating in the stem," he shouted.

All right—I didn't care if it spanked in the whole rump.

The excitement had made me feel better and I thought I'd dress, but everything had been left behind in my cabin, which was filled with water.

There was an unusually loud slam and that noise was over, for the rudder had broken off.

I got a blanket about me and crawled up to the saloon, where everyone was huddled together in terror. Outside they were lashing a big wooden spar, which they slipped over the stern so it would drag and give some steerageway. That was better for, finally, we got out of the trough of the sea and took the waves on the snout.

God, how I hate a ship! Everything smelt of rubber, machinery, and seasickness. The place was hermetically sealed and one gasped for air.

Forty-eight hours and the hurricane had passed, but the seas were still mountains high. Another twenty-four hours and the sun came out.

Three other men and myself were sitting in the lee of a lifeboat, getting warm, when the ship gave an extra lurch and threw the bathtub full of water, that had collected in the sagging canvas cover, all over us.

"Oh, God, be reasonable."

We were flying distress signals and finally were sighted by a freighter who towed us into Savannah, Georgia.

I went ashore in a clean blanket, for there was no one on board my size or shape. It was no snap getting a suit, even in Savannah, but they rigged me out after a fashion and we all took a midnight train for New York.

Chapter XXVI
ALADDIN'S PALACE

WE ARRIVED in New York in the morning.

All the shop windows were decorated with blue and gold and I thought the University of California must be in town, but I soon found it was only the opening night of the horse show.

One of the men on the boat was going to the new Astor on Broadway and Forty-fourth Street, so I trailed along. I wasn't familiar enough with the big town to know I was in the kidneys of the "Tenderloin" instead of the heart of "Mayfair."

Fortunately, I had left my trunk with all my goodies in San Francisco, and had written from Guatemala to forward it on to New York. I had lost the few things I had with me on the boat, except the pajamas I had on which, thank God, held my pocket-book. My contracts were with my shipments of antiques, which were in the hold of the steamer and finally arrived safely.

I sent the porter for my trunk and it took hours to get it, so there I sat in a hotel with a bed quilt wrapped around me waiting. What else could one do but telephone? I knew very few people in New York and I bethought me of Tessie Oelrichs, and the operator put me through. Tessie was delighted and asked me to lunch, but my clothes had not arrived so we compromised, and Tessie, who was going out to dinner, said she would send me over a ticket for her box at the horse show. It was three-thirty before I got my trunk and prettied up for a stroll about town.

All enthusiasm, I stepped into Broadway and was met by an icy blast that chilled my tropic, flower-like being to the bone. My wardrobe had never included an overcoat.

The room clerk was a "natty dresser," so I went back to ask him for his tailor's address and found it was a hand-me-down only a block away, but then he had a figure. At parting he said, "If I could afford good clothes I'd go to Bell or Wetzel."

I tried the ready-mades first and everybody got a laugh. For "corpulents" they had things that might fit a Bartlett pear; for all "men's" sizes were for fallen stomachs. Although I was frankly fat now, it was my shoulders and chest that baffled them. With a button hook they got one around my bosoms, but everywhere else it looked like a maternity wrapper, so I finally landed at a Fifth Avenue tailor shop, where beg and plead as I might it would take four days to have Omar sew up such a tent.

So I spent the next few days hopping from hansom to revolving doors and back.

When my cab, which was waiting in a line of magnificent carriages, finally drew up at the entrance to old Madison Square Garden, I tried to look too healthy for a top coat.

I had never seen the "Garden" before and for an instant must have looked just what I was—a country bumpkin. The glittering lights, the jam of people, the magnificent exhibition in the ring was all so much more glorious than I had imagined that for an instant I was bewildered.

Finally, an attendant showed me to the box. Tessie was already there with Harry Lee and two women. I was presented. The names were headliners in every social column in America; in fact, they were the two women that were tilting for the throne so lately vacated by old Lady Astor's retirement. For the first time I learned the difference between jewelry and jewels.

I had hit the social top and I was in the "seventh heaven" of astonishment and delight.

I had never been happy in my life that a fly did not light in the ointment, so I began wondering what it would be this time. I didn't have long to wait. Half way down the arena I spotted Wilson. He was a head taller than anyone else and was strolling my way. He was more exquisitely dressed than I can describe, with a gardenia in his buttonhole and a straight-brimmed silk hat.

I had left him five or six years ago in a Mackinaw coat on the beach at Nome, and now I was split between flight and a desire to get his address. Wilson has always been my chief weakness and dreaded menace. I was in a panic. My first idea was to hide, but finally decided to stand my ground and give him the signal to scram.

A hundred and fifty feet away he saw me and in a voice you could hear all over the building said, "Well, where in hell did you come from?"

I said in a hurry and all in one breath, "Just got in from South America. Where are you staying?"

"At the Rossmore."

Never having heard of it, and hoping for the best, I asked, "Where is that?"

"Oh, it's a bedhouse on Broadway near Forty-second Street."

"Why are you staying there?"

"Oh, I like it. Of course, they won't let you smoke opium in the elevator, and you do have to bury your own dead, but you'll like it."

"I'll look you up later," giving him the "office" to move on.

"Will you come out and have a drink?" he said, as he lifted his hat and moved away.

I shook my head and said, "I'll see you later."

Tessie had gone for a walk and Wilson had no clue as to whom I was with. I tried to look at ease, as both the ladies said in chorus, "Who was that?"

"I don't know; he was just one of the men on the shipwreck I was telling you about."

The lady with the mahogany hair said, "He's very good look-ing and is very amusing. Why don't you go out and bring him back? This is a very dull evening and we need something to cheer us up."

The other one joined in along the same lines. Finally, they almost threw me out of the box with insistency.

I found Wilson at the bar drinking "White Rock." We greeted one another effusively this time, and he asked, "What are you doing here?"

"I'm going to live here; I've moved on for good."

"Given up the idea of knowing the *right* people?" he said, with a derisive accent on the "right."

"No, not altogether. Why?"

"Well, don't you know that this is the most conspicuous place in the whole world you could bring a couple of old madams like those to? You're marked up for life in New York now."

I went back to the box and told my two "social leaders" that I couldn't find Wilson.

Freddie Wood drifted up and asked me to dine with him the next night. I was getting dated up. We had supper at Sherry's, which was the very right thing to do, and the party broke up.

The next night, Freddie and I dined rather early and he told me that Mrs. Goodsall and Mrs. Yerkes were meeting us at the Casino Theater to see the opening night of Lillian Russell in "Lady Teazle."

We took up our stand in the lobby. A great maroon electric buzzed up with two men on the box. The footman was down and at the door before it stopped. He handed out Mrs. Goodsall and then took out something that at first glance looked like a red velvet sofa. It was Mrs. Yerkes in an enormous velvet cloak with a foot of silver tip fur down the front and around the bottom, with a collar twice as wide. She had on a big black lace hat, with an enormous emerald holding in place a long white ostrich plume, which spread over the top and hung down to tickle her ear.

I was formally introduced and we moved on into the theater and were shown to a box inside the footlights; like in a French theater, there were little shutters in the railing to pull up to keep the light out of your eyes.

I took Mrs. Yerkes' wrap and hung it up. She was very lovely, all in white, very slender, and tall. She had on two strings of moth balls and an emerald pendant big enough for a creme de menthe for a cow.

177 | THE MANY MIZNERS

It was a big box and there was room for all four of us against the rail.

I spotted someone in the orchestra I knew, who was very chic, and I bowed. I got a dirty look in return and instinctively thought my pants were unbuttoned.

I looked again at Mrs. Yerkes and for the first time realized that she was tight as a drum. It was the middle of the second act that she started in.

"I got a picture of 'Lady Teazle' by Van Bears at home and she's got on a yellow dress. That woman has on a pink dress—she isn't 'Lady Teazle.'"

You could hear her all over the house. Drunken women have always embarrassed me, and in half a minute I was hiding in the back of the box.

The manager came in and told her if she would like to give the show he would ring down on Miss Russell and let her go on with it.

She began to pout and finally dropped off into a doze, awakening once in a while to make silly faces and then dropping off again.

I don't think I have ever been so relieved in my life as when we struck the pavement again.

Mrs. Yerkes insisted we were going to Sherry's for supper, where she had thirty people waiting for her. I've never been a very good liar, but I am a quick one and have never had a second thought in my life. So I told her I was so sorry, that I had sent word to friends that I was so ill that I was going to bed and couldn't join them at Sherry's. I had done all this just to be with her, and that I must go home. We bickered for ten minutes about it and finally she decided to move the entire party to her house. So in the great purple hack we glided up the avenue to Sixty-eighth Street, and the secretary was sent back to gather up the rest of the party.

At the house a powdered footman, in silk stockings with silver trappings over a green livery, opened the great doors.

The view was astonishing. A huge court rose two stories, with huge red marble columns supporting a glass dome.

Directly opposite was a cascade of water, dropping down one story from a beautiful garden of orange trees and palms that seemed infinite as it reflected its white marble peristyles in huge mirrors. On the right was a magnificent marble staircase; and beyond, a huge marble, two-story room over a hundred feet long, hung with priceless tapestries. At the end of this room a twenty-foot staircase led to the garden. At the back of the house supporting the hanging gardens there were two picture galleries, each one hundred and twenty-five feet long and thirty feet wide, hung solid with Rembrandts, Frans Hals, Van dykes, and many other old masters, taking in Italian primitives and early Spanish pictures. It was the first private gallery I had ever seen that wasn't two-thirds Barbizon horrors.

Who the hell was this woman? I held in the back of my mind "Yerkes" and the London tube, or underground. Were these the people?

While the ladies were powdering their noses, I pushed Freddie to the far end of one these galleries and asked, "Where the hell am I?"

"Don't you know? The old man took the rap in the penitentiary for two years for two of Pennsylvania's leading citizens," (he mentioned two names I would rather leave out), "and they gave him five million for doing it. He built the tube in London and owns all the traction in Chicago. They say he has run that five into fifty millions. This is his second wife and they aren't getting on any too well. He spends most of his time in Europe and has a stable of hot water bags in London and another one in Paris. He wants her to divorce him so he can marry one of them, but she won't do it and is as sore as a crab about it. They haven't made the social grade, but a lot of amusing people like free champagne. You'll have a laugh out of it."

I did, and the party broke up about six o'clock in the morning.

Mrs. Yerkes told me to call her Myra, and she called me Addison and everything was going fine. I didn't see her take a drink, but every little while she would disappear and I knew she had gone to dip her beak, for about three-thirty she fell down and someone dragged her onto a sofa and let her sleep quite quietly, while we went on with the festivities.

About noon the next day the telephone rang and Myra was on the line. For the next month she took full charge of me and I couldn't call my soul my own.

She told me I wasn't fat, but had one of the finest physiques she had ever seen, so I began to get worried and tried to dodge—but no use.

It was in the fifth week of my slavery that one afternoon the telephone rang. Wilson was in my room and I bethought me of a good excuse.

"Honest, Myra, I can't come for dinner tonight. A brother of mine, whom I haven't seen for five years, has just come to town and I must dine with him."

"No, I won't take that for an excuse," came back over the line. "I don't care if he has been in Alaska for five years and has a ring in his nose, you can bring him along. I don't care how awful he is; you've got to come."

I told her I would see if I could get Wilson to come and would ring her back in ten minutes and hung up while she was still babbling.

I had an awful argument with Wilson and finally convinced him it was not "high society," but that it was a circus, so he began to weaken just as the phone rang again.

"Why did you hang up? I won't take 'no' for an answer."

"You won't have to—my brother says he'll come, but I warn you he will probably put his moccasins on the piano, and he isn't 'house broken.'"

At eight-thirty we arrived. Myra greeted us and looked Wilson over.

"He's much better looking than you are; I don't see why you're ashamed of him."

She beckoned to a footman. "Change Mr. Wilson Mizner's card for Mr. Mizner's card."

She dragged Wilson to a sofa and shortly we went in to dinner. There were thirty-six of us and I was way down the table from Wilson, who was on Myra's right. During the game course,

I peered down the board to see how "Mama's Angel Birdie" was getting on and saw him patting her on the back and heard him say, "You're a good old sport; I'll have to see more of you." So I knew they were getting along all right.

As we all left the dining room I heard Wilson snarl at her, "For God's sake get back into your dog house and rattle your chains."

I saw at once that he could handle her better than I could, so as soon as possible I slipped out and went to "Jack's" on Sixth Avenue to enjoy the quiet and refinement.

My telephone was still.

I took an apartment on Twenty-fourth Street in the old Livingstone House on the second floor. The drawing room was enormous, and with a bedroom, bath, and kitchen, I was very comfortable. I fixed it up with my Guatemala loot and lighted it with huge church candles. I got myself a "brunette" to act as cook and valet, in the person of "Miss A. Louise Darry," and settled down.

On the twenty-third of November, 1904, I had a call from a lawyer who was representing Miss Warren in the Dolber will case.

For months I had not mentioned Bertha's name and tried to put any thought of her out of my mind. It was dragging out a very sad memory and it was hard to discuss.

Gerrett McEnurney was acting for Miss Warren and Hiram Johnson was acting for those who were trying to break the will. The emissary finally convinced me that my testimony would cinch the case and that it was my duty to go. I hated the thought of that seven-day trip out to California and seven days back just to be on the stand for a few hours, but the next afternoon I started.

I arrived in San Francisco on December second at seven in the morning. Mr. McEnurney met me at the train and told me I would go on the stand when court opened at ten.

He rode with me to the San Francis Hotel and followed me to my room, where he began to go over my story with me.

"Hiram Johnson is one of the cleverest and meanest cross-examiners in the state. First, he will try to kid you and make you ridiculous and if he can't do that, he will try to get you mad and when he does that it's easy to make you lose your head. Have you got any other clothes? Those won't do for court." He looked me over with a smile that made me feel very uncomfortable.

"No one ever saw a pair of those here," he said, pointing at my best new spats. "Have you got a plain black or blue suit?"

I looked regretfully at my smart new shepherd plaid.

"That makes you look too sporty."

He made me dress like a bank clerk and we started off.

I had never been elevated above a police station before and was scared stiff.

I was the first witness called and by the time I was handed over to Johnson my circulation had returned. It was as Mr. McEnurney had said; Johnson started with merry quips about the "Cynics' Calendar" and got jocular and personal.

Judge Coffee banged his gavel and told me fifty times to answer "yes" or "no." Try as I would, I had to slam back at Johnson with as good as he sent. By adjournment time the judge had broken the gavel, but Johnson hadn't broken my testimony.

The greatest compliment I ever received was when he was leaving the court room he said to a friend of mine, "I know Mizner is lying, but he's too smart for me."

I wonder if the great Senator Johnson of California will remember losing the Dolber case.

Really, I hadn't been lying and hadn't even edited it. That is, not much.

CHAPTER XXVII
ME AND THE POPE

BACK IN New York again things were running smoothly. I sold fifteen hundred yards of red damask for two dollars per yard; and two thousand yards of yellow for two dollars and a half; three hundred yards of Seventeenth Century blue velvet at three dollars and a half per yard; and a lot of red velvet at the same price; besides a quantity of priests' robes and oddments, and had over twenty-five thousand dollars in the bank, and three-fourths of my stock still on hand.

I had learned to take care of my money a little better, although it has taken me thirty years or more to learn the word "no."

I had spent a day in San Francisco with the directors of the company I had invested my Klondike money in and found that things had taken a sudden turn and that I was to get a good and steady income from that.

My ups and downs had been like riding on a seesaw. I had never had a desire to be one of the vulgar rich, but I liked nice things and comforts and always wanted to make presents—sort of a Santa Claus complex.

I felt I now could keep up my end, while I struggled with architecture again.

Through a lot of old family friends I met many of the "right" people and through Broadway acquaintances I met a great many who were not. I lived a dual existence, "sachetting" from Fifth Avenue to Broadway.

I first met Mrs. Stuyvesant Fish at a dinner given by Harry Lehr. (No one ever seemed to include Mrs. Lehr as hostess.) I had the beautiful Mrs. Joe Widener on one side and Mrs. Fish on the other. I started talking to Mrs. Widener and was having a grand time, when Mrs. Fish broke in:

"I have been listening to your chatter and am disappointed. Harry said you were amusing. I spent part of the afternoon looking over your 'Cynics' Calendar.' It's not bad, but there are a few that aren't very original. The one about Folley, for instance. Racine said that when he said—" And she quoted a half page of French.

I listened attentively and when she finished I gave her my most innocent blue eyes.

"Yes," I said, "but you must admit that at least I paraphrased it into one line."

I had no idea what the quotation was, as I didn't know a word of French.

"You know, Racine wasn't exactly original either, for Confucius said five hundred and fifty years B. C.—"

I counted up to one hundred in Chinese and ended with, "Of course, he was a little more flowery but he had such a beautiful way of putting things."

She gave me a hard look and turned her gaze across the table. "Nordica's got on too much paint, don't you think?"

I had crossed swords with the greatest wit in society and had gotten away with it. As I got to know her better I grew to love her terse humor and her direct way of putting things.

Several months later she said to me, "You are the only person I know who's not afraid of me and dares be impudent."

I had been lunching with her at her house. There were six others, with a footman behind each chair.

Adelle Stevens asked me to tell them a story I had told her about the Klondike and I had demurred, as it is hard to repeat a story. Everyone insisted so I started in. I hadn't gotten two sentences when everyone started talking about a "Silver Ball" that Tessie Oelrichs was going to give. I was spoiled perhaps, and California was old-fashioned enough to listen when they asked for something. I hesitated for an instant and then caught the eye of one of the footmen across the table and beckoned to him. As he leaned over me I clutched his lapel and said, "Now, if you will be polite enough to listen to the finish of this story, I'll give you five bucks."

I went on with the story. For a couple of minutes no one noticed what I was up to and then Mrs. Fish said, "What are you doing?"

"I'm going to pay this gentleman for hearing my story out," I finished.

Everyone glared at me and finally Mrs. Fish laughed, "You are the freshest thing I ever saw, but it's more or less a novelty to find someone else who dares do what they like."

I think this cemented our friendship, for we were friends for many years.

I joined the Lambs' Club, when it was still in Thirty-sixth Street, and met all the well known actors, playwrights, and a lot of amusing Bohemians.

One day Mrs. Fish told me that she wanted to get some entertainment for supper after a ball she was giving and asked me what I would suggest.

Marie Dressier had just opened in "Tillie's Nightmare" and I was at her feet with admiration, so I suggested her. "Miss Mamie," as we all called Mrs. Fish, asked me to see if I could get her, so I made arrangements.

Marie brought with her as accompanist Jerome Kern. It was a howling success, but no one thought of places at the table for the entertainers, so I hauled up chairs at Tessie's table and the laughter brought first one and then another to our table. I think Marie was the first lion from Broadway ever taken in by the "Four Hundred," and, of course, everyone adored her.

One night after Marie's show some of the company were kept to run through a new number. It must have been two A.M. when Marie and I walked up Broadway. It was when imitations were just becoming the rage and Marie didn't think the new number was such-a-much.

"Supposing I flounced out and said I was going to do bird imitations. My first imitation will be a canary," she tweet tweeted; "my next imitation will be a wood thrush," and queer, low notes issued from her throat. She went through a list, as we walked along; finally, she said, "I will now give an imitation of a macaw."

She let a squawk out of her that brought the police from several blocks. I have always wondered why she never did it on the stage, for it couldn't have been funnier.

In February of 1905 Tessie said if I would join little Herman and her in Paris she would take me motoring through Italy. I had never been in Italy and I was thrilled. I told her that I would join her on the steamer and keep right behind her until she was ready to motor. So I sailed on the first of March.

We left Paris a couple of weeks later and I spent half of my time in shops buying photographs of palaces and cathedrals, that I wasn't to use for many years, as I only got bungalows and warehouses to build at first.

The papal Countess Leary had given me a letter to the pope and we all made a date with him, when we reached Rome. The audience was for eleven in the morning and I felt like a fool all dolled up in evening clothes. Tessie looked lovely in her lace mantilla.

We all bought dozens of rosaries to have blessed and were saluted by the Vatican guard and handed over to an attendant and started up the many long flights of stairs to the Raphael loggia. At the last turning I saw a magnificent creature in red velvet brocade with a tall staff with a silver head. I thought it was the pope, but our courier said it was only one of the valets and stopped me making my first bow.

We were ushered into a magnificent anteroom, where there were about twenty others waiting. After a few minutes two great, carved walnut doors were opened by two valets and we were ushered into a much bigger room that was even more magnificent. It was very solemn and I should have been impressed, had I not suddenly remembered the great personage who spoke in Benicia that time and besides I was so busy taking it all in and didn't want to miss anything.

The pope sat at the far end of the room under a canopy. He had on a white cassock piped in red, with red buttons; a superb chain and cross were about his neck and a priceless ruby on his finger.

In batches we were led up. Kneeling down before him, we kissed his ring and then retired to stand against the wall until the others had gone through the same ceremony.

The pope then rose and gave his blessing in Latin. He was a fine looking old man with sad eyes. We were all kneeling again as he passed out, followed by dozens of attendants.

The audience was over.

Min had been living in Rome for a year and, of course, she barged into the hotel a few moments after our arrival, which was late in the afternoon. She and Tessie had a lot of gabbing to do and I was busy cleaning up after a dirty trip. Motoring wasn't the restful thing then that it is now and we were very tired.

A dead man would sit up to listen to Min, for she was the most amusing and witty woman I have ever known.

We all dined together in Tessie's apartment. After dinner Min insisted that my first impression of Rome should be the Colosseum. Even a drizzling rain wouldn't put her off and in the dark we entered a carriage and started out. Even if we didn't see much, we had a good laugh.

I had been away from the family so long that I found correction a bit irksome and Min had many suggestions to make along this line in the next ten days.

I enjoyed Rome least of my travels that year. We had had enough of an open car and went to Venice by rail and back to Paris.

One day on the Rue de la Paix I ran into Frank Goad from San Francisco and we decided to take a trip through Spain together, though it was out of season. I had always loved Spain, even when I was at Salamanca and was supposed to be studying hard.

Frank's sisters, Ella, Aileen, and Genevieve, were beautiful, but his parents had gone into the red with Frank. He had a big white face with almost albino eyelashes and brows and carroty hair. Spain had never seen anything like him before and all I had to do to keep a compartment was to tell Frank to look out of the window when we came into a station. He was the most delightful travelling companion one could have; full of laughs and had a wonderful new angle at looking at things.

On leaving Paris Mrs. George Law had given me, as a go away present, the first thermos bottles I had ever seen; in fact, they were just out in Germany. When we decided to go over to Morocco, I put them in my kit. They each held a quart and fitted into a leather case.

After a few days in Tangiers, we thought it too civilized and found there was a caravan going on to Fez, so we hired a courier, who made arrangements for us. Of course, I had to have a camel, which I threw up from, before we had gone ten miles. They were rightly called "the ships of the desert."

That night we halted near an oasis. The courier came up while I was still on board. As a matter of fact, I was too sick, tired, and sore to get down. Blearily I looked out on the many people passing and wondered why everyone had to spit just as they passed Frank and me; God knew how sick I was without that.

"Why aren't they unpacking our outfit?" I asked the courier.

"Shush!" he said, "You're only Christian dogs out here. We will have to wait until the sheik gives his permission."

I slipped off the kneeling animal and stiff as I was, I was ready to be indignant, when I got a warning word from the courier as the sheik came up.

Hanging on the saddle were the thermos bottles and I told the interpreter to ask the main guy if he would have some coffee. I had filled one bottle with hot coffee and the other with a white wine cup. The chief grunted something and the interpreter said, "Yes." So I poured out the screw top full and handed it to the sheik, who threw it down his throat as though it was a rat hole.

Instantly he spat it out and started spluttering curses. It was scalding hot and he had burned his mouth. I poured from the second flask and handed him the cup. Gingerly he took it and with the greatest care put it to his lips. Ice was still jingling in it and he sipped it gratefully. Then the damnedest clatter broke out, as the sheik made a speech salaaming to me at intervals.

I finally got the interpreter's ear.

"What's the matter?" I whispered.

"He says you have done a miracle. In an instant you have produced burning hot and biting cold."

It was a miracle well produced, for from Christian dogs, it had turned us into awe inspiring mysteries. The rest of the trip was wonderful, for we were treated with great respect and given the best of everything.

Wonderful old Fez—but I'm not going to get descriptive.

Crossing over the Straits to Gibraltar on our way back it was very rough and I found a bench on deck, where I lay on my back trying not to be seasick. I finally fell asleep.

An old maid school teacher, whom we had talked to at the hotel in Tangiers, saw some dolphins and woke me up to look at them. She could not have regretted anything more in her life.

CHAPTER XXVIII
I BECOME A NEW YORKER

IT WAS LATE summer when I got home again; so Newport and smart house parties were in order. I was a success, for I was considered a curiosity and a freak and above all a few of the very best people had taken me up. I went almost everywhere; besides, men were scarce. I was dated up for dinners weeks in advance. I never have understood why sex is so important while you are "feeding your face." Of course, you would have been ostracized if you had even asked the sex of a dog in those days.

To think I used to be considered shocking and now I'm just mid-Victorian. The world has passed me.

Through Tessie I met Stanford White and I fancy she annoyed him into giving me a few small jobs, which were too unimportant to go through his office. He asked me not to say he was sponsoring me, for he told me that every woman in New York with a protégé would run him ragged; though, perhaps, that isn't exactly the way he put it.

The first important job I had in town I got through Emma Eames, whom I had known in California. She introduced me to Mrs. Stephen Brown, who was unhappy about her house on Seventieth Street and had let the architect go before it was finished. I took the work over, completing it and did all the interiors.

At least it gave me something to show, for you couldn't point with pride to a few old brown stone fronts you had made over into apartments, or a brick front warehouse.

Unobtrusively, I was building up a small clientele. I never have been a book agent salesman, who could harass people into taking my wares and I have never asked a client to give me his work in my life, for I have always felt it might be embarrassing for him to tell me to go to hell. Besides, architecture is a dignified profession like law and medicine and I have never seen a doctor waiting on a stoop to see if someone was going to be ill.

I got to know Mr. White very well and as I was not pushing for jobs, he used to like to sit and talk architecture to someone who knew so little about it. I worshipped, for he was my god.

I was invited to several of his parties. I never saw one that wouldn't bore a present day debutante to tears. In the hall, at one of these affairs, Stanford stopped me to say, "I have discovered the beauty of the age. Now, Mizner, don't drag out any rough talk for she is only seventeen and a virgin."

So, as I was anxious to see one, I bolted into the studio and almost dropped dead when I came face to face with Evelyn Nesbit. She gave me a frightened and then a pleading look and I said "not a word," and passed on as though I had never seen her before and talked to some of the other guests.

Mr. White entered in a moment and called me over to present me. He always had the most courtly manners and believed in all the Old World courtesies.

The evening was so dull that I found myself longing for one of old Lady Astor's private afternoon musicales, where Melville Ellis played divinely for hours and Harry Lehr and a few others of us sat back in the shadows and drank tea. Truly, I was relieved when Mr. White bowed Evelyn into a carriage and sent her home with a maid in attendance.

It was a few days after this that I got a phone call from Joe Weston. I had not seen him for a year. At that time he had been on an awful "tear," and was just getting over it. I made him swear off for twelve months. I was delighted to hear from him and asked him to come over at once. He looked very well and started in on the subject uppermost in his mind.

"Ad, it is a year and two weeks since I have had a drink and I think it is time to begin again."

I roared out my derision and told him—"Why don't you then? You look so well in a gutter."

"Wait a minute; don't go off the handle until I tell you my scheme."

He hauled out a ream of paper covered with figures and selecting a sheet laid it down before me.

"This is the idea." He pointed at the paper which he had put on my desk, "I have divided liquor into four classes: 'A,' 'B,' 'C,' and 'D.' Now 'A' is hard liquor you see—cocktails, highballs, brandy, etc., they count twenty points; 'B' is champagne and counts fifteen points; 'C' is claret, white wine, and sherry—that's ten points; 'D' is beer and counts five points.

"Now, you see, with a card in my pocket with that list on it I can regulate my drinking, taking only one hundred points per day.

> At lunch, I can have a couple of glasses of white wine.....20 points
> In the afternoon, a highball.....20 points
> Before dinner, a cocktail.....20 points
> With dinner, a couple of glasses of champagne.....30 points
> And when I go to bed, I can have a couple glasses of beer to make me sleep.....10 points

You see that's not much; only a.....100 points"

Joe was an honorable little fellow and although I laughed over the scheme I knew he would live up to it. We bade each other goodbye and I didn't see him for a couple of weeks.

I had dined at home and was dressing to go to the opera with Mme. Nordica when "Miss A. Louise Darry" opened the door and helped Joe in. He was cockeyed. He steadied himself against the bedpost and looked plaintively at me, with glassy eyes. I started cursing him for a no good this-and-that and asked him why he hadn't kept his promise.

"I did keep it; only I underrated beer."

He collapsed on the floor with his legs braided around his hat. What a wreck twenty beers had wrought! I called up his regular hospital and had them take him away and hurried on to the "Diamond Horseshoe."

For light opera there was "The Merry Widow." It had only been running a couple of weeks and everyone had gone mad about it. It was Sunday afternoon and I sauntered up the Avenue in top hat and cutaway, whistling the waltz softly to myself. When I got to six hundred and sixty, I stopped in to have tea with Mrs. William K. Vanderbilt, Sr., who was always in Sunday afternoon. Lillie Havemeyer and Mrs. Eustis were there and they were all talking about "The Merry Widow." Mrs. Havemeyer asked me if I knew the dancing master who had put on the waltz, as she wanted to learn it. I told her I did not, but that I knew Donald Brian very well who was dancing it and that I could get him to teach it to her. At once I was the center of attraction. We finally decided on Thursday afternoon at four at my apartment and I went to the Lambs' Club to see if that would be all right with Donald.

Thursday afternoons were from then on "dancing class day." It started with only six of us and a piano player and within two months it had become too big for my apartment and we moved to Mrs. Vanderbilt's, Mrs. Harry Payne Whitney's, and several other houses, where they had ballrooms, and now it was quite the thing to belong to.

One night I was dining with some social climbers and was surprised to find myself at the hostess' left, especially as there were older and more important people present. She started in by telling me that her daughters had all gone to convents and had become Christians and that they were set.

"By-the-way, you haven't invited me to your dancing class."

She shoved a little slip of pink paper under my plate. Thinking it was a love token, I sneaked it under the table and unfolded it. It was a check for two thousand dollars. I passed it back, saying, "You haven't spelled my name right."

What an idiot I was in those days.

I think this was the first step towards modern dancing ever taken by the "Four Hundred," for it was only a short time before Birdie Vanderbilt and others were learning the "bunny hug."

Frank Munsey heard me telling some of my Klondike yarns one night and asked me to come and see him in the Flat Iron

Building, as he wanted to have me write some of them for his magazines. I told him I couldn't even spell, much less write, but he insisted and I went.

He rang a bell for Bob Davis, the editor of the "Munzie," whom I had known in San Francisco, and we went out to talk things over.

I got myself a secretary and we started in. "Tip" Mooney was a delightful ass with a great gift for poetry and a bottle of whiskey, but little perseverence. We ran up a story that I thought was pure enough for a Sunday school lesson, but when Munsey had blue-penciled it, you could have published it on the back of a postage stamp. We tried again with a little better result; but the magazine decided to re-write it themselves and when it was published, it was the most anemic, limp thing I ever read. That ended my literary aspirations.

When I made a holler about it, I was reminded that all the Munsey publications were read in the homes of America's backbone. Munsey told me himself that twice a year he had different people re-write "East Lynne," and published it under a new name. So you know the type of things published in those days.

He was the sort of man that if you had stabbed him he would have bled ice water.

I was so disgusted that I packed up my bag and went down to Baltimore to spend a week with Jimmie Breeze at Havre de Grace.

Douglas Wise (afterwards the Duchess de Richelieu) was just as amusing then as she is now and was one of the "Southern belles" in her debutante year. There were a lot of beauties in Baltimore that year and I hated to leave.

I wish I had Cholly Knickerbocker's memory! I can't remember a single name.

Back on Twenty-Fourth Street I saw a lot of "Tip," for I didn't have any place to lock up my liquor.

I let work interfere with my pleasures a little, but was on the go all the time. I was hell at a ball, for Mama Mizner had taught me that I must dance with some of the older women and this made a big hit with them and I was asked to some pretty stodgy parties.

Mama Mizner came on to spend a couple of months with me and I took the apartment across the hall and gave her mine. It was delightful to have her with me again and we had a lot of laughs. Her attitude was in thought if not in words: "My family is 'my damned liars' and 'my damned outlaws,' but they are nobody else's." Even one of us couldn't discuss the others too lightly with her; that is, unless it was funny.

One day she wanted to go shopping, so I took her to one of the best shops; they were all on Twenty-Third Street then, and she embarrassed me no end.

She wanted "undies" and the poor girl had to take down everything she had; mother would hold up a pair and talk through them to me and then decide they hadn't enough drafts and ribbon on them and go on to another pair. The place was full of people and I didn't know which way to look, I was so mortified. It took hours to select a dozen things and she said to send them. I could have put the lot in my ear, but I was so anxious to get out that I gave the address and dragged her away.

Mother had several old friends in New York; one was old lady Jay; I don't mean Mrs. Col. Jay, who was Lucy Oelrich, but her mother-in-law; well, anyway mother said she was a lady of the old school. She had taken mother for several drives in her great barouche and so I asked her for lunch with a couple of other old ladies. Lunch was served in the studio, which I am sure they thought was devilish. Before coffee was served I went into the next room so as to let them tell their naughty stories.

I was looking over the papers and didn't hear the first part of the conversation. When I found myself listening, Mrs. Jay was saying, "My daughter-in-law said she saw them with her own eyes; they had lace on them and insertions—even ribbons—and that, above all, they were made of thin silk stuff in pink. I told Lucy that no good women would wear things like those and I would surely cut her dead. In my whole life I have never heard of a lady wearing anything but cambric, with perhaps a little hand embroidery. No one but a fancy woman would wear such things."

I had to have a peek; especially, as I knew what Mama Mizner was sitting in. She had on her face the sweetest smile and her hands were clasped on her empire stomach.

"Do fast women wear them? I wonder if that's why men think them attractive?"

The lunch broke up and Mama Mizner got no more rides.

A few nights later I was taking mother to hear Nordica sing at the William Solomons'. She was dressing early and I went in to see how she was getting on. She was sitting before the mirror in a high neck, black velvet gown, which would have been quite right at an afternoon reception. So I went to a chest where I had some fine old lace I had bought for her in Guatemala and came back with it. "This is a present I was saving for your birthday, but you might as well have it now."

I threw it about her shoulders and told her maid to get me some pins. There was a pair of scissors on the dressing table so before she knew what I was doing, I slashed the back out of the dress and snipped around to the front.

"Good heavens, my son, what are you doing? You have ruined my best dress."

But I went around to the other side.

"Now, Suzanne, tuck in the edges and pin that lace around, letting the ends fall in front."

I went through her jewel box and got out a lovely old Spanish brooch and made her pin it on with a black velvet ribbon the maid found. We pinned on another jewel with a pendant and put it about her throat. She looked too lovely and I was delighted with my work, for I hadn't dressed anyone up since the old theatrical days in the barn at Benicia.

"How do you like it?"

"It's wonderful, but I'm an old woman. Do you realize that I will be seventy on the twenty-ninth of next February, and besides I feel half naked."

At the party she got so many compliments that I had an awful time keeping any clothes on her at all after that. She really was the most beautiful old lady I have ever seen, with her exquisite skin and snow-white hair.

Wilson was pretty regular in his attendance on Mama Mizner. Of course, he was the original sun dodger and couldn't get up until five P.M. He would come in about tea time and occasionally take mother out to dinner. He confessed to me that it wasn't any cheap sport doing it, for the old lady always ordered by the right-hand column and generally took the thing that stood out the farthest. Wilson always gave the grandiose impression of eminent wealth and mother had no idea it was a financial strain on her last born.

"We will have a little sherry with the soup; a pint of so-and-so; claret with the game course; and a pint of 1888 champagne with the roast."

I don't mean that the old lady was a souse, but in those days one generally had a sip of a different wine with each dish.

One night when I came in from the opera mother was reading in bed, as usual, with her lace boudoir cap and lace jacket on; she always looked like Marie Antoinette or some other great lady of the Eighteenth Century, even in bed.

"My son, I had a delightful dinner at Delmonico's. You brother knows how to order a very good dinner—"

(I knew Wilson had not had much of a chance with the menu.)

"But he hardly lets you finish dinner before he rushes you home in a hurry. I think he must be attending night school."

Among our friends Wilson and I were known as the "night" and "day" editions of the Mizners.

Edgar came on to attend to some business and took Mama Mizner back to San Francisco with him. I was terribly sorry to see her go. The only thing the entire tribe agreed on was a love for mother. She was certainly a grand old lady.

Old Zimmerman, from Cincinnati (you know the father of the Duchess of Manchester) was "gone" on the widow Martin and asked her to get up a party to go to the Mardi Gras at New . Orleans, in his private car. There were Mr. & Mrs. Jules Vetable; a nice woman from Atlanta; Clarence Follace; Zimmerman, and myself. We had a great time on the way down and as Mrs. Martin had a supreme sense of humor and a contagious giggle, we laughed all the way. The old man would wake up in the morning with the most dignified manners. It was "Mrs. Martin this," and "Mrs. Martin that." After lunch, when he had inhaled a few drinks, it was Florence; by dinner time it was Flora; then it drifted into Flo; and by bedtime it was just Fla.

Mr. Zimmerman had made no arrangements either for hotel accommodations, clubs, or the great ball. Fortunately, I knew a man named Poisevan and I rang him up to see if he could help us get rooms; for, of course, everything was jammed. He turned out to be the "whole cheese" in town and within an hour we were at the finest hotel, with cards to the best clubs; windows for the carnival; and tickets for the ball. I have never known such hospitality in my life. Everybody entertained us and we had the finest time imaginable.

It was the evening of the last day that old Zimmie came in to dinner with a telegram in his hand.

"An important directors' meeting is on for the day after tomorrow in Cincinnati and I have got to go up tonight."

We all gave a sigh of delight. Alas, too soon, however, for he steamed out on his private car and left us flat.

There were absolutely no accommodations for the North to be had for a week and we were in a fine mess. Finally, the porter told us we could take a train next day for Jacksonville, Florida, and change there for New York.

Everybody said in chorus, "Let's go to Palm Beach."

It was in this fashion, tired, dirty, having been on every local in the South, that I arrived in my future home to stay a week. But it was twelve years before I made it my permanent home. Today I am scribbling this in my mirador, which takes in a view of a myriad of tiled roofs and I am thinking of those few days we spent here, when there was nothing but two old wooden Flagler hotels.

Zimmerman had lost out, for Mrs. Martin married Preston Satterwhite a few months later.

Chapter XXIX
MARRIAGE

RETURNING from the South I had to make a decision, for my lease was up and they were talking of tearing down the building. Also, I had a new litter of Chow puppies and had to have a place with a yard.

I took a lovely old house on Eighth Street, backing up on Washington Square and expanded to a cook and butler, while "Miss A. Louise Darry" acted as parlor maid and valet and always social secretary.

Louise was a character and a leader in the best colored set. Every New Year's she appropriated last year's "Social Register" and could tell you all about everybody in it.

"Why, Mr. Addison, they ain't nobody; they ain't in The Book.'"

On the phone she would gush all over those that were "IN," and be very cold to those that were not.

Her sister worked for Adele Ritchie, who was at the top of the ladder in the musical comedy world and she was all right. Marie Dressier, John Drew, Trixie Friganza, Raymond Hitchcock, and other stars were on her list, but woe betide any understudies trying to crash the gates.

Louise and I used to quarrel as though we were married. One row was one morning when she came in pouting with my breakfast tray and slammed things around until I had to bawl her out.

"What the hell is the matter with you; you damned old fool. Stop that racket."

"I just can't help it; I'm so put out I just can't get calm."

"What about?"

"Read your paper and you'll see."

"For God's sake, see what?"

"Lord Astor has married a divorcée. You know as well as I do that'll just ruin his standing over there."

Her social status was shattered so I had to get up and take the dogs for a walk, for I knew there would be no peace in the home until she cooled down.

Some times I used to forcibly throw her out, but it was no use; she would be in the kitchen doorway before I could get there to bolt it.

One day Adele Ritchie asked me to dinner. Louise took the message and accepted for me.

"But I don't want to go."

"You must; she's just moved into her new apartment and I want you to see it. It's furnished with all the latest antiques."

So I had to go, and I found that it was.

For nearly two years I saw very little of Wilson except surrounded by a crowd. If they were theatrical people or writers, they would have scraps of paper and a pencil surreptitiously taking down his witticisms to be used later as their own. In these circumstances I never had a chance for any intimate conversation and besides the Mizners had an unwritten law, which was never to ask one another a direct question nor a leading one.

Indirectly, I heard that Mrs. Yerkes was in hot pursuit, but I thought he could take care of himself, and that any minute it might end as abruptly as my romance had, so I went my way without really giving it any thought.

One morning I saw by the paper that Mr. Charles T. Yerkes had "cooled off" at the Waldorf and vaguely wondered if that would make any difference and forgot it.

Just five weeks later "Miss A. Louise Darry" fluttered in with my breakfast before I had rung for it and I knew by her manner that something as pretentious as the Astor marriage had happened. She set the tray down with such a jolt that everything on it rattled. Without a word she took the paper from under her arm and with a dramatic crackle opened it before my startled eyes.

"MIZNER-YERKES' NUPTIALS,"

in red ink filled half of the front page. The smaller headlines were:

"Young Lochinvar from out of the West captures the widow of the late traction magnate, who so recently left her fifty million dollars."

Louise was pouting like an ape. "That will just about ruin your social career, Mr. Addison; she ain't in 'The Book.'"

She had more or less voiced my thoughts, though I was thinking more of my business career and what Mama Mizner would think.

Without touching my breakfast, I started dressing; grabbed a taxi and was on my way to the "Hut," as Wilson called the palace on the Avenue.

Wilson had attached to him as a valet one Johnnie Bray, who had been a "toddy tosser" in Tim McGrath's souse house in San Francisco. I would ask for him and get the details.

Johnnie was a soulful looking boy, with huge dark eyes, an olive skin, and red mouth—Morelli might have painted him; but, by those tokens you were not to judge him, for I knew that he was tougher than a bear's behind and would shoot his mother just to see which way she would fall.

By the time I had reached the house I was boiling mad. To hell with Johnnie, I would bolt right into the bridal chamber and tell him what I thought of him.

A footman with an iron mask opened the door.

"Is Mr. Mizner here?"

"Yes, Mr. Mizner; he has just rung for his breakfast and his man is about to carry it up."

"Is his wife with him?"

"No sir; she isn't awake yet. Madame is still in her own room."

"Will you show me right up? You needn't announce me."

From the upper gallery you looked down into the great court and across it to the orange grove; but I was too mad to be looking at scenery.

I was ushered into an antechamber, in the middle of which stood a silver table with the late lamented's ivory dressing set laid out.

There was a thick sliding door between this room and the bridegroom's room. The footman knocked and after a roar, which meant come in, he slid the door back part way.

A picture which is tattooed on my stomach for life greeted me. The size of the apartment, the magnificence of its appointments were all dwarfed by the bed. Upon a dais, with two green velvet steps, stood the nuptial couch. It had been made for the "Crazy King of Bavaria" and was of inlaid woods with bronze gilt appliques. At the head there was a swarm of gilt cupids covering up a semi-nude figure of "Night" and at the foot they were tearing the covers off her.

In the bed lay Wilson, with a woolen undershirt that had shrunk. A million dollars worth of point-lace covered him to his middle and he was rolling a Bull Durham cigarette in a brown paper.

I stood speechless just inside. Johnnie was trying to force his way through the half-open door. Evidently, he had never seen one that slid, for he was pushing it. He was hampered by the biggest silver tray possible, which was laden with a gold coffee set, silver covers of egg, dishes of rolled oats, sliced fruit, and racks of toast. His foot slipped and he crashed with the whole thing on top of him.

Wilson started cursing him, from his exalted position, and Johnnie struggled to his feet, wiping an egg out of one eye and rolled oats out of the other, gaping dazedly about.

"Honest to God, Wilse, I would have fallen down if I had come in here without a damned thing," he said.

My mad had vanished and I sat down to laugh. Oh, hell! What was the use. I started in to get the story by asking the tabooed questions.

"What is this; did you lose an election bet or what? You certainly have made a fine messy alliance."

It seemed things had gone along nicely until "C. T. Y." had broken off the branch and then Myra had insisted upon marriage. Wilson thought he could kid her out of it, but weakened only a few hours before the wedding.

Joe Weston had dug up a dumb-looking dissenting clergy-man and he and Emile Broguere had been the witnesses, while Mrs. Goodsall was maid of honor.

Johnnie had brought Wilson's bags, but was sent away to break an engagement with the chorus of the "Hippodrome," or some other small group. He had forgotten to leave the keys to the luggage and, hence, had almost spoiled the wedding, for Wilson's taste in pajamas was exotic and that was to have been the big number.

Wilson was rather coy about it all and said that he thought his bride was very beautiful and didn't look twenty years older than he, which was true. And then he wound up with, "Things are very comfortable here and the service is excellent."

In fact, the service was so good that an army had cleaned up Johnnie's misadventure and served a fresh breakfast for Wilson and me.

I think Wilson was sincere when he said that he was going to try to make a go of it. As he put it, "Everyone is already trying to gyp her out of everything 'C. T. Y.' had left." He hadn't spoken to her for two years.

The old man had a lawyer, who had instructions to leave her penniless, and had left a son by his first wife who wasn't going to be left out in the cold.

"Myra will sign anything they stick under her nose and even if she read it, she wouldn't know what it meant. So you see I can protect her and see that she doesn't land on her neck across the street over there in Central Park."

But, alas, the other side was thinking the same thing and they weren't going to have a young man, who had met a few bad ones in his life, sitting at Myra's ear and pen hand.

There was an ominous calm for about ten days and then the storm began to break. First, it came in little gusts of anonymous letters, warning Myra what a terrible character she had married. Each one meant a scene and an endless explanation. Then news-papers with scurrilous articles about him.

I tried to trace these and found that in two cases no such paper existed and we never could find out who was at the bottom of it. Wilson had only seen the old lady once spread the web feet and wade into the liquor and he gave her such hell that it had never happened again. Now that she had the knot tied, she defied him and had the nose bag on all the time, which made all the mail that much more intolerable. Within three weeks life was a sizzling hell and the joke was on Wilson.

One night I met a man, who said he had been chief of police in San Francisco and was a great friend of Edgar's. He made himself out very important and bragged about the great influence he had with the leading paper here in New York and offered to help stop the constant publicity Wilson was getting and run down its source. We exchanged cards and he said he would keep me in touch with his findings.

The next afternoon Wilson came in.

"I've had a showdown with the old lady," he told me. "I can't stand that rowing any longer and besides she's as full as a tom-tit on a pump handle all the time. I'm on my way to Washington to have a rest. I told her I wouldn't come back if she opened any more mail. So that's that. I've lived right in the cage with her for five weeks and am about to go nutty. I'll telephone you from Washington."

The next night I was going to dine at home alone. A few minutes before dinner Louise showed in the "ex-police chief." (To save my life I can't remember his name.) I asked him to sit down and ordered him a cocktail and asked him to stay for dinner, which he said he would be delighted to do.

He started in little by little telling me what they had on Wilson. I asked him if the other side was getting anonymous letters like Myra was.

"I don't know Mrs. Yerkes." No one ever called her Mrs. Mizner, least of all a Mizner.

"No," he said, "this seems to be pretty straight stuff. I don't know where it is coming from, but it looks tough. You had better tell Wilson to keep out of town for a while."

All the time I had been listening politely, as he got bolder and bolder. I was getting an ear full. Suddenly, the telephone rang from the New Willard in Washington and Wilson said, "Hello, how are things going?" "Not very smoothly I fear. 'Mr. Blank' is here and howling to speak to you."

"I don't want to talk to that rat; I think he is the one that's making most of the trouble. Look out for him." We talked for a few minutes more, while "Blank" was saying over my shoulder every second, "Let me talk to Wilson. Let me speak to him."

I hung up and turned on "Mr. Blank."

"Now you listen for a while. You have accused my brother of everything you could think of while you drank my wine and ate my food. You know as well as I do that there isn't any truth in a word you say. He's been a little spoiled and a bit fast, but so are most young fellows we know. What of it? With the exception of that girl he murdered in Honolulu in 1900 they haven't anything on him, and he was acquitted for that and you can't try a man a second time, so what the hell difference does it make?"

"Now, Addison, don't fly off the handle. I was just telling you what they think they have. Don't get mad; I'm trying to help you. I am your friend—don't you see?"

He finally managed to bow himself out as the clock was striking nine o'clock.

Just before the clock struck the half hour the telephone rang again. It was Myra speaking in an excited voice.

"That you, Addison? Oh, my God! They have found out all about Wilson murdering a girl in Honolulu and they are after him. We have got to get him out of the country tonight—Mexico, South America, somewhere, anywhere, but quick."

She was working herself into hysterics.

"I'll meet you in half an hour at the side door of the Fifth Avenue Hotel; you know, on Twenty-fourth Street. I'll be just inside the door with a heavy veil on and I will bring all my jewels and you can pawn them and get the money to help him escape. Fifth Avenue Hotel—Twenty-fourth Street entrance—ten o'clock."

It was the first time she had run out of breath long enough for me to get a word in edgewise.

"Listen, Myra; how much did the hack cost you from here to your house? So that big boob swallowed it, hook, line and sinker, did he?"

She tried to break in with, "I don't know what you're talking about. Meet me at the Twenty-fourth Street entrance."

I cut her short with, "Tell that dirty stinker and all the rest of them that Wilson has never been in Honolulu in his life and that in 1900 he had been in Alaska for three years without leaving. I'm glad to know where you're getting your stuff."

I hung up. The telephone rang and rang until I had to stick a match under the clapper. That was the last time I ever heard from Myra, but I got a good punch at "Mr. Blank," which cheered me up a good deal.

It was the next morning that Mr. Simmons, who was Nordica's accompanist, came in to tell me Nordica wanted to see me right away. I went with him, thinking that she must be on her deathbed at least.

She received me in the music room and introduced me to Mr. George Young. He was very nice and asked me to go to Daytona Beach with him on a private car. He had purchased a new big racing car and had entered it for the great race. I must come—just a small party—and he had an extra room for me. Of course, I was flattered and wanted to go, but somehow his insistence seemed a bit queer and I hesitated, saying I was sorry, that I had several engagements and couldn't very well break them. But, I wound up by going.

It was a strangely assorted party, all men, and listed as follows: Robert Graves, Louis Sherry, Samuel Untermeyer, Young's brother, George, and myself.

Before we had passed Philadelphia I was on.

It started with how funny he had heard Wilson was and how much he would like to meet him.

Before we reached Florida he had given me three feet of gold snake chain and in Ormond he found a thin gold watch that he thought "looked like me."

The papers did not know that the "love birds" had split up and I was doing so well that I didn't mention it; on the contrary, the more he talked the more stupid and innocent I looked.

"Who was Wilson having advise him. What he needed was some good business connection who could manage his affairs. Just put everything in their hands and forget it and have a good time. I want to meet him as soon as we get back."

"Yes, I am sure he will give you a lot of laughs," I said, and looked dumber than ever.

With a new watch, a new chain, and a beautiful fitted travelling bag, I stepped off the ferryboat at the foot of Twenty-third Street. The newsboys were screaming:

"MIZNER-YERKES ROMANCE LANDS ON ROCKS."

I jumped into a taxi and waved goodbye. "I have had a lovely time," I called.

I felt just like a tart, with all my "pretties," but after all, that isn't such a bad feeling.

The divorce was rather tame and Wilson didn't ask for anything but freedom. All I got out of it was a modern Russian enamel spoon—I don't think it is even silver.

Although there were a few squawks out of Min as to her social position, Mama Mizner never mentioned the "incident."

It wasn't long until I was brother-in-law twice removed; once by divorce and once by death.

They turned the poor old lady into a wine cellar and she drank herself to death.

Chapter XXX
PORT WASHINGTON

I HAD BEEN up on top for a couple of years and that was too long. On the morning of April 18, 1906, down I crashed again. San Francisco had suffered its disastrous earthquake.

The telephone had wakened me. Tessie was on the wire. There never were any preliminaries with her.

"San Francisco has been shaken down by a terrible earthquake and is burning up."

"Are you joking?" I gasped.

"No. Just got a telegram from our Oakland agent. He says that from his office he can see fifty fires across the bay. You had better come up here. I have made arrangements with the papers to give me the latest news. We ought to send out money at once. Come up here!" She hung up.

Almost instantly the newsboys were shrieking "extras" on the street. I was stunned and sick at my stomach. I don't know how I got my clothes on or stumbled into the street. Everyone was buying papers and I had a hard time getting a boy.

The *Journal* was the best for they were also the San Francisco *Examiner*.

At Tessie's there were already a dozen Californians cluttering up her library. Some were in silent tears; others just dazed, while still others were hysterical.

Each new edition was more ghastly than the last.

"THOUSANDS KILLED!"

"Chimney of California Hotel collapses, killing Edgar Mizner, well known clubman."

"Fire spreading!"

"The disaster is complete."

It was awful; the banks couldn't get any money through and there were no connections by wire with the stricken city. The only news was coming through by boats to Oakland and this was meager.

Mama Mizner, Lan, Edgar, and William were all in San Francisco.

Everyone at Tessie's had relations there and her house became one of terror.

"The fire is sweeping the entire city."

"The dead may number a hundred thousand!"

Each edition was worse than the last.

The day dragged through and night came on and we still sat with our hands tied, for we could do nothing. The railroads refused tickets to any but officials or those carrying money for more than twenty people.

The telephone company had installed ten phones and given Tessie a switchboard with a girl. By now the house was crowded and the phones going continually, for the news had gotten out that the house was one of the headquarters for information.

Cold, gray dawn came on and we sat staring at one another.

At eleven-thirty the second day I got the following telegram from Oakland:

"All family safe," signed, "William."

So I went home and fell on the bed without undressing.

I had moved from Eighth Street to Forty-fourth Street some six months before and was now just across from the entrance to Sherry's.

It must have been about six o'clock in the evening when I came to. There was whispering in the living room and I went to see what was going on. Marie Dressier was leaving a message with "Miss A. Louise Darry."

She hugged me and patted me on the back. I showed her my telegram; then she cried and told me to meet her at Rector's as soon as I had bathed and shaved. She said it was very important.

A half hour later we were seated at a table and she was telling me about the relief drive she was in. I was terribly hungry, not having had anything for two days, so Marie let me gorge for a while, as she tackled everyone that entered the place.

"Come on; you've had enough. We'll grab a sandwich later."

She dragged me out and from restaurant to theater, with me carrying a small hamper. We trudged for days. She worked like a trooper; we didn't even have time to count the money; she took it away from people in such hunks and so fast. I have forgotten how much it all was, but I know that it was over seventy-five thousand dollars.

My hat's off to New York—the way they gave is something beyond belief.

Finally, the following letter came from Mama Mizner. It was so brave and yet so precise and typical. It started out on hotel paper and then switched to anything she could get:

"Hotel Pleasenton
"Sutter Street, San Francisco,
"April 18, 1906.

"My dear Son,

"At fourteen minutes after five o'clock this morning San Francisco experienced one of the most severe earthquakes I have ever known.

"I at once arose and opened my door to prevent it from jamming, should we have a second shock. Fortunately, I had on one of my nicest nightgowns with hand embroidery, for in the halls people were running about in very common lingerie. One lady I knew had on a cotton affair that was quite horrid.

"I was hurrying to the window, when the second shock came. A chimney across the street fell on a poor man trying to escape and crushed him. It was a very dreadful sight.

"As no one was answering bells or telephone calls and as Suzanne had not appeared, I decided to get dressed and go to see if she had been hurt. When I had completed my toilet, a bell boy (that I had always tipped handsomely) knocked at my open door to see if he could do anything for me. I told him I would like him to see if anything serious had happened to my maid. I was greatly astonished when he told me he had seen Suzanne dragging a steamer trunk into the street some time before. For a moment I was almost sorry that the chimney had not taken her, rather than the worthy man who had just lost his life. Of course, I did not tell the bell boy this, as you know I never gossip with servants. The young man, however, spoke of how ungrateful it was for Suzanne to act that way.

"But, I have no one to blame but myself, for after the way those French sailors acted on 'La Bourgogne,' I should have known better than to have engaged her.

"By this time, ladies I had met here in the hotel were rushing in and out in different stages of panic and it struck me how much better it would be for them to remain calm.

"I had a large trunk in my parlor with my fine old laces. This was covered over with some old Guatemala brocade and looked very genteel. It acted as an extra piece of furniture and gave me a place to keep more books and other articles on top. I also had a smaller trunk in my bedroom treated in the same way. When one lady came in to tell me that the city was on fire in several places, I decided that I had better sort out my finest things, as I had been told by the management that the fire was coming our way very rapidly and that it would be possible to take only one trunk.

"Edgar came in about nine and thought the trunk I had selected was too large and that I had better take the smaller one, so again I sorted and packed, for hours. Sutter Street was jammed with people trying to save their belongings. Every known kind of conveyance was being used; trucks, baby carriages, and one family had piled their treasures on a brass bed and were pulling and pushing it along.

"Edgar left me, saying he would return for me within a couple of hours with some sort of trap.

"Lansing came in just as Edgar was leaving and we were all delighted to hear from Lansing that William was quite safe and trying to save some of his more valuable instruments from his office. All doctors would need them to take care of the many injured.

"As Edgar had promised to take care of me, Lansing thought he would take a walk with Frank Michaels and see the fire from some elevation. He said it was a splendid sight. They had only been gone half an hour when the manager rushed in to tell me the hotel was on fire. Fortunately, I was only on the third floor, for the elevators had been jammed in the first shock.

"The cape of sables and the large ermine wrap I had made from the skins you brought me from Alaska I had to leave behind, as I could not even get anyone to carry my small trunk. Fortunately, I had packed a small bag with several changes and some toilet articles and as this was not too heavy, I took it with me.

"You must remember that I am getting old and that I have never thought it very elegant for a woman to be seen alone on the streets, so you will see I was very much out of practice. But it was Hobson's choice. Everyone was so laden down with their own things that I did not have the heart to ask anyone to help me. By changing the bag from hand to hand and walking quite slowly I could make two or three blocks at a time without resting.

"I am sure you would have laughed, had you seen your mother sitting on odd people's steps from time to time. I had only gone ten streets when I saw a fire engine coming slowly up the hill, so I hurried out into the street and called to the driver to give me a lift. He was a very respectable young man, who told me that he had a mother himself, which he seemed to think odd. So I had him drive me to Mrs. Bourns" (a matter of about four miles). "I got my gown quite soiled, as the engine seemed to be covered with soot; but as it was better than walking with a heavy bag I said nothing. The driver was such a nice man and had been so polite that when he set me down, I offered him a dollar" (a taxi would have been at least two dollars), "which he would not accept. He said that he still remembered his mother, who had only died two years ago.

"Now, my dear son, I do not wish to distress you and I do not think we should think of it when everyone is suffering so, but we have lost everything we have. It was, as you know, downtown property, which was the first to burn. God has seen fit to take it away and as we are all safe and well we should send up a thanksgiving and not a wail.

"Mrs. Bourn seemed very glad to receive me. She was very composed, although her daughters were rather flurried. As I had neither breakfasted nor lunched, I was delighted when Mrs. Bourn ordered tea for me. She is always so thoughtful.

"Tonight we watched the fire, which was burning furiously and made a magnificent sight; that is, if one could forget for a moment the agony of those who had been injured or the ones that have lost their dear ones.

"I have yet to see one person who is not taking everything magnificently. There is even a spirit of banter as one man jokes with another as to whose house has made the finest fire.

"We were fortunate in having some cold things in the house and had a very nice dinner. No one is allowed to have a fire, for fear the chimney may be cracked. There is no light and no water. The real cause of the fire is that the water mains were severed near Burlingame, which cut off the entire supply of water in the City.

"Most of this letter has been written from time to time and I fear I will not have an opportunity to write another. Will you please send this one to Henry and Wilson?

"It is now long past midnight and writing this by one flickering candle hurts my eyes; besides, I begin to feel a little tired and beginning to realize that I have had a full day.

"Goodnight, my darling sons, with all a mother's love.

"ELLA WATSON MIZNER.

"April nineteenth.

"The fire is still burning. I heard through some people that Edgar was at the head of the dynamite division, so was able to let him know where I was, as I knew he would be worried.

"I hear that the general at the Presidio has taken charge and that the army is doing splendid work, giving people tents and other supplies.

"All morning there have been terrible explosions and I hear they are dynamiting all buildings east of Van Ness Avenue, trying to halt the fire there. They say that all communication is cut off from the docks and ferryboats, so that there is no escape in that direction. This also has cut off all food supplies from across the bay.

"Later—twelve-thirty.

"Lansing came in just a few moments ago with Mr. —" (name obliterated) "and he has put his fine steam yacht at my disposal and we are leaving from the Presidio dock at three o'clock.

"Five-thirty P.M.

"We left as arranged and as I was very anxious to see the full extent of the fire, I instructed the captain to steam down the bay. Most disasters are always so grossly exaggerated that I wanted to see for myself. I fear, my dear sons, that this one can hardly be overstated. It is the fire and not the earthquake that has made such dreadful havoc,' for if the water mains had not burst they could have put out the fires in their incipiency.

"The damage by earthquake, they say, was very slight.

"Many, many years ago I sailed into this beautiful bay, without anything, after a great tragedy of the sea, and now I am leaving it in the same way, after a tragedy of fire. It was then only a little settlement and I have watched it grow into a great city and I know that I will live to see it arise from its ashes, greater and more beautiful than ever.

"We have now turned around and are on our way to Vallejo, where Minnie is going to meet us and we will go to Stags Leap. Fortunately, I have several trunks there. Hereafter I am never going to save anything and what I have left of my lace collection, I am going to wear everywhere, even on my 'panties.'

"I am sorry to leave my boys behind" (At this time her oldest boy, who was left behind, was forty-five and her youngest, forty), "but I feel that God has taken care of them through so many hardships that he will still guard over them.

"I will mail this in Vallejo and hope that it may reach you safely and soon, for I know how you will be worried. Remember that we are all safe and unscathed, and this is enough to make us all very thankful.

"With a heart full of love for Henry, Wilson, and you, I am, as always, your devoted mother.

"ELLA WATSON MIZNER."

In my new flat I only had one bedroom. I started looking for something where I could have mother with me. This was difficult, as I knew I had to conserve my dough and had already sent some to the family.

It was Spring and I spent the weekend with the Burke Cochranes at Port Washington. I discovered an old house on the edge of the village, on the Sands Point side. It had a millpond, no heat or plumbing, but was lovely. So I bought it with a dollar down and "chase me" for the rest.

With three new bathrooms, heat, and repairs it soon was very comfortable and, being a Californian and a godson of Burbank's, I had a garden going in no time.

Mother was arranging to start East and was to stay over in St. Louis for three months, where Henry had a mission in the slums. Then she was to make her permanent home with me, which gave me plenty of time to get things ready.

Henry brought mother on in the spring of 1907 and stayed a couple of weeks. I hardly knew him, as I had only seen him twice in twenty years and then only for a few days. I am afraid I had gone far afield in the meantime, for I found myself minding my "P's" and "Q's" and stopping just on the verge of saying something that might shock him. But he was on to me.

"Don't you know that I have worked in the slums for years and am used to anything," he said with a smile that put me more at ease.

He could be very witty and funny without being profane, or hiding, which more or less awed me, but he never minded what anyone else said, as long as you didn't drag in the Holy Family. He was a peach and I began to realize the wonderful work he had been doing.

He had gone down into the worst part of St. Louis and, beginning with two rooms in a tenement, had built up a marvelous community center, with a chapel, baths, clubs, a theater, gymnasium, and schools and everyone adored him. Only lately I have heard that twenty percent of the younger men in responsible positions in the City had come into their own with Henry's recommendation. At last, one Mizner had accomplished something.

He left mother with me and after a few weeks she had forgotten the cathedral back-drop influence of Henry and became worldly. She could fit herself into any situation.

1907 was the year of the great panic. Banks were slamming doors in everybody's face and failures were the order of the day, but I had enough tucked away to pull through with and we were happy.

The George Lees lived at the Essex and I knew them very well. One day when I dropped in to see them I found that the situation had crushed them flat and that they were being ousted from their magnificent apartment. I was terribly sorry for them and especially for their four sons, who ranged from ten to seventeen years. It looked as though they would be banished to a little up state town to languish for the rest of their lives. Merwyn, the oldest, was terribly in love with a little girl named Dorothy Whitehead and was broken-hearted at being torn away. So I said, "Mr. Lee, why don't you let the boys come down and stay with mother and me for a week or two until you make up your mind what you are going to do?"

So the kids moved in and stayed eight years. The second and the youngest moved up to Sodus to be with their mother, but Merwyn and Wyburn became part of my family. I can never thank them enough for the love and devotion they gave Mama Mizner. They certainly brought life and youth into a house that might have otherwise been drear. Merwyn managed to hang onto a fine automobile he owned and they raced around the country until my hair stood on end, but they could never frighten mother, who rather urged them to go faster.

My office was on Fifth Avenue between Thirty-ninth and Fortieth Streets. I left Port Washington on an early train each morning and didn't return until six in the evening.

Two or three years flew by.

Merwyn was becoming a young man and although he was supposed to be working in my office, he did not take it seriously, for his father, who was coming back a little, furnished the boys with spending money and the best tailor and best haberdasher.

The doctors had warned me that mother had heart trouble, so I always slept with the door open between our rooms.

She had formed the habit of reading in bed and waiting for her boys to come home. Now she felt that Merwyn and Wyburn were worthy of the same attention. The boys always stopped in to kiss her goodnight.

One could tell when Merwyn had anything to drink and exactly how much by the way he shot his cuffs. If his arms were near his side, then he was all right; the higher he lifted them the more he had. So this particular night they were evidently straight in the air, for he made enough noise to wake me before he got upstairs. He had been to a party in New York and it must have been three o'clock when he arrived in mother's room.

"Had a fine time," he yelled. (Mother was getting deaf.)

"So I see. You're drunker than usual tonight; you'd better go up to bed and have a good sleep," mother said with a little chuckle.

"Yes, and I'm awfully tired. I think I'll go to sleep right here."

With this he dove from the foot of the bed into the big four-poster and snuggled up on mother's arm. There was a moment's silence and then I heard mother trying to wake him.

"Merwyn, wake up; you can't sleep here. What would the servants think, if they found you here in the morning?"

So time flashed by, as my business increased.

Mama Mizner was a luxury and from time to time I had to dip into my savings, but things went on without event and we were all happy.

Wilson, who had never written a postal card in his life, turned playwright and had had produced "The Only Law," "Alias Jimmie Valentine," "The Deep Purple," and others, and I was terribly proud of him.

Lansing came on to visit. He was the strangest character of the lot. We were alone one night, sitting before the fire, and I asked him why he never practiced his law.

He twisted the stump of his cigar to the other side of his mouth and contemplated the dying embers.

"I do not think it a very honorable profession. If a man has a good case, he does not need a lawyer, and if he hasn't one would be party to his crime if he should take the case."

What a wasted life. He was the most beautifully educated, well informed, and the wittiest man it has ever been my fortune to know, but his ambitions were as twisted and futile as the broken stump of his dead cigar butt.

Great lawyers, like Delmas, had told me that his was the greatest legal mind they had ever come in contact with. But there he sat smiling contentedly, gazing at the dying fire.

He just wouldn't work.

Chapter XXXI
A BACHELOR'S HOUSEHOLD

I WAS pretty well tied down all day trying to get bread for that damn butter. In the evenings I was generally tired enough to be content to stay home and besides there was a little hurt look that came into mother's eyes when I said I was "stepping out."

The house was full of dogs, for on my first trip to China I had bought three Chow puppies and I had always had at least one of the strain with me, when possible.

I found it lucrative and amusing to run a kennel and used to sell forty or fifty puppies each year. Animals of any sort made friends with me and although I have been bitten and scratched, it was generally my own fault.

Born on a ranch, I had become a fair veterinarian by the time I had reached my teens and now the half hour in the kennels in the evening was a joy.

I had a Buick car and drove in and out of the city now, instead of going by train, and enjoyed it, as it gave me a chance to stop in on a few friends on my way out; that is, if I got away early.

One Saturday afternoon I turned into the Raymond Hitchcock's and found Flora Zabelle down in the cellar with the sickest looking animal I ever saw.

"Oh, Addison, do you know how to give chloroform? I haven't got the heart to do it and the poor thing is suffering so."

She was in tears.

I knelt down beside the poor little thing.

"What is it?" I asked.

"It's one of Prince Trubetski's wolves; you know he brought a pair back from Russia a year ago and they were so vicious that he couldn't keep them and gave them to the Bronx Zoo, with the understanding that if there was a whelp he would get half the litter. Six weeks ago they had ten and he gave me one and Irene Castle one and kept one himself."

While she was talking I was going over (shall we call it the "puppy") and found it in the last stages of worms and having convulsions. There was one chance in ten of saving it.

"Zazie, you know I am like you are, I can't kill anything. I tell you what I'll do, let me take him home and if I can save it, it's mine; is it a bargain?"

"Yes, anything—but don't let it suffer."

I got a bit of brandy and poured it down its throat. Wrapping it up in some blankets, I put it in my car and raced home. After I had doctored it I put it next to my bed. I was up most of the night and all day Sunday and I saved him. Skoy grew to be thirty-two inches high and became the most beautiful thing you ever saw, with an enormous brush and huge gaping jaws and fangs. To think that in a second generation you could make a pure bred Russian wolf into the gentlest, sweetest, and most affectionate pet, is remarkable.

He slept on my bed and, generally, on top of me, until he got to weigh ninety pounds and then I had to banish him to the kennels at night, where he got even with me by howling his queer wolfish song. He only had two drawbacks. No dog would have anything to do with him. They didn't fight him, they simply ignored him. The second fault was a nervous timidity with strangers. He roamed the country for miles and I never heard of him doing any damage.

There were monkeys, cats, and an anteater—it was a strange household, with an Italian butler, a French maid, an Irish parlor maid, and a Spanish cook, whose husband was the gardener.

One morning I came down to breakfast and found nothing ready and heard a vast row going on in the kitchen. The cook had eloped with the butler and the gardener was putting on the third act of a melodrama.

I took the day off and got a six-foot four Alsatian and a snooty looking cook.

As things seemed to be running smoothly on my side of the pantry door, I was surprised one Saturday afternoon to find my Alsatian on the floor of the pantry, amid a pile of broken dishes, with the cook, poker in hand, standing over him. I gave her an unexpected boot in the pants, which so astonished her that she dropped her scepter, which made "her royal highness" easy to eject. Of course, she brought the police and tried to have me arrested for assault, but I was in local politics and had the officer help her pack up and we shipped her to parts unknown.

Sunday was a hard day to get a cook, but Joe Dondaro, who ran a saloon in the village, told me of "Mrs. Beatrice Alvera Johnson," who went out to cook special meals. She was a big black negro and a wonderful cook.

The "ship of domesticity" sailed on a smooth sea for two weeks and I decided to give a swell dinner for ten of the vulgar rich. I called Alvera into my study and we made out a menu.

"Mr. Mizner, my baby is having a birthday tomorrow and this being Saturday and I ben here two weeks, would it be all right for me to ask for a little money on account of my wages, cause I wants to buy a present and a nice midday dinner."

We compromised on twenty bucks and everything was fine. Sunday morning there was no breakfast and I found Alvera on the floor under the kitchen table. We put the buggy robe and ashes under her and still couldn't get her on her feet, for she seemed to be cast, like a horse on a frozen pavement. Finally, I called the boys and with our combined efforts we got her up. She smelled of pure alcohol and Wyburn suggested sticking a wick in her mouth and said, "I think she'd burn a week."

She only lived a little way up a side street, so we started her on her way. I tried everywhere and couldn't find anyone, so I spent the afternoon in the kitchen. She had made a plum pudding, which only needed to be heated, and the ice box was full. I stuffed the turkey, prepared the vegetables, and the boys made the ice cream. The butler and the maid fixed the salad and set the table.

219 | THE MANY MIZNERS

The boys left about seven, as they were dining in New York and the Alsatian said he would serve all right, with the maid to help in the kitchen. So between bastings, I went upstairs to shave and dress. Just in my undies, with a dressing gown over them, I thought I would dash down and see how things were going.

Alvera was coming in the door as I entered the kitchen. "I left my rubbers," she said, as I put her out and locked the glass door. She put up an awful wail and I paid no attention to her. Finally, she broke a pane and reaching in turned the key and came in again, with fire in her eye.

"They ain't no one going to throw me out 'til I get my rubbers," she bellowed.

She threw her two hundred pounds against me and defied me to lay a finger on her. I had had about all I could stand of her and I grabbed her and forced her to the door as she grappled and clawed, but outside the door there was a step and as she embraced me we both tripped and fell rolling over and over down the steep walk to the road. It was a magnificent war, while it lasted; though, to an onlooker it might have had a comic side. For a moment it looked as though we were going into the mill-pond. This seemed to scare her, for she started screaming that I was trying to drown her. In her fright, she let go of me and I pushed her away and we got up together. She started to run and I chased her down to the main road and then went back to the house.

I was a mess, covered with mud and blood. I went up to repair the damage. The only thing that showed at all above the collar line was half of the mark she had left when she bit me on the neck, but anybody might get bitten on the neck.

I was re-bathed and dressed and coming down the stairs just as my first guests arrived. They looked a bit bewildered. Another car was rolling up in front and then I heard the tirade.

"You dirty big, fat, this-and-that; why don't you pay the butcher what you owe him? You dirty, big, potbellied 'summer squash,' why don't you pay the grocer what you owe him?"

The voice was so loud and clear I thought she had a mega-phone.

"I wonder who that drunken woman is?" was all I could think of to say.

I led them all into the back room and turned on the pianola. Nothing would drown the racket. In desperation, I called my friends, the police, and told them my troubles.

"Alvera Johnson?" came back the awed voice. "Don't have anything to do with her; she's just out of Mineola jail, where she's been serving six months for stabbing a couple of men. She's the meanest negro in the world and goes crazy when she's drunk. Lock the doors and wait until I get three or four men to help me arrest her."

By the time we went in to dinner the row had subsided and I thought an arrest had been made.

The dinner passed off smoothly. I had had a trying day and it was with pleasure that I bade my guests goodnight.

All was quiet on the battle front and I don't know what made me go into the kitchen, unless it was the broken door. Just outside there was a bright, flickering glow, so I stepped out to find what it was. Alvera had set fire to the woodpile, which was against the house.

This time I overlooked the police and called the fire brigade. Together we put out the blaze, which had already begun to lick up the side of the house and then went Alvera hunting.

She got another six months' "rest cure."

One night I was dining in town, going to the theater and supper after, so I decided to stay the night at a hotel.

I hadn't seen "Tip" for years and had only heard that he was broke in London, or that some woman was buying his cigarettes and opium. I was surprised to meet him as I strolled up Broad-way. He looked like a million dollars; his clothes were perfect, and altogether he gave the appearance of affluence. He was a magnificent looking fellow—six feet two, with wide shoulders and no hips and I didn't wonder the girls were crazy about him.

He was very glad to see me and asked me if we couldn't go somewhere for a talk.

"I tell you what; I've got an apartment in that new building on Fifty-second Street, just off Broadway, let's go up and have a horizontal smoke and a chat."

As I had never tried opium, I said, "Fine." On the way up the street I asked "Tip" where he had gotten all the scenery. "You look like the ready money."

"Oh, I've got a new girl; she's the best dip in town; picks a man's pockets without even touching him. She cleans up a thousand per week, after she splits with the cops. She's a beauty—you'll go crazy about Mazie."

As he was fitting the key in his lock the door of the next flat opened and two girls looked out.

"Hello, Tip! Thought you were alone."

They started to close the door.

Tip said, "That's all right; it's an old pal of mine; he's all right. Come on in."

So we were all properly introduced and entered. There was a great big mattress and springs in one corner, piled high with cushions. Tip brought the "layout" and set it down in the middle of it and we all gathered around, propping ourselves up with cushions so that lying on one elbow was made comfortable.

Tip was evidently a little overdue, for he rolled one "pill" after another for himself and then "cooked" one each for the girls. He had just dipped the yenhock in the "stuff" ready to fix me up, when the door opened and in walked a delicate and lovely girl. I got an awful shock; for I imagined, as the knob turned, police and headlines in the morning papers, "Addison Mizner found in pickpocket's apartment smoking hop."

It was Mazie, who was looking with great disdain on Tip's two lady guests. She bade them an icy goodnight as they slunk out and I was introduced.

Her manner changed at once.

"Oh, is this Ad you have been telling me so much about? I know all about you—I'm awfully glad to meet you."

She hesitated a moment and then went on.

222 | ADDISON MIZNER

"I hope you won't think that those cheap chippies are friends of mine. I don't associate with that kind and I don't want to have you think I'm one of those."

A common dip, supporting a worthless, able-bodied man, was drawing the social line with fine distinction. Even Mrs. Astor could not have passed up a social climber with more dignity. I told her that I understood Tip thoroughly and not to think that I didn't know a lady when I saw one. Tip pruned the wick of the peanut oil lamp and said, "Are you ready for a pipe?"

He had lost his nervous, jerky movements, and now seemed perfectly normal.

"Did you come home with the bacon, dearie?" he inquired.

"Not much—only a lot of Rah boys and a guy in a hack."

She pulled a handkerchief out of the neck of her gown and unknotted the corner. There were two pairs of cuff buttons and eighty dollars in bills.

"Where did you get the cuff buttons?" I gasped.

"Out of the cuffs of a couple of suckers," she replied.

When I had first come in I had followed Tip's suit and as I had seen him take off his coat and hang it up, I did the same. I was in evening dress and had on a hardboiled shirt that had taken me ten minutes and an awful struggle to put my diamond-edged buttons in. I gave them a quick glance and decided it would take an electric drill to get them out again, so I forgot them, while I watched the dainty way that Mazie handled the pipe. She had beautiful hands.

They all had been so hungry for their "smokes" that they hadn't rolled me one yet. As Mazie laid down the pipe she turned to me and said, "Did you lose this?" She handed me one of my buttons. I didn't know she had touched me. I finally got a couple of pills and went home walking on air.

It was a horrid sensation and how anyone could deliberately take it up, seems so vicious that it is beyond belief; for it takes three months before you even like it and six to ten months before you crave it.

It was several years after that, that I heard that girls had given out and that Tip had stuck his head in an oven and turned on the gas.

So, the easiest way leads but to the kitchen stove.

And that reminds me that I think cooks go crazy stewing their brains over a range all day, for in a bachelor's household they are always the fountain head of trouble.

I would love, some day, to write a book on "A Bachelor's Housekeeping." For nearly forty years I have had many and varied experiences and I regretted at times that I had left "Miss A. Louise Darry" behind in New York. But she wouldn't leave her "rooster."

In 1913 I went out to St. Louis to stand up with Henry at his wedding. He had been engaged to Margot Postelwaite for fourteen years and because he wouldn't give up his mission and come uptown to be a fashionable clergyman and be elected bishop, her aunt, Mrs. Castleman, opposed the marriage. I met the old girl, only for a moment, the day before the wedding and I don't think I ever took such an instantaneous dislike to anyone in my life.

At the ceremony, which was in the cathedral, I was to give Mrs. "C." my arm after the knot was tied and we were to walk down the aisle together. In the chancel, she made some dirty crack about Henry and we started a fight that lasted until I cut it short by slamming the car door on it. I don't think she ever came nearer getting her face slapped than she did that day.

Mother was devoted to Margot and it didn't take me long to love her also.

In due time, a baby arrived. It was a girl.

Min had two children, but they were Chases. There was no one to carry on the name. I guess it's just as well.

So the years sped by—until the war broke out, and then people were so intent on Belgian relief they didn't think of building. For the first time I was having a struggle to keep things going.

Chapter XXXII
THE LAST TIE

I WAS FURIOUS at Wilson. For six weeks he had not been out to see Mama Mizner and every night on my drive home I had to make up an excuse for him, for I knew the first question mother would ask would be, "Did you see Wilson? When is he coming out? You are sure he is not ill?"

I would have to have my lie ready and glib. Of course, I had not seen him and I knew of his new and violent attachment, but even at that I hated lying to the old lady, because she loved him so; therefore, I wouldn't hurt her for millions.

One morning I went into her room as usual to say goodbye for the day and found her sitting up in bed looking off into space. She had a letter in her hand.

"What's the matter, mother? What are you dreaming about?"

She gave a deep sigh and answered, "I have just received a letter from the girls and I feel that I ought to go out and spend a couple of months with them. We are all getting along in years and I may not see them all again if I wait much longer."

"I don't know who the hell 'the girls' are, but you are not going. We'll send for them to come here."

"The girls" were her three sisters, who lived in Erie, Pennsylvania.

Aunt Mary Leach was eighty-two; then came mother in her eightieth year; and the "maiden ladies," Isa and Elsie Watson, a year or two younger.

It took me ten days to make arrangements to have them shipped down. Mama Mizner was as busy as a bird dog and twice as excited.

It was bad luck, but a very important business appointment made it impossible for me to be at the station and anyway I had never seen them before in my life. So the boys volunteered to go in to the Grand Central and bring them out.

Mother looked up daguerreotypes and photographs for identification. The latest was taken twenty years ago.

I wouldn't let mother go and stand around a station, with her bad heart. Wyburn said there couldn't be three old ladies together, all looking like Mama Mizner's sisters and have him miss them.

"Anyway, I'll brace every woman that looks as though she was over thirty-five."

It was tea time before I got home and found the girls sitting in a row on the sofa, with Mama Mizner sitting bolt upright in a chair before them. In the forty-five years that I knew mother I never knew whether she knew what the back of a chair was made for.

Mother never criticized any of my friends unless I pinned her down in cross-examination; for instance, I had been bragging about a woman who had lived abroad most of her life and I thought very chic. She came for dinner one night and I thought she had made a great hit.

"What did you think of her, mother?"

"She's very pleasant."

I always hated that word "pleasant," so I insisted on a more specific description.

"Well, first of all, my son, she doesn't even know how to enter a room. Her dress probably was the latest thing in Paris, but it looked like a napkin ring and she never kept it in the middle; first, she pulled it up and everything stuck out below, but when she pulled it down, it was worse."

She enjoyed her own description so much that she laughed until the tears ran down her face.

Hanging onto a few old-fashioned ideas, she knew the world was passing in review and loved it all. After all, she was a woman of the world and although she had a few old set rules for herself, she never expected the world to stop still for her and she loved every minute of the parade.

I think she was shocked and amused at her sisters, for they were from a different planet. Mary read papers at a literary club and they all belonged to Woman's Clubs and were "high up" in church circles.

After I had been introduced and they had settled down again, mother said, "We were talking over the last time I visited your Aunt Mary and what a lovely time we all had. By-the-way, what ever happened to Mrs. —? Remember? She gave me such a lovely tea and I thought her so young and pretty?"

"My dear Ella," said Mary.

The girls all looked at one another and folded their hands neatly in their laps.

"I'm sorry you asked. We don't see much of her any more. You know one night at the Country Club when I was leaving early I went out to get in the car and I saw her, myself, smoking a cigarette with her husband on the porch."

Again they all looked at one another and sighed in resignation.

Mother had time to give me a little twinkle, and I had to iron out my face to keep from laughing.

Finally, another name came up and the old ladies all looked away. Finally, Mary said, "Girls, I think we might as well tell Ella."

She stiffened up for the big drama.

"They say she drinks cocktails."

This time mother was afraid to look at me.

It was only a few minutes later that Anthony came in with a tray of martinis. He passed them first to the girls, who smiled sweetly and said, "No, I thank you," one after the other. Mother was talking and I knew that she was just making conversation. As the tray was passed to her my heart missed a beat. Mother took one as though she had never heard of anyone disapproving of them and sipped it at the commas of her chattiness.

"Merwyn, dear, do give me another one—I see there are several left. That makes a second one for each of us." I had never seen her ask for a dividend and knew it was just devilment.

After dinner we went back into the living room for coffee and liqueurs.

"Wyburn, please give me a cigarette. I haven't my case with me." (She had never owned a case and never had a puff of smoke in her life.)

I was afraid the boys would give it away, but Wyburn said, "Shall I light it for you, Mama Mizner?"

"Please do; I haven't my lighter."

She took two or three nonchalant puffs and laid it down. Merwyn gave her a creme de menthe to take the taste out of her mouth. The "girls" were being shown the world.

It was like a breath out of a long forgotten past and instead of being a bore was delightful. Even the boys enjoyed them and joined mother in teasing them like three kids, always scheming what to do next. All three of them were just as naughty as they could be. One evening I caught the boys making Aunt Isa taste a cocktail. They had enticed her into the library and away from the rest.

"Why, it's delicious. I don't see why Mary is so opposed to them."

She took another sip.

"Do you suppose it would hurt me to finish it?"

A lovely color came into her faded cheeks.

"It makes me feel young again. I'm afraid I have missed a great deal in life, now that I have seen Ella in her world. You promised me, boys, that you wouldn't tell Mary and Elsie!"

A sort of frightened look came into her eyes and we all pledged again to keep her vile secret.

After that, every night before dinner Isa joined the boys. She was more like mother and might have had a different life, had she not been check-mated with her sisters.

They stayed a month and went home with enough to keep them thinking the rest of their lives. Mother adored having them with her and I think it did them all good. Perhaps Mary went away with the idea that mother was fast; but even at that, it gave her something to think about.

They couldn't have been sweeter, and so typical of what ladies should be, according to "Godey's Lady Book" of 1860.

Mother was very well all winter. The boys had invented a chair with sedan handles to carry her upstairs in, and in no way was she allowed to strain her heart.

She had nothing to worry about except the war. Her whole makeup was peace and tranquillity.

We all hung up our stockings for Christmas; had a tree, and carried it out with the same custom that we had known in Benicia years ago.

The last day of February she celebrated her eightieth birthday.

She always kept Lent and we had hot cakes on Ash Wednesday and hot cross buns on Good Friday.

That Friday she complained of a slight cold and headache. I called the doctor. The next day he pronounced it to be a very light case of la grippe.

Easter morning she felt much better and was so interested in the wonderful flowers everybody sent her that I thought she was nearly well again.

Monday morning she asked me if I had heard from Wilson and wondered why he hadn't been out for Easter. (As though he had any way of knowing when Easter came!) As a matter of fact, he hadn't been out for two weeks. The doctor came about noon. He looked a little worried and beckoned me into the living room.

"I don't want to alarm you, but your mother is not quite so well; it's her heart; the grip has been very slight, but enough of a strain to make things more or less serious. Are there any of your family you want to have with you, just in case anything does happen?"

I shook my head. I was thinking of Wilson. He was the only one I knew and loved in the world and yet I felt a little spiteful and thought I would make him suffer for the lies I had told. I knew that he adored mother as much as I did; that he was careless and a little thoughtless; and that he would be brokenhearted if anything did happen and he hadn't known.

Spite or discipline could not last long under the circumstances, so I rang him up. A sleepy voice answered the phone and then sprang into life as I asked him to come out.

Mother was propped up on pillows. She had been looking at a new *Vogue*, and laid it down with her finger still marking the place.

"I shouldn't think those new-fangled things would be very comfortable," she said. "Everything in just one garment."

I took the book and looked on the page she was marking and knew that if she lived she would try them.

Wilson's car dashed into the backyard and he came quietly up the steps and into the room, mopping his brow.

"Hello, mother. Jiminy, I have been sick for the last ten days. Never felt worse in my life." He got no further, for mother laughed 'til she cried.

For forty odd years she had backed up her "Angel Birdie" and now, for the first time, she let us know that she had been on to him all the time.

He hadn't asked her how she felt; just the same old stall and for the first time he hadn't gotten away with it.

At eight o'clock that night the greatest spirit in the world had slipped away to keep a love tryst with Papa Mizner.

And this being the last tie binding the "tribe" together, we can call it the end of "The Many Mizners."

THE END

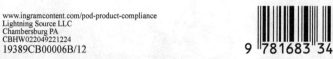